The Daily Telegraph

A–Z GUIDE TO THE
INTERNET

The Daily Telegraph

A–Z GUIDE TO THE
INTERNET

WENDY M. GROSSMAN

MACMILLAN

First published 2001 by Macmillan
an imprint of Macmillan Publishers Ltd
25 Eccleston Place, London SW1W 9NF
Basingstoke and Oxford
Associated companies throughout the world
www.macmillan.com

In association with the *Daily Telegraph*

ISBN 0 333 90557 1

1 3 5 7 9 8 6 4 2

A CIP catalogue record for this book is available from
the British Library.

Typeset by SetSystems Ltd, Saffron Walden, Essex
Printed and bound in Great Britain by
Mackays of Chatham plc, Chatham, Kent

In memory of John Henshall
(1953–2000)

Contents

Acknowledgements

Thanks as always to my agents, Diana Finch and Bill Hamilton, and my assistant, Rachel Carthy.

No one can be an expert on every topic, and several people have helped flesh out listings for topics that are normally obscure to me. Thanks to Guy Clapperton for help with wine, Ian Ridpath for astronomy, Robert Schifreen for security and hacking, Ben Rooney for recruitment and David Morton for sending me all those strange URLs all these years.

I'd also like to thank a number of people at the *Telegraph*: Susannah Charlton, who came up with the idea for this book and made the right slavedriver moves actually to get it written; Becky Barrow and Michael Becket, who I write for regularly; and James Delingpole (especially for gardening) and Georgia Cameron-Clarke (now at the *Industry Standard*) from whose weekly columns I cribbed many ideas and sites.

Preface

I've been online since the summer of 1991 – not early enough to qualify as one of the genuine pioneers, but early enough to have been in on the Net as it's grown into the mass medium we're seeing today. It has been a lot of fun.

However, if there's one characteristic of long-time Net users it's impatience. Very quickly, you lose interest in flashy graphics or dysfunctional animations and gravitate towards sites that are quick to load and slick to use, and don't talk back when you tell them you aren't interested in receiving follow-up email.

This book very definitely reflects these biases, along with more general biases dictated by my personal interests (I know far more about aquarium fish than dogs, tennis than football). Wherever possible, I've tried to indicate if a site is going to be slow or uses special software that is demanding in terms of connection speed or computing power. The Web is great fun – but not if you have to spend half an hour waiting to use it.

A few other biases you should know about. I am strongly in favour of sites that make it easy for people with old hardware or physical disabilities to use them, and I love text-based discussion groups that can be automated using good-quality software so that reading them involves wasting little time on uninteresting bits and responses are sent efficiently where they're supposed to go. You will, therefore, see a number of references to Usenet, which is often ignored in favour of Web-based conferencing (which, even with a fast connection, can be agonizingly slow).

Many sites mentioned in this book are ones that I have used personally, often repeatedly. I am, for example, a regular shopper at Amazon.com and CDNow, a frequent bidder on used DVDs at eBay UK, and a daily hanger-outer on the Usenet newsgroup rec.sport.tennis. Without being too intrusive, I've tried to indicate when I know a site well: if I call someone's customer service superb, it's because I've used it and found it to be so.

As difficult as the technology was when I first got online, I think it was still easier to start then than it is today. This is principally because, although the face the Net presents to users is prettier and nominally easier, the Net is much more gigantic now. But I hope this book makes the process of getting started less painful. And if you do come across a common term with which you're not familiar, and it doesn't have an A-Z entry, then refer to the **Glossary** at the back of the book (see p. 363).

Have fun, and remember to check your email.

Wendy M. Grossman
Kew, October 2000

Introduction

HOW THIS BOOK WILL HELP YOU

The short explanation: speed.

This book is intended for busy people who do not need to know how the Internet works but just want to know how to use it to perform ordinary tasks such as buying a car, tracking down a long-lost friend, or helping the kids with their homework. Despite the Internet's techie origins, this is its future – just as you don't need to read a textbook on the inner workings of circuit switching in order to make a telephone call, so you don't need to know all the technical intricacies of the Internet to be able to use it effectively.

It's not much comfort to say to newcomers overwhelmed by the vast complexity that is the Internet, 'You should have seen it in the old days.' It's almost impossible to convey what using the Net was like before graphical interfaces made everything a point-and-click away, or before search engines made it possible to find sites efficiently. Those who were around in those days take a certain amount of pleasure in their technical knowledge, and can still make their computers do things that the rest of us can't.

Even so, the fact is that the Internet is still vastly confusing. Generally not now because of its technical difficulty, but because of its size and variety. This book focuses on helping you get things done.

GETTING STARTED

If you don't want to bother with any of the rest of the introduction, just read this. To use the Internet from home you need:

- a computer

- with a modem attached to it (for alternatives see the section on **Alternative Connections**, p. xx)

- which is plugged into your phone line

- with an account from an Internet service provider

- and the software (usually provided by your ISP) for handling email and browsing the Web

If you have all these things and you can log on successfully, turn to **Quick Start** in the A-Z section. If you want to know more about getting online, read **What You Need to Get Connected**, p. xvii. If you have all this set up but are having trouble connecting, turn to the **Trouble(shooting)** section or call the help desk of your ISP. If you have even a tiny amount of patience, read the sections on **Security** and **Privacy** before logging on for the first time. Read the section on **Browsing Tips** after your first online session. Also glance at the **Trouble(shooting)** section, even if your connection is working, as it contains some information about common browser errors that can be very confusing if you don't know what's happening.

WHY GET ONLINE?

There are many reasons why it's worth getting online. If you have distant relatives or friends, being online means that you can communicate with them by email far more cheaply and quickly than before – even daily contact is affordable (see **Email**). Email is also, if anything, more flexible than traditional forms of communication – you can send photos of the school play or recordings of the new baby's voice as easily as a casual two-line note, just checking in where a phone call would be too formal. If you have kids, knowing how to use the Internet as a research tool and as a way of networking (in the social sense) with like-minded people are going to be vital skills as they grow up and enter the workforce. If you want to buy insurance or a car, need to find out how to contact the manufacturer of, say, an electrical appliance to replace a broken part, or aren't sure how to fill out the VAT form you're working on after hours, the Internet can help you save money and make a better informed purchase, get that phone number, or find the answer so you can finish on time. That is not to say that the Internet is the only way of doing these tasks, but, increasingly, it is the easiest and most efficient way for those who know how to use it. Best of all, it is always available.

WHAT IS THE INTERNET?

The Internet is a giant computer network that interlinks other computer networks. Although the US usually gets the credit for it, in fact significant parts of the technology that makes the Internet work were developed elsewhere. The basic bits of software that let computers of all types talk to each other to create the Internet, for example, uses ideas that came from networking pioneers in France and Britain, and the World Wide Web itself was invented by British physicist Tim Berners-Lee during a sojourn as a physicist at CERN in Switzerland.

When you access the Internet, the machine you're using becomes part of this network, allowing you to access any other part of the network as if you were directly connected to it. The upshot is that it costs no more to access a Web site in Australia than it does to access one that's next door in the UK. This is wholly unlike the more familiar design of the global telephone and postal systems, where the further your communication has to go the more you pay to get it there, and it is one of the most important principles that has made the Internet into such a rapidly growing phenomenon.

Internet facilities like the World Wide Web, email, and other less well-known services are applications that run across the Internet just like a word processor runs on a home or business computer. Each relies on two complementary pieces of software, a *client* that runs on your computer and a *server* that runs on the distant computer you're contacting. In the case of a Web site, the client is the software that displays Web pages, known as a Web browser, and the server is a program that sends you the pages you ask for. The Web server may also perform specialized tasks on behalf of its owner, such as manage security so your credit card details are protected in transit, run small programs known as scripts that take data you enter in forms and feed the pieces of information into a database, or run small programs known as applets on your computer using a system called Java so that you can interact effectively with the page. Similarly, the email software you run on your machine is the client, while the distant program that stores the email on your behalf and delivers it when you ask is the server.

WHO OWNS THE INTERNET?

Basically, no one and everyone, a bit like real life. The Internet, unlike most other communications systems, grew more or less organically, with people paying for their own part of it. You, for example, pay for your connection to your Internet service provider, which in turn pays for its connection to either a larger ISP upstream or to a centralized routing point. ISPs work cooperatively, carrying each other's traffic for free in an arrangement known as 'peering'. This is ultimately the reason why it costs no more to access a Web site in Australia than one in your next-door-neighbour's house. The postal and telephone networks, by contrast, use a process known as settlement, an arrangement whereby the comparable services in other countries get paid for delivering your letter or call to its ultimate destination.

Of course, this isn't the whole story. What makes the Internet work is standards to which everyone adheres. The standards that govern the Internet are developed via a series of published documents known as RFCs, for Request for Comments. Essentially, anyone who wants to propose a new standard or a new way of doing things writes up the proposal and circulates it freely. Other technical people then analyze it, and it gets revised. If the proposal finds enough backers, it gets adopted. There are standards governing all kinds of Internet elements you never think about, such as the formatting of email headers (the information at the top of the message that identifies where it goes and who it's from), or the inner workings of MIME, a system for encoding non-text content such as music or pictures. Even the most basic of the Internet's building blocks, the protocols (TCP/IP) that allow all different types of computers to 'talk' to one another, is an open standard.

Although governments and other organizations sometimes try to block access to objectionable material, the diversity of the Net has so far made it impossible to control what material is out there. This reality has consequences for consumer protection, the confidence with which parents let their children explore online and personal privacy.

(See also **Children**, **Privacy** and **Security**.)

WHAT YOU NEED TO GET CONNECTED

To get connected to the Internet from home you need a computer with a modem attached, a phone line your computer can use, an account with an Internet service provider and client software to access the different functions of the Internet you want to use, such as email and the Web. The computer does not need to be anything special, and it does not need to be the latest, whizziest model. However, in using the Web you will find that a fast processor and lots of memory will speed things up immensely. If you want to be able to keep archive copies of the information you find, particularly if you want to collect bulky files such as music or video, you will need some empty disk space. The most important thing, however, is to make sure you have the fastest modem you can get. If you are paying per-minute phone charges, the faster the modem the more quickly you can get the information you want and disconnect. You will easily make back any extra money you spend on modem speed in reduced phone bills. More important as unmetered services come to dominate Internet access, the faster pages load from the Internet on to your computer the less of your own time you waste waiting.

Picking an Internet service provider for home use isn't that difficult either. There are more complex considerations for businesses or if you want to make your own Web page (see **Businesses** and **Web Pages, Make Your Own**).

When it comes to choosing an Internet service provider,

you have three basic choices. The first is a 'traditional' dial-up account where you pay a monthly fee (usually £10 to £15) to your ISP, plus telephone charges for connecting. ISPs that have this kind of setup include Demon Internet, Pipex, and many others. The second is a so-called 'free' ISP, such as Freeserve, where you still pay telephone charges for access but the account with the ISP is free. The third, which should become much more pervasive during 2001, is an unmetered service, which includes all telephone and ISP charges and costs a flat rate. AOL, for example, offers such a deal at £14.99 a month. Wherever possible, go for the unmetered service if you can get it, because telephone charges add up very quickly once you get in the habit of using the Internet. One important difference to bear in mind is that some of the fee-charging services – AOL, Compu-Serve, and the Surbiton-based electronic conferencing system CIX – have their own content in the form of online communities, news, and other information services (see **Communities**).

Many ISPs offer free trials, and it's worth trying one of these before committing yourself. You can pick up a Freeserve CD at any Dixons, for example, and AOL gives away free trial disks in many magazines. Either way, you install the software and follow the instructions. One word of warning: fee-charging services (such as AOL) typically take your credit card number at the beginning of the trial. You must actively cancel your trial account before the end of the trial period if you do not want to be charged.

Once you've developed a feel for what it's like being online, you can make a much better-informed decision about what sort of ISP you want to be with long-term. Ideally, you want a company that responds promptly to customer support queries (because if your email ever goes down you want a fast response), that operates a telephone helpline as well as answering customer questions by email (because if your email isn't working how will you get help?), that has good reliability, and offers good online speed. In addition, assuming you're setting up a dial-up account, you want an ISP that has enough capacity that you can get through in the evenings, typically the busiest time of the day. Several Internet magazines do monthly surveys of the leading ISPs, and, before settling on an ISP permanently, check out one of these surveys for the most recent information. Bear in mind that although changing ISPs isn't a big deal in terms of Web access, you do want to stick with the same email address as consistently as possible, because changing becomes more and more difficult as your address becomes established in the minds of everyone you know.

Finally, you would also be well advised to install and run anti–virus software. The longer you are online, the more likely you are to download files, and although most sites are meticulous about checking that the files they make available are not infected with these often malicious bits of software, you should still do your own checking. See the **Virus** section for more details about where to find and how to use such software.

ALTERNATIVE CONNECTIONS

Particularly if you live in a large city, you do not have to have a computer at home or even at work to use the Internet. Most places these days have Internet cafés or other shops which make terminals available to the public for a modest fee. In London, for example, £1 buys you up to an hour's access. Sign up for a free, Web-based email service such as Hotmail (http://www.hotmail.com), My Own Email (http://www.myownemail.com, though your address will be one of two hundred quirky domains such as dangerous-minds.com and antisocial.com) or Yahoo! (http://www.yahoo.co.uk) by going to the site and filling out the registration form, and you'll be able to send and receive email from any machine that has a Web browser.

More widespread computer-less access is likely to become a reality as mobile phone companies begin rolling out new data services and phones that can take advantage of them. These new products ('WAP') will give mobile phone users access to the Internet via connections that will be much faster and cheaper than today's slow, expensive link-ups. The Internet will not look to these users the way it does now to those who log on via computers, but expectations are that the so-called 'wireless Web' will become bigger than the computer-based Web.

ADVANCED CONNECTIONS

The popularity of the Internet is driving the deployment of faster and better connections generally lumped together under the term 'broadband'. The two main contenders for 2001–2003 are likely to be ADSL and cable modems, followed closely by radio links and the next generation of mobile telephony. ADSL, which stands for 'asymmetric digital subscriber line', is a service that allows fast connections over ordinary telephone lines, and it should become available via the leading ISPs. To begin with, the service will be provided by British Telecom; ISPs such as Demon, Freeserve and Easynet will essentially be rebadging it. Cable modems, which are supplied by the regional cable companies, work somewhat differently, but produce the same effect: fast, always-on access.

Beyond those technologies, don't be surprised if that antiquated technology of the last century, radio, makes a reappearance. Several new radio technologies are going to make it possible to put in place broadband wireless connections, filling in the gaps where ADSL and cable are impractical. In addition, digital audio broadcast, a technology largely overlooked because of the high cost of receivers, is likely to become a viable alternative for letting extremely popular and timely material get sent out with far greater efficiency than we saw when many millions of Internet users all logged on at the same time to get the Starr report, slowing the Net to a crawl. In another five years, you could be watching TV over radio connections while the results of the latest report into a government scandal downloads in the background into a portable reader.

Just as important as the faster access, however, is the fact that pricing for these services is flat-rate – that is, you pay a monthly fee for your connection and it remains on permanently. The Internet becomes like electricity: it's just always there.

Constant availability has been a major issue with the unmetered dial-up services, as users generally want to stay logged on but ISPs want to maximize the efficiency of their system capacity by keeping users' hours down. It remains to be seen how this will develop as Flat Rate Internet Access Call Origination (FRIACO) becomes available. For the moment, at the time of writing, most unmetered dial-up services are complaining loudly about users 'abusing' the service by trying to maintain constant connections. Limits on the number of hours you may remain continuously connected are generally acceptable for most ordinary home users, but wholly inadequate for businesses, which increasingly depend on email and Web research.

At the same time as all this is going on, BT is being required by Oftel to open its exchanges to competition ('unbundle the local loop') so that other telephone operators such as Energis can run their own lines to residential and business customers. The upshot of both these initiatives will be to open the UK telecommunications market to genuine competition and to drastically cut phone costs on all levels.

By 2001, unmetered Internet access should be widely available in several forms, from AOL's £14.99 a month all-you-can-eat dial-up connection to business-oriented ADSL services costing £99–£200 a month. Although a novice may not understand the appeal of an always-on connection, as your familiarity with and use of the Net grows, the low cost and high convenience of always-on will become increasingly important to you. Wherever possible, go for unmetered. It is rare for online use to do anything but increase over time.

Additional sites

ADSL Guide (http://www.adslguide.org.uk): regularly up-dated listing of ADSL services available in the UK, with costs and other information.

Usenet: uk.telecom, uk.net, uk.telecom.broadband.

ON THE ROAD

A major part of the point of being online at all is that you can continue to run your life more or less seamlessly wher-ever you happen to be. Like most things connected with the Internet, making this happen requires some planning. For detailed instructions to ensure that you'll be able to get on the Internet while you're on the road look under the entry **Mobile Users.**

USING THE INTERNET

Once you have your Internet connection and you have set up the software your ISP supplied, the obvious question is, Now what? The usual drill is to send someone an email message announcing your arrival and to try browsing a Web site. Send the email. Then read **Browsing Tips** and **Quick Start** and visit the book's Web site (see the Connected section of telegrah.co.uk), where you should be able to find something to interest you.

Remember to log off when you're done.

Remember to log back on in a day or two to look for a response to your email.

Disclaimer: Please note that the Internet is fast-moving and ever-changing, and although every Web address and site was checked at the time of going to press, it's inevitable that some pages will have been moved, changed or deleted. Check the book's Web site for updates (see above).

A

ABBREVIATIONS

People who use the Internet or even just email a lot get sick of typing the same phrases over and over again. These are some of the most common abbreviations. In use, they are not always capitalized.

AAMOI: as a matter of interest.

AFAIAA: as far as I am aware.

AIR: as I remember.

BTDT: been there, done that. Variant: BTDTBTTS: been there, done that, bought the T-shirt.

BTW: by the way.

FWIW: for what it's worth. (Probably not much, but you never know.)

IANAL: I am not a lawyer. (But he's going to tell you what he thinks the legal position is anyway.)

IIRC: if I remember correctly. (Useful; it saves you the trouble of going and checking for sure.)

IME: in my experience.

IMHO: in my humble opinion. (As if anyone who uses this phrase is ever actually humble.)

IYSWIM: if you see what I mean.

OTOH: on the other hand.

ROFL: roll on the floor laughing. Variant: ROTFL.
SFAICS: so far as I can see.
TANSTAAFL: there ain't no such thing as a free lunch.
TEOTWAWKI: the end of the world as we know it.

Very quickly, these become more natural than the original phrases.

ADVANCED INTERNET STUFF

There are many other Internet services that preceded the Web, such as Gopher, FTP, IRC, and Telnet. All of these still exist, but they have been subsumed into the Web, which acts as a unifying interface. You may occasionally run across systems that mention these services, however, and in the rare instance that you are advised to find a client for one of them, you should have no trouble doing so (a good source is http://www.stroud.com). In order, Gopher is a Net-wide, text-based menuing system; FTP stands for file transfer protocol and is a way of directly sending and receiving files; IRC stands for Internet Relay Chat and allows you to send and receive typed messages in real time; and Telnet lets you log on to a distant computer and operate it as though you were seated at a directly connected terminal. For IRC and Telnet you will need an extra piece of software that works with your browser. FTP and Gopher are both built into Web browsers.

ANTIQUES

People who like to go shopping for antiques seem to spend a lot of time in junk shops poring over odds and ends (sometimes very odd). The Internet is certainly home to lots of junk, but it has its top-class antiques too.

Antiques World (http://www. antiquesworld.co.uk) is a well-researched site and a good place to start. The site claims to be the best guide to UK fairs and markets, and it runs magazine features on collecting by experts in various fields along with contacts for collecting clubs and listings for exhibitions. It's considerably less commercial than the market-place auction sites, with the emphasis being on advice for collecting rather than shopping.

If what you want is to find an expert or a specialist, Antiques Directory UK (http://www.antiques-directory. co.uk/) has a searchable listing of over 17,000 dealers, auctioneers, restorers, art galleries and museums all over the UK, even including stamp dealers, bookbinders and other specialities. The site includes discussion forums and gives dealers the option of putting up their own pages.

You may be surprised to learn that the *Antiques Road Show* (http://www.pbs.org/wgbh/pages/roadshow/index. html) is the top-rated show – on PBS in the US. The American version of the programme has a comprehensive Web site with tips on appraising items, stories from the show's travels and features on specific types of collectables (October 2000: baseballs). The original BBC programme also has a site (http://www.bbc.co.uk/antiques/whatson/

onair_ars.shtml) which is a bit more genteel – more experts, less DIY. This site provides specialist guides on topics such as porcelain, silver, furniture, toys and clocks as well as buyers' guides and an 'antique of the week' feature highlighting a particular sale and a few of its more interesting items.

These few sites don't even scratch the surface; but the best option with such a broad subject is to search on the topics that interest you using more specific terms (see **Search Engines**). If you're interested in using the Internet to buy antiques, besides the sites listed here you should get into the habit of monitoring the main auction sites (see **Auctions**). You can find some good deals on these sites, but you need to be careful and knowledgeable; it also pays to be familiar with the general run of prices before jumping in.

ARGUE
(Discussion Groups, Message Boards, Conferences)

One of the chief recreations of the early Internet was chewing over every topic under the sun, and in many ways it still is, with discussion boards and public chat rooms and channels proliferating like mad. All of these are ways for groups of people to type messages that will be seen by all of them – like video conferencing, only typed.

In this context, discussion groups are defined as asynchronous: that is, the participants in the discussion do not all have to be present at the same time for the conversation to proceed. This is the essence of many types of online discussion areas, from the old-style bulletin board systems that users dialled into directly with modems in the 1980s to CompuServe forums, electronic conferencing systems like London's CIX, AOL message boards, Web-based 'community' boards and Usenet.

The fact that users can log in, read messages and add comments when they have time or the inclination gives a breadth of participation that wouldn't be possible otherwise. For a parent sequestered at home with small children, being able to dip into adult conversation for a few minutes now and then throughout the day can help diminish the sense of isolation where scheduling a phone call or live chat session might be too difficult. Even a person who is deaf, blind, limited in mobility or slow at thinking and typing can participate equally in this type of online discussion. Over time, any type of online discussion that attracts regular participants develops a strong community feel. You may not appreciate this the first time you log in as a casual observer beyond noting that the regulars seem to have a lot of in-jokes, but that fellow feeling is what leads eventually to the formation of strong offline friendships among people who first met as disembodied words.

Web-based conferencing

If you're used to reading discussion groups in a threaded newsreader off a computer hard disk, Web-based conferencing is agonizingly slow and painful. You spend acres of time waiting for single messages to load, and if you want to archive anything your only option is to print it out – you can't easily save it into a searchable database as a reference archive. Even so, this is the trend: conferencing built into the Web sites of all types to complement their official content. To be fair, it does have a number of advantages. For one thing, users don't need special software beyond their Web browsers. For another, the Web's unified interface makes it easy for members to share files, point each other to other Web sites, and post pictures and sound files for each other. These things are all possible on text-based systems, but they are not as easily integrated.

To find Web-based conferencing areas, essentially all you need to do is look around the Web sites you already use. Most magazine sites have at least rudimentary discussion facilities for their users and/or subscribers, though many of these are underpopulated and the quality of the discussions isn't impressive. A few of the good ones are the Table Talk area at *Salon* (http://www.salon.com), Café Utne at the Utne Reader (http://www.utne.com), the stock market-oriented message boards at the Motley Fool (http://www.fool.com), and the extensive message boards at Yahoo! (http://www.yahoo.co.uk). For all of these, the rule is that anyone can read the boards but you must become a member in order to post.

One site that offers a convenient compromise is eGroups (http://www.egroups.com), now owned by Yahoo!. The site has two distinguishing features: anyone may set up a discussion group on eGroups and either make it completely public or limit who may subscribe, and any discussion group may be read either through the site's Web interface or as an electronic **Mailing List** (see under **Email**). This hybrid design gives users a lot of flexibility. If you have a fast connection or just want to dip into the discussion group occasionally, you can use the Web interface, clicking on links as you come across them and enjoying all the benefits of the Web. If, however, you have a slow connection or want to read the group daily, you can ensure you don't miss any messages and make the most efficient use of your online time.

To find out what groups eGroups hosts, go to the site and use the search engine on the front page to look for groups on the topics that interest you. To subscribe to them, you will have to register with the site, but this is fairly painless. Individual groups may require you to email the moderator for permission to join.

Usenet

Usenet, which is the most universally available of all these systems, pre-dates the Internet.

Usenet is the town square of the Internet. Public, free and largely uncontrolled, it has all the good and bad qualities that implies: freedom from speech-limiting rules like those on the moderator-controlled commercial systems, but lots of noise and useless junk those commercial systems don't have. Because Usenet has been in intensive use for twenty years, it has developed a set of community standards known as **Netiquette** (see entry). No one can throw you off Usenet for not following these rules, but if you want to get the best out of Usenet, it pays to behave in ways that will encourage

other people to want to help and/or deal with you. The rules
may seem arbitrary, but like manners in the physical world,
they evolved as a way of making it comfortable for people
with different tastes and abilities to share the same space.
The rule that you quote selectively from the message you're
responding to, for example, is a reflection of the reality that
Usenet does not propagate predictably (so some readers may
see your response before they see the original message) and
that many people's software may not correctly display the
messages in relation to one another (so your response may
not hook directly below the original comment). Every online
discussion system has a set of community standards, and
although there are many common factors, such as keeping
messages on-topic, details do differ. Any time you join a new
area, therefore, you should read it for a couple of weeks
before jumping in, just as you would wait to see what was
going on in a strange situation in the physical world.

To read Usenet, you need an Internet connection (or
a connection to some other service that carries news) and a
newsreader. You do not need to be able to handle graphics,
you do not need a big, fancy computer with lots of memory
and disk space, and you do not need a fast connection.
Newsreaders come in all types, from text-only DOS programs to full-featured Windows software that automatically
decodes pictures and sound files. The most important dis-
tinction is whether they are used online or offline. Online
readers include the newsreader built into your Web browser
and Web-based services that carry Usenet such as Deja
(http://www.deja.com) or Altavista (http://www.altavista.
co.uk). If all you want to do is search Usenet as a reference

source akin to the Web itself, you want to use one of the Web-based services. If you just want to get a taste of a newsgroup to see what it's like, the built-in browser news-readers are adequate. But if you want to read a newsgroup on a regular basis – say, daily – you will be much happier with an offline reader.

Offline readers allow you to go online just long enough to collect new messages and send the ones you've written, saving you money if you're paying metered phone bills to connect. More important, they load messages from your hard drive, which is much faster than waiting for the Web, and they have proper threading so that messages on the same subject are displayed in the correct relationship to each other, saving you time. Using a threaded newsreader, it's very easy to skip over an entire thread that's of no interest, or to spot the ones most important to you. Better newsreaders also have facilities for flagging topics of special importance to you and blocking out ('killfiling') users whose postings are annoying or abusive.

Start by looking at the software your ISP supplied; it may very well include an offline Usenet reader. If not, you will have to download one from the Internet. Of the independent newsreaders for Windows, probably the best known is Agent (http://www.forteinc.com/agent/index.htm), which comes in a free version (Free Agent) and a commercial version ($29). Turnpike (http://www.turnpike.com) is a full-featured offline news and email reader supplied free to Demon subscribers; it costs £17.62 (including VAT) to users of other ISPs, although unlike the other software listed here you have to wait for it to arrive by post. Also a good possibility even if you're not a subscriber to the Surbiton-based electronic conferencing system CIX is Ameol (http://www.ameol.com), free software originally developed for CIX's own internal conferences that handles email and Usenet no matter which ISP you use.

The most important rule of Usenet is: choose the right newsgroup. There are several reasons why this is important. The first is that if you start complaining about the BBC's golf coverage in a newsgroup dedicated to politics, people will get annoyed with you – and on Usenet when people get annoyed with you they let you know in no uncertain terms. You won't get any useful response, but you will get a reputation as an idiot. The second is that not all newsgroups are carried by all service providers, so that if you pick the wrong newsgroup you may not reach the right people.

To make it easy for computers to sort newsgroups and for people to find the topics they're interested in, Usenet is sorted into hierarchies: rec (for recreation), sci (for science), talk, misc (for miscellaneous), soc (for social), comp (for computer-related), news (for Usenet administrative groups, not for news in the broader sense), and biz. These so-called 'Big Eight' have formal voting procedures that are invoked whenever anyone wants to start a new newsgroup. Then there's alt (for alternative), which was founded in response to all that formality: anyone can start a newsgroup in alt at any time, although they can't make anyone post in it. There are many alt newsgroups (such as alt.barney.dinosaur.die.die.die) that were probably created at least partly just to propagate the joke in the title. In addition, there are country-specific hierarchies (such as uk),

ISP-specific hierarchies (such as demon or easynet) that are used for posting technical information or to let users exchange technical notes, and even internal corporate hierarchies. One additional hierarchy you may see a lot is clari, for Clarinet. This is a chargeable subscription news wire service, and you will only have access to it if your ISP has chosen to pay the fee to subscribe.

Within all hierarchies, you may see groups with 'binaries' in their title; this means the newsgroup accepts non-text files in the appropriate category. So alt.binaries.signatures, for example, is for posting scanned-in images of autographs, and alt.binaries.sounds.radio.oldtime is for sound files of shows from the early days of radio. Don't post binary files to non-binary newsgroups (or you'll get a computerful of abuse). If you read Usenet over the Web, image files will display automatically. But that belies the added complexity for binaries newsgroups that Usenet carries only text messages of up to a certain size. So in order to post such a file it needs to be broken up into smaller pieces and converted into text using encoding software such as MIME or UUencode. To look at, listen to, or run the files (some programs get exchanged this way) you will need to have decoding software that can stitch the pieces back together and turn them back into a binary file. This should be built into your newsreader, but it can get complicated if, for example, the radio show you want is uploaded in fifty-five pieces and you only have fifty-four of them. It is an effective system for exchanging this type of material, but you can see why we needed the Web.

The list numbers in the tens of thousands at least and

varies according to the news service you use; your ISP should be able to provide a searchable list of the newsgroups available to you. Then it's merely a matter of finding the relevant ones and subscribing so your software will download the ones you've selected. A good newsreader should let you download either whole messages or just headers you can scan and tag to get only the messages you want.

(See the entry on **Netiquette** before posting to Usenet.)

ART

There are four things to do connected with art on the Internet: buy it, learn about it, find images for reproduction and create it.

To some extent buying it and learning about it (or appreciating it) overlap: many of the sites that sell art also run features and provide background information on the subject. (See also **Museums** for sites that display art but don't sell it.)

Online versions of art magazines, such as the *Art Review* (http://www.art-review.co.uk), have links to galleries around the country as well as some clever ideas, such as an Art under £1,000 section. Half of the paintings shown are paid-for advertising, but if you want some critical evaluation of these less expensive pieces, there is also an editorial section covering topics like Dublin's sudden mania for Francis Bacon and artists' profiles. One of the most useful bits of the *Art Review* site is its annual directory (http://www.

art-review.co.uk/ARTREV/99awd/welcome.asp), which lists
art organizations, galleries both commercial and public,
artists and education resources. The directory is slow to use
because you have to load each category, letter and entry
separately, but the quality of the information is good,
including full contact details and even notes along the lines
of 'serves light lunches daily'.

Art Review also directs you to the very impressive Invaluable site (http://www.invaluable.com), which carries daily
news from the art world, a comprehensive database of
auction lots, and features on collectables such as Stafford-
shire pottery, along with specialist sections ('channels')
including furniture, antique cars and sports memorabilia.
All very nicely done, with links to relevant books for sale,
listings of upcoming events and auctions and useful guides
to recent prices.

For twentieth-century work, it's also worth looking at Art
For Sale (http://www.artforsale.co.uk), the Web arm of London's Cross Street Gallery. Besides searching for artists'
work by name, you can search the works by medium
(charcoal, etching and aquatint, oil on canvas) or by price,
and you'll find work by artists such as Patrick Caulfield,
Frank Auerbach and Ivon Hitchens.

You can also find collections of artists using the Internet
instead of renting expensive physical space to promote
their work. One example is Starving Wife (http://www.
starvingwife.co.uk), the name being taken from the Bernard
Shaw quotation: 'The true artist will let his wife starve sooner
than work at anything but his art.' Some of the works shown
here are available for sale online, while some are just for

show; for a number of works (notably some of the glass sculptures) you need to contact the site's organizer by email. It's not a massively complicated site. It loads quickly with small examples of each artist's work, some description of the work from the artist, an email address and a phone number. Other struggling artists should get their act together and do the same – it's the cheapest marketing around.

Finally, one of the things the geeks originally brought with them when they were creating the Net was a love of science fiction. It is, therefore, no surprise that science-fiction art should be well organized online. If weird landscapes and stranger characters appeal to you, take a look at the extensive listings of artists and galleries, both physical and digital, on the science-fiction art site (http://home. interstat.net/~slawcio/artsf.html). This is a guide to nearly eight hundred science-fiction artists and galleries. In part, it's a promotional site for the owner, but the listings lead to some wonderful stuff, such as Jim Burns's cover paintings.

Additional sites

Art AIDS (http://www.illumin.co.uk/artaids): an ongoing Internet project to commemorate and celebrate the fight against AIDS (it says on the top), with contributions from people such as electronic and installations artist Susan Collins (whose own site is at http://www.ucl.ac.uk/slade/sac/ and includes images, video clips and commentary).

Quilt National Prize Winners (http://fuzzytop.cats.ohiou. edu/quilt/gallery_prize.htm): if you think of quilts as crafts rather than art, you may never have seen really great quilts.

Creating art

As the Net develops as an interactive medium, chances are
you will see more and more new types of art evolving to
take advantage of the Net's unique capabilities: its support
for collaborative enterprise, as well as its inexpensive worldwide reach.

Some of the most interesting British computer art of the
last decade comes from techno-artist William Latham,
whose instantly recognizable images also evoke science
fiction: some people find them disturbingly like alien life-
forms. Latham's company, Computer Artworks (http://
www.artworks.co.uk), runs a site with examples of his work
that also sells screensavers, PC games and movies, and
software that generates complex images using techniques
based on biological evolution. Latham got fascinated by
evolution and computers as a student at the Royal College
of Art, and in 1985 began working on 3D images using
software techniques to pick, marry and breed images to
form complex mutations. He was a Research Fellow at IBM
from 1988 to 1994, where he worked with mathematician
Stephen Todd to develop this work further; for IBM it
eventually fed into architectural design software and financial modelling. Computer Artworks, the company he helped
found in 1993, focuses on moving his art into popular
culture. The site requires Flash.

If after seeing Latham's work you want more, you
can explore the possibilities from the comprehensive
listing of Artificial Life/Art sites (http://www.dmoz.org/
Computers/Artificial_Life/Art/) that use evolutionary programs to create not only art but music. From there, it's but

a short step to virtual pets (see **Pets**) and other artificial life programs that use evolutionary techniques. In fact, there are a number of sites where you can experiment with this type of genetic selection. GeneticArt III (http://www.cs.cmu.edu/~jmount/g3.html) is an example. You'll need Java for the site, which offers you ten pictures that you can mate any way you like, replacing one picture on each pass.

Finding and reproducing images

If you find images – photographs or graphics – online that you want to use, either on your own Web site or in a printed project such as your company newsletter or slides for a presentation, check on their copyright status. Briefly, unless the Web site's copyright policy says specifically that the image is available for use, it is probably safest to assume that you need permission. Of course, an image's appearance on a Web site is not a guarantee that its presence there is authorized.

The problem of protecting images online is one reason there are relatively few good photography or art sites: photographers and graphic artists tend to think that, even though it's illegal to do so, any image placed on the Web is likely to get copied.

So far, most people's solution has been to keep the best quality images off the Web, either by only posting versions whose resolution is too low for high-quality reproduction or by simply not posting them in the first place. The limitations of the equipment we use to access the Web foster this choice anyway, as too large and detailed an image won't be viewable on a PC's screen, and the dial-up connections in common use today are too slow to make large images acceptable anyway. As time goes on and bandwidth and screen size increase, however, this may change. Certainly, for professionals being able to ship images around via online connections speeds up delivery times to the point where a photographer with a digital camera, a mobile phone and a Mac had pictures of William Hague's wedding announcement on newspaper screens within eleven and a half minutes.

That situation, however, brings us back to the issue of identifying images' owners. In the old days, you had the negatives. Today, when your photograph begins and ends its life as a bundle of bits, it's difficult to prove it's yours. In addition, software such as Photoshop makes it comparatively easy to alter images any way the user likes. Like sampled music, this also poses a challenge to traditional ideas of copyright.

This is not to say that technology companies and others haven't been working on solutions. They have, but none is ideal. Corbis (http://www.corbis.com), for example, sells commercially licensed, personally licensed and royalty-free images on the professional side of its Web site. Buyers search the site on keywords and are shown low-resolution versions of the images, and then pay reproduction fees according to the resolution or size of the final image, downloading it then and there. On the consumer side of its site, Corbis offers smaller, free versions of the images for personal use, but marks them visibly with the word 'Corbis' in the background, turning them into advertisements for the service. In many cases that works as enough of a deterrent.

Less obtrusive is digital watermarking. This technique involves encrypting information such as the name of the copyright owner, the creator, the date and the source or buyer and hiding it all unnoticeably in the picture file. Software downloadable from vyou.com, for example, lets you package files and restrict the right to display or print them. Digimarc marks material so that it's identifiable and traceable; it also has software known as MediaBridge that works with a Webcam to let users go directly from a printed page to a related Web page.

Digital watermarking sounds good, but has two flaws. First is the fact that there are plenty of geeks out there dedicated to cracking such systems, many of which have already been shown to have technical limitations. Some of these systems can, for example, be defeated by methods as easy as saving a file in a slightly more compressed format, discarding the same noise in which the digital watermarking is hidden. In general, the consensus is that so far these systems promise more security than they can deliver. The second problem is that even at their best digital watermarking systems don't block copying; they merely make it provable and traceable. While it may be comforting to think about being able to prove that the images distributed across the Net are yours, that doesn't give you back control.

Unless you are sure the image you want is royalty-free, ask before distributing copies. If you are posting images of your own, remember they can be copied.

The Free Clip Art site (http://royaltyfreeclipart.com/) offers a collection of images – photos, graphic elements for Web pages, cursors and so on – you can use freely. To save an image to your computer for reuse, move the cursor over the image (tricky when it's a small bullet) and right-click; choose 'Save image as' from the menu that pops up.

ASTRONOMY

Did you watch the one hundredth launch of the space shuttle on TV? If you weren't happy with the coverage or commercials, you could have watched it on NASA TV (http://www.space.com/news/spaceagencies/nasatv_sched.html), which Webcasts several hours a day both live launches and other space-related programmes on streaming video. (For this you will need the plug-in Real Player – see **Plug-ins**). This is the kind of thing that is really best if you have a broadband connection, as over dial-up you're talking a small box of grainy, jerky video, but it is the way of the future: niche, single-purpose channels available throughout the world.

Astronomers were among the Internet's earliest heavy users because of the need to alert people as quickly as possible when something new is discovered. Pictures from, for example, space telescopes and space missions are posted straight up and are available before they're printed in the newspapers, and of course there are many more of them than can fit in the limited space available in print or even on TV.

Besides ready access to images, there are many useful sites for working astronomers and amateurs. Of course the first port of call is NASA (http://www.nasa.gov). Its charter requires it to make the data it collects available to the public, and its Web site is comprehensive, educational and informative; have a look, for example, at the Marshall Space Flight Center's science pages (http://www1.msfc.nasa.gov/ NEWMSFC/science.html) with their solid background on the science of astronomy. One other consequence of NASA's charter: the images it produces are generally freely reproducible as long as NASA is identified as the source.

One of the most useful sites, because the information isn't available elsewhere, is the German Heavens Above site (http://www.heavens-above.com) that publishes predictions of satellite movements. The site has a huge database, so even if you don't know your actual latitude and longitude it will tell you if you enter your town's name. Once the site knows where you are, it will give you very accurate predictions for man-made satellites like the Mir space station and, now passing into history as the satellites are taken out of orbit, flares from the Iridium satellites. These had very big antenna panels which caught the sun like windows, so for a second you would see a very bright star flare up and then fade away again, causing untold numbers of UFO reports. The Web site would calculate their appearance very accurately for your location.

For finding out what's naturally up in the sky, the best bet is a planetarium program – software you can find on the Net and download to run offline. There are a number of these, some commercial, some shareware (which you can try before you buy). The best-known shareware planetarium program for PCs is SkyGlobe, but there are many others available (http://www.seds.org/billa/astrosoftware.html), and there are Web-based ones as well (http://www.mystarslive.com/). (See also **Shareware**.)

Often the best way to learn about a subject is to unlearn common misconceptions – it can be more instructive than learning things that are true. The Bad Astronomy page (http://www.badastronomy.com) is both great fun and educational. Run by astronomer Phil Platt, who works at Goddard Space Flight Center, the site is devoted to misconceptions about the sky.

Additional sites

Refutations – (http://www.math.washington.edu/~hillman/Relativity/wrong.html) – of some incorrect/erroneous/vacuous claims about Cosmology and Relativity.

Darwin Space Infrared Interferometer Project (http://ast.star.rl.ac.uk/darwin/Welcome.html): British project to search for planets outside our Solar System. Most press write-ups of any kind of progress in astronomical understanding revolve around the US; this project is one exception where the ground-breaking work is actually being done in the UK.

Sky and Telescope (http://www.skyandtelescope.com): breaking news, notes on what to look for in the sky each week, software, astrophotography basics and all sorts of technical advice, including tips on buying telescopes.

Space Telescope Science Institute (http://www.stsci.edu/): huge collection of pictures from the Hubble Space Telescope.

Usenet newsgroups: sci.astronomy, sci.space.news. Both good sources of news and discussion, as well as advice and assistance.

ATHLETICS

See under **Sports.**

AUCTIONS

It may seem soulless to chase items by auction online instead of in a real-world room full of excited strangers, but online auctions have one thing real-world ones don't always: critical mass. You can assemble a much larger gathering of potential bidders and a much larger collection of items online. According to experienced buyers, the best bargains are in two areas: office-type electronics (computers, printers and scanners), and **Art** and **Antiques** (see entries on both these sections). Of course, you may need to use a very broad definition of these categories. The antiques section of eBay has been known to include stuffed Donald Ducks.

eBay (http://www.ebay.co.uk), which invented online auctions and is the biggest service, is like a giant, rolling flea market where you can find everything from a human soul (once, withdrawn before the auction was completed) to

Peter Rabbit baby suits. The company, founded in the US by a French entrepreneur named Pierre Omidyar whose wife collects Pez dispensers, is one of the few ecommerce companies to get profitable quickly and stay that way. eBay now runs sites in several European countries as well as the US and UK, and has many imitators, including the British services QXL (http://www.qxl.com) and eBid (http://www.ebid.co.uk), as well as auction areas on Yahoo! (http://uk.auctions.yahoo.com/uk/) and Amazon (http://www.amazon.co.uk and click on the Auctions tab). In 2000 the traditional British auctioneers Sothebys (http://www.sothebys.co.uk) and Christies (http://www.christies.com) joined these companies online with catalogues for their current offline auctions as well as specialized online auctions; rare book collectors may also like to take a look at Bloomsbury Book Auctions (http://www.bloomsbury-book-auct.com/index_ex.htm). Probably 2000's best online auction was the joint Amazon/Sothebys affair selling off Spitting Image puppets, wonderful just to browse.

With the person-to-person trading sites (as opposed to the official sites run by professional auctioneers), critical mass is of major importance: buyers will get better prices and sellers will garner a larger audience. Beyond that, though, one reason eBay continues to be the most popular service (it's quickly passing its native competition, QXL, in the size of its user base) is that it is by far the best designed and easiest to use. All auction sites let you search for items by type and category. But eBay is designed so that you can, for example, bookmark the page of DVD auctions expiring in the next 24 hours (http://local-listings.ebay.co.

uk/aw/listings-local/endtoday/all/category2288/index.html),
making it much easier to do a daily scan to see if there's
anything you want in your category (see **Bookmarks**). The
other person-to-person sites are all much clunkier and
slower to use and lack these efficient features, and that in
itself is a deterrent to using them. Sothebys and Christies
are, of course, a different matter, as they are professional
auctioneers and their sites reflect the quality and careful
selection of merchandise they're known for offline.

Before you begin bidding on any of these sites, you should
read – carefully – the FAQ for the service you're planning to
use (see **FAQS**). Pay careful note to the terms and conditions,
any charges that may apply, and the instructions on how to
handle disputes. Make sure you're comfortable with all the
procedures. Before you can bid, you will have to set up an
account on the service, supplying whatever information the
site asks for, typically your real name, email address, and
home address. A few ask to store a credit card number. You
do not need to register just to browse or search items. Bear
in mind that except in the case of professional auctioneers
you are not buying from the site itself; you are buying from
individuals like you who list goods on the site.

For that reason, each item's terms and conditions may
differ. Accordingly, before you bid, read the item description carefully, noting any shipping costs that are going to
apply and ensuring that you'll be able to make the payment
terms. For example, if the seller is based in the US and will
only accept a personal cheque drawn on a US bank in US
dollars, make sure you have a way of supplying that before
you bid.

Once you've digested all this background information, buying in online auctions is surprisingly painless. You find the items you're interested in either by browsing among the categories of merchandise or by searching for specific items. Each item has its own page, which typically shows the amount of time left in the auction, the current price, the name of the highest bidder, the name of the seller, and any information the seller has made available. For a second-hand DVD, for example, the seller might give a summary of the movie's plot, list the stars, describe the condition of the disc, and note how much postage will cost on top of the bid price. In some cases, you may want to do background research to ensure the item is what you expect it to be – you can email the seller to ask specific questions or search the wider Internet or specialist sites for more information about the item you're interested in. In the case of a DVD, that might mean looking up film reviews and technical details (see also **Films**). Once you're confident you know what you're buying, to actually bid on the item you enter the amount in the bidding window provided, enter your user ID and password, and press the button to proceed. On eBay bids are in increments of 50p; on QXL it's £1. Typically you'll be offered the chance to review the bid and confirm it before it becomes final. Submitting bids is subject to the same strictures as in the physical world: once you have made your bid you are committed to buy the item unless someone outbids you before the auction expires.

Unless the auction is specifically labelled as 'live', bids are asynchronous – that is, an item will be listed with a fixed time and date when the auction ends, and people bid at any time during that period that's convenient for them. Say, for example, that a DVD has an expiry date of ten days after its original listing. Bidders can view the item any time during those ten days, and bid at any time. Depending on how you configure your account, you can have the system email you to let you know if someone outbids you on an item. Some services even offer SMS alerts or email to your mobile phone.

To make the whole business easier, sites offer proxy bidding services. Essentially, you enter the maximum amount you're willing to pay, and when other users come in and bid on the item, raising its price, the site's computer automatically bids on your behalf up to the maximum you've specified. If you're the kind of person who gets carried away at auctions, this can be a useful method for enforcing discipline. The maximum amounts and bidding history are hidden until the auction ends.

Once the auction is concluded, the system sends out email messages alerting both buyer and seller. At that point, it is up to the parties involved to contact each other to arrange payment and shipping (see **Payments**). Typically, the buyer pays and then the seller ships. If both buyer and seller are in the UK and the item is small, paying by cheque is usually acceptable. Trade sellers who use eBay (and many do, partly to garner sales and partly to publicize their businesses to a well-targeted audience) frequently accept credit cards. In addition, there are a number of payment schemes such as Billpoint (built into eBay) and Paypal (a credit card aggregator) that allow you to pay even individual sellers by credit card. For large items, investigate whether the site runs an 'escrow' service – these offer you protection by holding your money in trust until the item has arrived safely and is working as advertised.

One of the important ways these sites counteract the possibility of fraud and deception is a customer feedback facility. Essentially, these are short reviews buyers and sellers post about each other after deals have been concluded. The results are readily available to bidders by clicking on the appropriate link, and, especially for large items, it's always a good idea to follow through and check the seller's reputation before proceeding. Whenever you complete a transaction satisfactorily, it's considered polite to post positive feedback.

Organizations that combat Internet fraud say online auctions are the most common source of complaints, and it pays to be somewhat careful. In one incident in 2000, a thirteen-year-old boy from New Jersey, offered his best friend as a lot in an online auction, and when there were no bids followed up by using his parents' credit card to bid $3 million on classic cars, a replica Viking ship and a Van Gogh. The auction house concerned, eBay UK (http://www.ebay.co.uk), was certainly embarrassed, and the resulting publicity focused on the incident as a way of illustrating the importance of trust in 'Person to person trading communities', as Internet auctions have become known. But the story probably raised more security concerns than it should have: although the items had to be re-listed and the boy himself was banned from using the Internet by his angry parents, we're not talking about a criminal case where a thief made off with millions of dollars' worth of goods. The services themselves are aware of the issue of security, and work to combat fraud; for example, eBay insures most items up to £120 through a policy with Lloyds.

But, to put all that in perspective, most people are honest, and many thousands of transactions go through daily without trouble (says a veteran buyer of umpteen second-hand DVDs). However, it does happen that winning bids fail – as a sample, I've probably bought about thirty second-hand DVDs through auction sites, almost all through eBay, and have bid unsuccessfully on something like twice that number, and I've never had any trouble getting the goods I've paid for. In two of the unsuccessful bids I've received email from the seller saying the winning bid had fallen through (once because the bidder was apparently a vagrant and once because the bidder had not paid attention to the payment conditions), and in both cases I've paid the amount of my last bid and received the goods without trouble.

B

BABIES

One of the few things you actually can do when you have an insomniac baby on your lap at 3 a.m. is log on to the Internet. You might find appropriate advice or someone to talk to who's in the same boat, or you might just save a little time the next day by ordering supplies that would be too much trouble to carry home.

It's odd that books on child health aren't more popular baby gifts: most new parents could use better information and a lot of reassurance. The Child Health Guide (http://www.kidsource.com/kidsource/content/hg/), compiled by the US Department of Health, can help here, with growth charts, information about immunizations, and general guidance on subjects like development, dental health, and nutrition. The site that hosts it, Kidsource (http://www.kidsource.com) provides information for parents of kids of all ages, covering subjects like health and safety, discipline, education and so on. Closer to home, you can find some nicely hypochondriac reading on the Patient UK site, which has an excellent page on child health (http://www.patient.co.uk/child_health.htm), including explanations of many common problems such as glue ear and asthma, and links and references to other resources including not just

Web sites but videos and books. One subject rarely covered on any of these sites is bullying – see Bully Online (http://www.successunlimited.co.uk/index.htm).

Baby shopping

For practical stuff, the familiar name wins: Mothercare (http://www.mothercare.co.uk) has opened a shopping site that covers what seems to be its entire range – search by keyword or catalogue number. New parents can set up giftlists so their friends can choose what to get them in an organized way, and a 'help me choose' feature guides you through the intricacies of pushchairs and car seats. Message boards and even a live advice channel complement the mix, so all together it's a well-designed and useful site.

For the upmarket newly baby-obsessed who can stand lots of flashing, animated graphics, the Urchin catalogue is online (http://www.urchin.co.uk), with hundreds of things your baby really doesn't need, like a Dalmation bib, penguin table lamp, or leopard-print bean-bag armchair. This stuff is by no means necessary – but it is fun. To be fair to Urchin, it does some more practical items as well, things like car seats and all-terrain pushchairs. However, the site is slow to navigate and for most people it will be easier to order from the offline catalogue. If you're looking for outdoor clothes for kids, however, you might want to take a look instead at Outdoor Kids (http://www.outdoorkids.co.uk), which is much faster to load and has a wider range – though it's certainly no cheaper. This is another of those areas where looking at US sites – such as Land's End (http://www.landsend.com), which has a selection of good-quality children and baby clothes and Babycenter (http://www.babycenter.com) – is very tempting, as the prices seem so much lower. But remember to add shipping, customs duty and VAT before comparing.

Even if you don't want to buy stuff there, Babycenter is well worth visiting – it will happily send you a free email newsletter weekly telling you what developmental stage your baby is at, and also has a terrific baby name finder. Want a Basque boy's name with three syllables? How about Ramiro? The site also tells us that in about twenty years the US is going to be awash with Jacobs and Emilys – those were the most popular names of 1999. Also Briannas, the number three for girls. If you're not sure whether you want to become pregnant, this is also the place for you: just check out the New Parents Passion Predictor calculator, which, based on a survey of 2,800-plus parents, notes that two months after the baby is born you'll be down to once a month.

Also worth consulting as a resource is Parents Place (http://www.parentsplace.com/), which covers the gamut from children's health to calculating how much they're going to cost by the time they're grown up.

For toys, there's the Early Learning Centre (http://www. elc.co.uk) – you can specify an age range, category of toy, manufacturer, or price range, and get back a list of possibilities – very helpful for gift-givers. The quality and brands are familiar, and the site is reasonably straightforward to use.

(See also **Toys**.)

BACKUP

It's often said that there are two kinds of people: people who have lost their data, and people who are going to lose their data. Backups are safety copies that give you a way of getting your data back when it gets lost. Most home users don't bother backing up their data. But if your computer's hard drive contains your banking records, the pictures of your grandchildren and your music collection, keeping copies means it's less of a disaster if the machine gets stolen or breaks down.

At their simplest, backups are simply files copied on to a floppy disk. This works fine for small files, such as word-processed letters. It's not hard these days, however, to create data files larger than a floppy disk's 1.44Mb limit. Most MP3 files, for example, are 3Mb or above. A convenient solution for many people is a Zip drive, which takes removable, rewritable disks holding up to 250Mb of data. Another possibility is writable CD-ROM; the drives themselves have become relatively inexpensive and the discs are cheap, costing less than £1 each (although they can only be written once). With these types of disks, it's relatively easy to create copies of the directories that hold data. You can even use CD-ROMs to create off-site backups because they're so cheap; just write a couple of extra copies of the disc and post them to friends.

If, however, you use software that's been heavily customized, just backing up the data won't save you hours of reconfiguring if there's a crash. In such a case, where you may have gigabytes to back up, the best solution is a backup device such as a tape drive and specialized software (usually bundled with it) to manage the backups. Such software can save a lot of time by only backing up files that have changed (known as 'incremental backups'). However, it is vital to test the backups periodically and make sure they restore correctly.

Online backups

The Internet has brought a new alternative: back up your data online, so your backups are stored offsite, where they won't be affected in the event of a robbery or fire. In its simplest form, this might just mean copying your critical files into the free Web space provided with many ISP accounts or emailing yourself a really important file that you can't afford to lose.

The more secure solution is using a service like Connected (http://www.backupmystuff.com). While this can be a very slow process over a dial-up connection, especially the first time, when there is the most new data to store, those who have newer broadband connections such as cable or ADSL are likely to find it both convenient and fast, since they can set a daily schedule and forget about it. For mobile users, online backup stores may be less convenient if you have to pay hotel rates for the call to your ISP, but at least the backups are accessible from anywhere.

To use an online backup service, you begin by downloading their software and installing it on your computer. The software then backs up all the data you specify, up to everything on your system, to the company's servers.

Thereafter, you tell the software how often you want your system backed up, and it handles the whole thing automatically. You pay by the month. For an extra fee, most sites will also send you a CD copy of your data. Security on the site is handled by encrypting your data before it leaves your machine, so that it can't be read by unauthorized people. Most sites try to cut down on the amount of time it takes to transmit the data by using compression and techniques that check for changed files and copy only the changes.

For most consumers this sort of service is probably over-kill. But for small businesses, especially those run from home by sole traders, it can be invaluable, as they rarely have the funding for spare machines with complete copies of their systems or trained administrators. In the worst possible case – a burglary or a fire in which all the equipment is stolen or destroyed – an across-the-Internet backup can make the difference between staying in business or going bust. Just buy a new machine and restore the data. It cannot be said too often: the value of a computer is trivial compared to the value of the data on it. Computers are easily replaceable with one just as good or better as another. Data, when lost, is gone for ever.

Backup services
@Backup (http://www.backup.com): prices begin at $99/year for 100Mb total storage space. A 30-day free trial is available. Windows only. The service maintains copies of common software, so that backing up your software means only saving your personal configuration.

BackJack (http://www.backjack.com/): Mac-based backup service. Prices start at $93.50 a year with additional charges for storage above 40Mb.

Connected (http://www.backupmystuff.com): prices start at $6.95 a month for up to 100Mb of data. The free trial gives you 30 days or 100Mb, whichever limit you reach first. Windows only. The service maintains copies of common software, so that backing up your software means only saving your personal configuration.

Driveway (http://www.driveway.com): requires no special software, just a Web browser. Your Driveway account appears as a folder on your desktop, and backing up files is a matter of dragging them across and dropping them on the icon. Works on any system that Netscape or Internet Explorer supports (in other words, almost all, via Netscape). The first 25Mb is free; above that, users pay $29.95 for three months for 100Mb.

BADMINTON

See under **Sports**.

BANKING

The first point about Internet banking is that within the next
few years every bank will be offering Internet access to its
accounts and selling the full range of financial products,
from insurance to mortgages, online. The only reason to
open an account with an Internet bank, therefore, is if you
think that its service has something special to offer. If you
already have an account with a bank you're happy with, it
may make more sense to wait for your existing bank to add
Internet access than to go through all the hassle of changing
it now.

For most people, the big draw for the cutely named
Internet outfits – Cahoot (http://www.cahoot.co.uk), Smile
(http://www.smile.co.uk) or Egg (http://www.egg.com) – is
competitive pricing. To attract customers to their fledgling
services, these companies are typically paying higher
interest rates on savings accounts and ISAs, and charging
lower ones on overdrafts, credit card balances and mortgages. Halifax's Intelligent Finance (http://www.if.co.uk),
Cahoot (backed by Abbey National), Egg (Prudential), and
Smile (the Cooperative Bank) are all Internet-only arms of
physical-world banks. The leading Internet bank, however,
is none of those above, but is Barclay's, with 1.2 million
accounts as of October 2000. Second in the running is Egg,
the first to be launched out of all the Internet banks. Oddly
enough, First Direct, which pioneered telephone banking,
has yet to launch a really good Internet service.

Exactly what services these banks offer and at what rates

varies. Each is adding services as fast as it can in order to stay competitive. However, the general consensus is that the Internet-only banks, particularly the ones that, like Egg, have been floated independently on the stock exchange, are going to have to adjust their rates toward those of the high-street banks if they are to make a profit and stay solvent. As shareholders become more demanding of Internet stocks, expect today's pricing advantage to diminish. When that time comes, what will matter is service: how good the bank is at responding to queries and correcting errors, what range of financial products it offers and what extra fees it tacks on to your account.

Shopping around for an online bank account is just like shopping around for a physical-world one. If you're considering opening a new or online account, the most obvious thing to do first is look at the comparative interest rate tables published in the newspapers. Also take a look at the comparative ratings on Gomez (http://www.uk.gomez. com), which updates its ratings regularly and uses a set of criteria that include ease of use, customer satisfaction, on-site resources and ongoing services as well as overall cost. Gomez's ratings also attempt to take into account different levels of Internet expertise and types of banking, so that a first-time Internet banker will get a different list than a long-term saver. As always, you should also explore the site and see how comfortable you are with it before proceeding. Smile, for example, uses a lot of the Flash plug-in (though there is a Flash-free version), and will load very slowly for most people (see **Plug-ins**).

Of course the big question is security. No one wants to

risk putting their money into a bank account that's vulnerable to hackers. This sort of fear was fed by high-profile incidents in 2000. Barclay's Bank, for example, had to rejig its Web site when customers logging in were able to see details of the last customers' accounts. Similarly, Egg got a lot of bad publicity when several men were accused of attempting to defraud its systems. Both these cases, while alarming, were in fact not particularly dangerous. In the Barclay's case, a software fix solved the problem, and while it is of course worrying to think that someone has read your bank account details, that is far less of a danger than a stranger being able to manipulate your account and divert your funds. In Egg's case, security experts say that the type of fraud attempted – submitting multiple mortgage applications – could just as well have been on paper, and the issue was nothing to do with the Internet. It's important not to confuse the security of the bank's own internal systems with the security of the Web interface that gives you access to your account. (See also **Security**.)

Nonetheless, more than any other Internet application, you should be extremely careful to guard the security of your accounts. Someone gaining access to your credit card account, for example, will have all the information needed to impersonate you and put through fraudulent charges, just as someone gaining access to your brokerage account could put through transactions in your name. The banks are extremely conscious of the risks, and have designed their security systems accordingly.

Most of the security you'll find on these accounts is the same mix you'll find on ecommerce sites: encryption to protect your confidential information in transit between your browser and the site itself and password-restricted access. However, like any security system, one of the most important components is the users. You must guard the user ID and password to your Internet bank acount as carefully as you guard your cheque book, Switch/ATM card or credit card now. Again, the biggest risk of compromised security is not that someone can read your information, as dismaying as that is, but that they can put through transactions on your account and there will be no way for the bank to discern that the transactions did not come from you. If you have any reason to suspect that the security of your account has been compromised, you must contact your bank immediately. In addition, before opening any online account, you should read the terms and conditions and all the help files on the site very carefully.

Having said all this, there is no denying that Internet bank accounts offer a lot of convenience. You can check your bank or credit card balance, review recent transactions, pay bills, and even apply for loans without worrying about what time of day it is.

The Barclaycard site (http://www.barclaycard.co.uk) is a good example of how these accounts work. If you're a Barclaycard holder, you ask the site for a user ID (an unmemorable number) and select a six-digit PIN. Like an ecommerce site, the Barclaycard site will offer to 'remember' your ID number (which you should write down in case this memory fails at some point); unlike an ecommerce site, the Barclaycard site raises the security level by insisting you enter your PIN each time you want access. Once you're logged in, you click to see the most recent statement or transactions you've put through, and you can even pay your bill online with your Switch card – convenient if you're travelling and getting uncomfortably near your credit limit.

Final security tips: remember to log out correctly when you've finished using the site. If you access a bank or other financial account from a terminal in a public location (such as an Internet café) make sure no one's reading what you type over your shoulder as you enter your user ID and password. Also, if you've been accessing your account from public locations or from abroad, it wouldn't hurt to change your password when you get home.

(See also **Investment**, **Personal Finance** and **Security**.)

BARGAIN HUNTING

One of the things Web sites can do is compare prices with great efficiency. Not all shopping sites like you to do this, however, so a number of them block this type of access. But even so, you can save a lot of time by letting comparison sites do your research for you.

One place to start is My Taxi (http://www.mytaxi.co.uk), a shopping directory and comparison shopper combined. A search on My Taxi will return a list of merchants stocking the item and also comparative prices. You will still have to check carefully to compare shipping costs, but it can be a big help. For a book-specific price comparison search that does include shipping charges to the UK, try Add All (http:

//www.addall.com). For DVDs, use DVD Price Search (http: //www.dvdpricesearch.com), but before searching remember to click on the Preferences tab and set your country to Great Britain. Then, when you search on a title or portion thereof, the results will include the top ten best prices from the online shops the site covers, plus shipping and handling to the UK, along with an idea of how long delivery will take. Doubtless as time goes on and other categories of goods increase in popularity on the Net there will be more of these things.

For US stuff, there are two really excellent sites. One is My Simon (http://www.mysimon.com), which is owned by the news service C | Net and searches across a really large range of shops for all kinds of items. Useful as much to find out where something is sold as to compare prices, My Simon is impressively good. Unfortunately, it lacks a UK-specific site, though Bravo Nestor (http://www.bravonestor.com) has licensed My Simon's technology and opened French and German ones and plans to open up in the UK (the site may be available by the time you read this). It's also a pity that Yahoo! (http://shopping.yahoo.co.uk), whose shopping portal searches across its range of partner shops, isn't bigger, but the UK range of partner stores is tiny (see **Yahoo! and Other Portals**). Price and source searching works great on the US side (http://www.shopping.yahoo.com), but unfortunately the range of partners on the UK service is too small to give much of a choice.

BETTING

Gambling (see also **Games**) is, of course, one of the most regulated industries offline. Every national and local government likes to set its own rules about who may gamble within their jurisdictions. Nonetheless, online gambling is growing fast. Traditional betting shops, like William Hill (http://www.willhill.com), are moving online quickly, taking advantage of the Web's international reach to offer tax-free betting.

William Hill's site has several good ideas. For one thing, you can try out the system by placing bets without logging in – those don't get charged to your account, so they're simply practice. Once you know you want to proceed, you join up by filling out the registration form and place funds in your account using a credit card or Switch card, or by sending a cheque or arranging a wire transfer. You can start betting as soon as the funds clear, which in the case of credit card and Switch payments means more or less immediately (see **Payments**). The site accepts bets on all the popular British sports plus some American sports such as football, basketball and ice hockey; you can even bet on golf or special events such as the US presidential election or who will be voted the British sports personality of the year. Losses are debited automatically. Winnings are paid into your account, and can be extracted either as a credit to the card you used to set up the account or paid by cheque or wire.

The range is a bit smaller at Ladbrokes' Bet.co.uk (http://

www.bet.co.uk), limited to football, golf, and horses. On the other hand, you get special features like Sir Peter O'Sullevan, who was the voice of the Grand National for fifty years. Although he retired from racing commentary in 1997, Ladbrokes persuaded him to do an Internet broadcast for the 2000 National. Oddly, Ladbrokes' site closes between midnight and 9 a.m. every day; apparently they haven't quite realized that the Internet never sleeps.

Betting across the Internet is likely to appeal to a different crowd than those betting in shops; it's ideal for people who feel like idiots for not knowing the right betting terms (the William Hill site has a helpful explanation of types of bets). Even though betting online isn't actually anonymous (after all, they have to have your real name and address), it feels more private and intimate to place a bet without having to run the gamut of a human bookie. Internet-based betting seems to appeal more to women, for example, who may feel uncomfortable in betting shops, traditionally all-male precincts.

BIRDWATCHING

Anyone who goes out birdwatching is probably going to want a book they can take with them. But if you're trying to find out more about the birds nesting in your garden, *Birds of Britain* magazine offers an online guide (http://www.birdsofbritain.co.uk/index.htm). The site runs a monthly mystery bird quiz and various features. The one disappointment is that there's no way of searching on the characteristics of the bird you just saw to find out what it is.

The Life of Birds (http://www.pbs.org/lifeofbirds/) is the site that accompanies the US broadcast of the David Attenborough television programme of the same name made by the BBC. PBS did a good job. There is material intended for teachers to use in classes, and multimedia essays cover topics such as brains, evolution and birdsong, as well as some practical advice about interpreting whether one bird is trying to attract or repel another. The one problem is that the site can be very slow to load.

If you want to hear some of those songs, check out the Wildlife Sound Holdings at the British National Library of Sound (http://www.bl.uk/collections/sound-archive/wildex. html) – plans are to make a selection of the library's collection of bird and animal sounds available on the site. In the meantime, some bird songs – although this requires Java – are available at Cornell University's Ornithology Lab's site (http://www.ornith.cornell.edu/index.html).

For more, see the terrific list of ornithology resources at NetVet (http://netvet.wustl.edu/birds.htm).

BOOKMARKS

When you're talking about the Web, a bookmark is a saved Web address – and when you look at the length of some Web addresses you can see why you would need the computer to save them. In techspeak, Web addresses are called URLs, for 'uniform resource locator', and although the intention was to give every site an easily memorable name, the size and complexity of commercial Web sites, along with the necessity of tracking individual shopping sessions, have made many URLs almost as long as a garden hose (the *Electronic Telegraph* being one of the worst offenders). The upshot is that any time you land on a page full of information you actually want to be able to find again, the safest thing to do is to save the address inside your Web browser or hit CTRL-D in both Netscape and recent versions of Internet Explorer, even though Internet Explorer calls bookmarks 'favorites').

Organizing bookmarks is one of those housekeeping chores that isn't any fun, but makes life a lot easier. In Netscape, your bookmarks are saved into a Web page called BOOKMARK.HTM, and it's easy enough to open that file as a page in the Composer and organize them into folders and arrange them so the most frequently used ones appear at the top. In Internet Explorer, the 'favorites' are stored inside the program, making it difficult to keep backup copies of the page, important as you get more and more dependent on that list of carefully saved addresses. To extract your bookmarks from Internet Explorer, you'll need to download and run FAVTOOL.EXE (http://www. microsoft.com/msdownload/ieplatform/favtool/favtool. asp), a little program Microsoft has created for the purpose. You can, of course, rearrange them into folders and put the most commonly used ones at the top without extracting them, and you should: it makes finding your favourite sites so much easier.

One alternative, especially helpful if you're going to be on the road and accessing the Net from a café, is to store the bookmarks online using a service like Backflip (see below). There are several advantages to this besides making sure that you have a safety copy. One is that you can access the bookmarks from anywhere; if you work at home, on the road and in the office, this can be a great time-saver. Another, however, is that you can both keep your bookmarks private if you share a computer and share them with friends. Yes, you could do that by putting up the list of sites on your Web page – and, in fact, many of the earliest Web pages were nothing more than lists like that – but not all bookmarks these days should be public. You shouldn't, for example, give public access to URLs that encode your user ID and password to give you quick access to your account on a site, and of course there may be sites you visit regularly that you don't want the whole world to know about. Backflip lets you save all your bookmarks online in organized folders, and choose whether to make those folders available and specify to whom. You can, for example, let your boss see the links to your favourite research sites while keeping hidden the folder that houses the links to the recruitment sites. Other such services tend to be variations on the same theme.

Additional sites

Backflip (http://www.backflip.com): creates your own personal search engine and directory; imports bookmarks from your Web browser and lets you create multiple folders, which you can share or keep private on an individual basis.

A link you add to your toolbar makes it easy to save new items to your Backflip pages. Also has a wireless service.

Blink (http://www.blink.com): imports bookmarks from Internet Explorer and/or Netscape, and gives you a button for your browser toolbar that you click on to store future bookmarks. Free, supported by sponsors; clicking on links the service supplies gets you BlinkReward points that can be used for gift certificates or donated to charities like the HungerSite.

Favorites Anywhere (http://www.favoritesanywhere.com): 'the Web site that remembers all your Web sites'. Store and manage bookmarks from any computer. Free.

My Bookmarks (http://www.mybookmarks.com): can import and organize all your bookmarks from Internet Explorer, Netscape and AOL 'Favorite Places'. Free. And the number one most commonly stored bookmark, according to the site's Top 20 list is: Real Audio (http://www.real.com).

Web Address Book (http://www.webaddressbook.com): stores bookmarks, but also offers free email, streamlined email retrieval from other (POP3) services, and a host of personal information manager services such as calendaring, reminders, and storage for information on companies you do business with as well as files. Free for individuals; for businesses prices start at $1 per month per user.

BOOKS

The last thing anyone expected when the World Wide Web was invented was that it would be used to sell physical books: big, heavy, physical books. What everyone thought would be the 'killer application' was electronic books. Five years after Amazon.com opened up its site to massive scepticism, physical books are selling in mass numbers, but electronic books are still trying to find an audience, slowed in deployment by incompatible, competing formats, panic on the part of copyright owners and electronic reader designs that are still far less versatile than a traditional paperback and much harder on the eyes.

Buying books online, however, is popular for a number of reasons. No physical-world store carries every title, so book buyers spend large amounts of time searching for the books they want and waiting for special orders to arrive. Books are duty-free just about everywhere in the world. Books are heavy, and a nuisance to carry home in large quantities. They are not easily damaged in transit. Finally, books are sturdy commodity products: you don't need to squeeze the book to tell if it's ripe or examine the print quality. The exception, collectors who want to make absolutely sure they have the first printing of the first edition with a perfect dust jacket, are a relatively small subset of the book-buying population.

All these things are even more true of used books, which are even harder and more time-consuming to locate. The small, independent stores that specialize in second-hand books are even more limited by physical constraints as to what they can keep in stock at any given time. One of the best developments for book collectors, therefore, has been the arrival of aggregating sites that search the stock of thousands of small bookstores and act as a broker between them and individual buyers. True, searching an online data-base does not give the same pleasure as serendipitously finding a long-lost book from your childhood on the shelves of a book dealer in some distant holiday town – but your purchases still support small independents, and you get the book a lot sooner. The one thing lacking in online second-hand bookstores is information about the books' contents, rather than just their physical condition. Doubtless this will become easier as time goes on.

Retail booksellers

Alphabetstreet (http://www.alphabetstreet.co.uk): books, and also, through related sites, DVDs, videos, games and an exchange service. Awards loyalty points for reviewing titles on the site.

Amazon UK (http://www.amazon.co.uk): Amazon.com's UK operation began life as one of two competing British online bookstores, Bookpages. Currently sells books, CDs, videos, DVDs, and also plays host to a range of small shops and private auctions. Amazon.com (http://www.amazon.com) is the larger US equivalent, and besides the above items it also sells games, consumer electronics, tools, kitchen supplies, and patio furniture, and is even experimenting with selling cars. Amazon.com offers an out-of-print search service, but although it does sometimes find books, the general recommendation is not to buy second-hand books through Amazon. The company sources them from the same bookshops you have access to via the second-hand sites listed below, and, naturally enough, adds a surcharge to cover its costs. It is therefore considerably cheaper for you to do your own searching. Amazon's big claim to fame – aside from the comprehensiveness of its range – is its customer service, which is generally superb.

W.H. Smith (http://www.bookshop.co.uk): the first British online bookstore, the Internet Bookshop, got bought up by W.H. Smith. Comprehensive database of books in print. Attempting to copy Amazon with features such as author comments, user reviews and the like. If you care about the privacy of your customer data, however, W.H. Smith's being a UK company should guarantee you protection consistent with European data protection law.

Second-hand books

Alibris (http://www.alibris.com): single search engine for thousands of bookshops across the US. The site handles all payments; books are shipped directly from the individual shops.

Bibliofind (http://www.bibliofind.com): single search engine for thousands of booksellers worldwide; the site estimates it indexes some 20 million used books and periodicals. No search service, but the site lets you post a want list of up to ten titles, which will get you email notification if the book you're looking for pops into Bibliofind's database. Bibliofind does not handle payments; it merely sends your order on to the supplying bookseller, so read the information the bookseller supplies carefully to make sure you can comply with its terms. Some smaller US booksellers may, for example, insist on payment in US dollars.

Powells (http://www.powells.com): ask any book lover who's ever been to Portland, Oregon (and a lot who haven't), and they will tell you about Powell's. The size of a city block and four or five stories high, Powell's sells both used and new books and is the kind of place no one ever manages to get all the way through. Powell's online store indexes the entire stock of the physical store, features staff picks and a 'rare book room', and offers good prices with the satisfaction of knowing you're buying from an independent bookseller instead of a chain. The kind of bookstore, in other words, that you always wanted to live near: and now you do.

Print and Used Book Metalinks (http://milton.mse.jhu.edu/library/opbooksnew.html): helpful set of links to useful bibliographic sites including the Library of Congress, a number of additional search sites not mentioned above, sources for foreign language out-of-print books, tips on searching and more.

Electronic books

253 (http://www.ryman-novel.com): Geoff Ryman's interactive Web novel was one of the first of its kind. You may have seen the print remix as released by HarperCollins. This is the original.

Project Gutenberg (http://promo.net/pg/): library of digitized classics, all cleared for distribution and intended to make these books universally accessible and readable. There is a search engine on the site for the project's existing titles, which are stored in mirror archives all over the world. For copyright reasons, the project is limited to books published before about 1923; the collection includes works from Dante, Sir Arthur Conan Doyle, Edgar Rice Burroughs, Edgar Allan Poe, Lewis Carroll and Shakespeare, as well as thousands of others. The project is constantly looking for volunteers and donations to help add classics to the growing collection.

Stephen King (http://www.stephenking.com): Stephen King made news in mid-2000 when he announced that he would try an experiment in online publishing. The plan: he would publish a section of a new novel called *The Plant* at more or less monthly intervals, asking $1 to $2 in payment for each section, on the 'honour system'. As long as 75 per cent of downloaders paid for the downloads, he would keep writing. King's quota was reached, at least for the early sections, but the experiment proved only that if you're already a big name you can get some people to pay for your stuff on the Web. King wound up cancelling the experiment after a few instalments.

BOWLS

See under **Sports**.

BOXING

See under **Sports**.

BROWSING TIPS

A large part of your online use will be browsing the Web –
that is, looking at information on pages placed on computers
all over the world for everyone to see. The idea is simple:
you click on a highlighted link and it takes you to a page
that's related to the one you're looking at. But the reality is
less simple, because to browse the Web you must use
software known as a Web browser and this software doesn't
always behave in the way you would like or expect. What
follows are some suggestions for smoothing your path
around the Web.

General customizing

Whenever you install new software – especially Web browser
or email packages – take a little time to go methodically
through all the customization options, these days often
called Preferences. In Netscape, these are accessible from the
Edit menu; in Internet Explorer you'll find them listed as
Internet Options on the Tools menu. Some of the security
options are quite technical, and basically if you don't understand a setting you probably shouldn't change it. But you
can specify content filters and ratings to block out material

you might find offensive, as well as default background colours, link styles and fonts, and generally make your browsing experience more comfortable.

Setting the home page

A lot of people don't realize that the page that loads automatically when they open their Web browser doesn't have to do that. Almost any Web browser you're likely to encounter will have a 'Home' button which, when you click on it, will always take you to a preset, familiar page; if a page loads automatically when you open the browser, this is usually the one, though they can be different pages. The people who make Web browsers typically set the home page to one they've created for the purpose that advertises their companies and may also include news headlines, discussion forums, a search function, and other useful elements for someone just getting started. In some cases, your ISP will set the default to load its own front page.

This kind of thing can be annoying, particularly if you're in a hurry to get on with doing something on the Web and the browser insists on painfully loading its preset home page. You do not have to let it do this, however. In Netscape, click on Preferences on the Edit menu; in Internet Explorer, look for Options on the Tools menu and pick the Navigation tab. Either way, you can set your home page to anything you want – your own page if you have one, a search engine, the weather report, a page you particularly like, or no page at all. To do this, either delete the Web address showing in the dialog box or replace it with the one of your choice by typing the URL you want into the box and clicking OK to save the change. One possibility is the Web address for the page designed for this book (visit the Connected section of telegraph.co.uk).

My own browser loads a blank page, and my home page is set to an extra page of bookmarks from an old browser installation.

Stop animations

If there's one thing that's more annoying than any other, it's having something blink or flash at you while you're trying to read a news story filled with detail. You can make it stop. In Netscape, you stop them on the fly by hitting ALT-V (to bring up the View menu) and A (to stop them). In Internet Explorer, you turn them off permanently by going to Tools I Internet Options I Advanced and clearing one or more of the boxes for playing animations, video or sounds. Ahhhh.

Get rid of pop-up windows

Unfortunately, you're stuck with those unless you install extra software to block them. The usual choice is AdSubtract (formerly Intermute) (http://www.adsubtract.com), which lets you set a variety of options to free yourself of online advertising and enhance **Privacy** (see entry). Or try Adfilter (http://www.adfilter.com).

Find text within a page

You've done your search and you've loaded a page that's supposed to contain the information you want, but the page is miles long and densely packed with text. Hit CTRL-F in

Netscape or Internet Explorer and type the word you're looking for in the box and hit Enter. You'll be taken right to it, if it's there. In Netscape hit F3 to find the next occurrence, if any.

BUSINESS ONLINE
(Setting One Up)

Setting up a business online, like most things, can be as simple or as complicated as you like. In its simplest form, all you need is a basic Web page (see **Web Page, Make Your Own**), a description of the products or services you sell, and a phone number. If you don't believe me, take a look at LateSail (http://www.latesail.com) or Gazetteer (http://www.gazetteer.co.uk). Both these sites are minimalist all-text affairs, and to buy anything from them you have to make a phone call. But the sites' owners make a profit because the overheads are low and the products they're selling – last-minute yacht charters and demographic data, respectively – require some personal service. The yachts, for example, are typically owned by a guy sitting in a Greek taverna with a pencil and paper, not by jet-setting business folks with WAP phones and satellite hook-ups. Although most businesses setting up online will need online payment and ordering facilities, these sites still serve as a reminder that it is pointless to use more technology than you need.

That said, it's undeniably true that online customers

generally write off businesses that expect them to phone or fax orders in; the general feeling is that if Web users wanted to shop that way they'd be browsing mail order catalogues, not Web sites. Accordingly, the average business setting up online will need at least some form of payment mechanism (see **Payment**) and at least one email address that is monitored daily – not weekly or when Sue in accounting gets around to it, but daily. The importance of this cannot be overstressed: email users are impatient, and they generally believe that if they haven't had an answer in 24 hours the business is either defunct or too deficient in Net-savvy to do business with. This prejudice is often, though not always, correct.

Setting up your Web site

Think carefully about who your target audience is. Don't deploy fancy-looking technology just because it looks cool. In general, you should avoid Flash and Shockwave introductions (hint: any time you have to put a button on your front page that says 'Skip intro' you are almost certainly doing something wrong); music or other noise (think of users logging in from libraries or crowded offices); useless pages that do no more than display a company logo and invite visitors to click on a button to 'Enter' the site; and pop-up windows that for all you know will stress your visitor's computer until it crashes. Use Java and scrolling news headlines only if they're genuinely needed (a better option is to use text headlines and let users click if they want a Java scroll, as Java really slows down some computers), and put the link to your product and price list – or the search window that leads to them – right up front on the site. Also – and this should go without saying but apparently doesn't – include your company address, contact numbers, and contact email addresses in a prominent and easily findable location. Don't worry: 100 million Web users will not all phone you. But would you buy from someone who wouldn't even tell you what city they were in?

Do make sure that your Web site conforms to the accessibility guidelines published by the W3 Consortium (http://www.w3.org/WAI/), as some of your customers may be using text-to-speech programs or other aids to assist them. Ensure that it runs correctly on both Internet Explorer and Netscape, and, if possible, Opera and other minority browsers. Do include a privacy policy to tell customers what you will do with transaction and other data they may leave on the site. If it's relevant, specify your delivery area up front: it is extremely annoying to wade through a site for 45 minutes constructing an order only to find out at the last minute that it only delivers to France, or the US, or outside the M25. Do provide an information file to tell your customers how you handle common problems such as returns, queries and technical support, as well as the details of any guarantees or shipping fees.

If you are having your Web site put together by an outside developer, do not let the developer demonstrate the site for you, or at least, not at first. Get the developer to put the Web site up in a secure location and assign the least Web-savvy person in your firm to log on to it using a standard dial-up account and try to complete a transaction. Time how long it takes pages to load and how long it takes the transaction to complete. Studies show that people get frustrated on the Web within about 80 seconds, and that some 72 per cent of transactions are abandoned partway through. If your non-Nethead staffer has trouble working out how to use the site, the design of the site may not work for your customers either. Bear in mind that Web site design has more in common with software design than anything else – and remember how hard most software is to learn and use.

If you are writing your own Web page (see **Web Page, Make Your Own**) make sure to test the page as above. Also have it proofread for typos and spelling errors by someone with an eye for the written word, and make sure you check all links regularly and fix any that are broken. Finally, keep the page up to date and make it plain that you are doing so – by putting a date on news, for example.

One of the big questions facing many businesses online is how to accept payment for goods and services. For all but the smallest businesses, the answer is likely to be credit cards and possibly Switch. The standard, SSL (for secure sockets layer, a secure channel facility built into Web servers and browsers), is built into many ecommerce software packages that set up basic stores.

For sole traders, individuals selling goods via services like eBay, and other tiny businesses a number of payment schemes have sprung up on the Web to make life easier. Probably the best-known is PayPal (http://www.paypal. com, but don't be surprised if your browser is redirected to www.x.com, Paypal's owner), which handles credit card transactions on behalf of small businesses, accepting payments from buyers and aggregating and holding them in accounts for sellers. For consumers, the service is free; businesses pay 1.9 per cent on payments received. A similar payment scheme, known as Billpoint, is built into eBay.

(See also **Payment**.)

Registering a domain name

Most times, a business should register a domain name to give it a distinctive identity on the Net – the 'telegraph' part of telegraph.co.uk or telegraph.com is the name that gets registered. Domain names are designed hierarchically, to make them easy for computers to sort and humans to understand. The right-most bit, .uk or .com, is the broadest hierarchy, known as the top-level domain. Many people think that because .com is the best-known top-level domain it's the right one to register in, but think carefully before you proceed. If your business is limited to the UK or is strongly British in flavour – for example, a property site that only covers the UK – you will be better off reflecting that by registering in .uk. Conversely, if you are a genuinely international business, registering in .com just makes sense.

The joker in the pack is that the organization that oversees the domain name system, the Internet Corporation for Assigned Names and Numbers (ICANN), approved seven new top-level domains in late 2000. These have a great deal of bureaucracy to go through before they are actually created, but the idea is that you will have a much better chance of getting a name you like.

Lawyers often advise businesses to check carefully for trademark conflicts before registering a name and beginning to market it. The Net traditionally has worked on a first-come, first-served basis. However, it is still true that some large companies lack a sense of humour when they discover conflicts. Under ICANN's new system, this type of dispute will go to arbitration, and the risk is that the arbitrator may tend to favour large businesses (one of the authorized arbitrators is the World Intellectual Property Organization).

In general, try to pick a domain name that reflects your business. However, don't get too obsessive about this: it's more important that your site pops up in relevant searches (see **Search Engines**) and is included on all your company information as part of your marketing efforts than it is that your site has an obvious name.

Marketing your site

Once your site has been set up, you will need to tell people about it so they can find it. Since the most important route by which many people will find your site is searching, you should make sure your site is registered with the main ones (see **Search Engines**). Of course, they may find it anyway, but you can greatly assist this process by going to the main engines and filling out the form for adding a link. This should ensure the search engine will index your pages.

You can also weight your page so that it's more likely to pop up on relevant searches by using what are known as 'metatags'. These are part of HTML, the coding used to write Web pages, that specify keywords for the search engines to relate to your page, as well as an author's name and a description of the page for a search engine to use when it displays the page as part of a list of hits. The

Search Engine Watch site has a good explanation of how to use these (http://searchenginewatch.com/webmasters/meta.html).

In addition, you should include your site's address on all marketing materials, company stationery and products, and in all advertising. Finally, you can advertise your site by buying banner space on related sites or by signing up affiliates who will get a tiny commission in return for directing sales your way (this technique has been very successful for both Amazon and CD Now).

C

CARS

Buying a car online seems a crazy thing to do: after all, since this is the second most expensive purchase a family makes after a house, surely you want to drive it and see it before buying?

True, but the automobile industry is plagued by high prices and dubious salesmanship; the perfect situation to make online sales look appealing. Vauxhall's (http://www.vauxhall.co.uk) answer to the conundrum is to display cars and information on its site, but to direct Internet users to their nearest dealer when it comes time to close a sale. In fact, Vauxhall was the first UK car manufacturer to sell cars online, and the company is surprised so few others have followed suit. Most, like Nissan (http://www.nissan.co.uk) or Toyota (http://www.toyota.co.uk), settle for the equivalent of fancy brochures and price lists.

Autobytel (http://www.autobytel.co.uk), by contrast, seeks to change the motor industry by making it easy to buy a car online. Autobytel doesn't actually sell you the car; it matches you with a supplier. Essentially, you pick a car, new or used, and the dealer makes you an offer including price, specification and availability. If you accept the offer, you make a partial payment, usually by credit card. The site then orders the car, and contacts you to discuss how you will be paying for it; payment is due seven days before the car is expected to arrive. The savings can be substantial.

Buying for import

According to European Commission reports, the UK is the most expensive country in Europe in which to buy a new car, with prices running at a premium of as much as 20 per cent over countries within the Euro-zone. Why do it? The unification of Europe means you can buy a car in another country and bring it back without having to pay customs duty (though you will have to pay VAT). The expectation is that over time prices in Britain will drop as British car dealers find themselves competing with their cheaper counterparts in Europe. In the meantime, the Internet makes it a lot easier to buy a car from another country, both by making it easier to find the necessary information on how to proceed and by making it inexpensive to compare prices between countries and locate dealers who cater to international customers.

According to EU reports – you should check the most recent information on pan-European car pricing for yourself (http://europa.eu.int/comm/competition/car_sector/) as doubtless things will change over time – as of late 2000 the cheapest markets in Europe in which to buy a car were the Netherlands, Finland and Spain. Why? Because car manufacturers deliberately set their prices lower in those countries to offset higher tax rates, presuming that otherwise their cars would be too expensive. For UK citizens, however, those lower prices represent an opportunity.

Import information sites

Car importing into the UK from Europe (http://www. carimporting.co.uk): walks you through the entire process, from finding a dealer or broker to calculating prices, where to buy an extended warranty and get insurance, and even maps and information on travelling to the country. You still have to do the legwork yourself, but that's a whole lot easier when you can start with this much background.

HM Customs and Excise Notice 728, 'Motor vehicles, boats, aircraft: intra-EC movements by persons not registrable for VAT' (http://www.hmce.gov.uk/public/info/index.htm): the horse's mouth on the subject of VAT and duty payable on new motorized transports (NMTs) imported into the UK. Read carefully – and look for updates – before proceeding.

CELEBRITIES

Want to engage in a pointless and slightly malicious pastime? Go to the directory site Goto.com (http://www. goto.com) and compare celebrity rankings. Here you can see how much advertisers are willing to pay per search to come top of the list in celebrity searches. Drew Barrymore, for example, costs five cents, Natalie Portman, Pamela Anderson Lee (who certainly used to be the most downloaded babe on the Net), Jennifer Aniston, and Anna Kournikova (http://www.annak.org) cost seven cents each, as does Mel Gibson. Julia Roberts, the top Hollywood box-office star, costs a whopping fourteen cents, paid by BigShow DVD to advertise the DVD of *Erin Brockovich*. A penny got the UK reviews site ManyAGem (http://www.manyagem.co.uk) Nigella Lawson. (My publisher got me for free.) One can imagine celebrities checking their prices just as some authors bookmark the pages for their own books at Amazon.com, to watch their place in the sales rankings go up and down.

More fannishly, lots of celebrities set up their own Web pages, so it's perfectly reasonable to try the celebrity's name with .com after it and see what you get. Not all will be official sites – lots of fans set up sites that way, too. No one would, for example, mistake the anti-fan site at http://www.juliaroberts.com with its feature on 'Baby animals whose heads Julia Roberts has bitten off or eaten whole as snacks' for an official site. Your best bet is to search using the celebrity's name with the term 'official' if you're looking for the official site (see **Search Engines**). But often the fan sites are more interesting than the official ones, which can be very bland. One exception is Douglas Adams (http://www.h2g2.com), whose company runs, among other things, a site for individuals to collaborate on an online *Hitchhiker's Guide to the Galaxy* – not a celebrity site as we know it, but fun. Also worth looking at are the sites belonging to the Grateful Dead (http://www.gratefuldead.com), magicians Penn and Teller (http://www.pennandteller.com), and writer Stephen King (http://www.stephenking.com).

One thing you can certainly do is find sound samples of your favourite celebrities from movies and TV shows – you'll have to search for these, but there must be millions of short snippets out there (see **Search Engines**). Also take a look at Fandom (http://www.fandom.com), which is host to a lot of unofficial fan sites.

This is one area where looking for Usenet newsgroups is bound to pay dividends. Look for the celebrity's name in your newsgroup list. For more general celebrity news, try alt.gossip.celebrities. Also try searching eGroups (http://www.egroups.com).

CHARITIES

For a comprehensive list of UK charities, see the directory BUBL's page (http://www.bubl.ac.uk/uk/charities) – it links to everybody you could possibly want.

If you want to donate money, the Charities Aid Foundation, which operates accounts to channel donors' money to the charities of their choice, will take donations online (http://www.charitycard.org). The good side of doing it this way is that you can give anonymously – no follow-up begging letters! In addition, until April 2003 the government will kick in an extra 10 per cent for all donations made through a programme called Give As You Earn, in which your donations are deducted tax-free from your pay cheque. You can also donate stocks and shares, free of capital gains tax, to your CAF account.

Web charities
The three sites below all rely on sponsors to pay for the charity they offer when you click. They also have

ecommerce links that net them some revenue and sell T-shirts and other merchandise.

The Hunger Site (http://www.hungersite.org): click on the button to donate a cup of food.

The Kids' Aids Site (http://www.thekidsaidssite.com): click on the button to contribute 15 seconds of free care to children with AIDS.

The Rainforest Site (http://www.therainforestsite.org): click on the button to contribute to buying back and managing rain forest land.

CHILDREN

Like books for children, there are two kinds of children's Web sites – the ones kids like and the ones parents like. The ones parents like are often glitzy, cartoonish and sweet; the ones children like are often gross, crude and even edgy. One site both groups can probably agree on is the unofficial Harry Potter fan site (http://www.fandom.com/harrypotter/) – there's also an official site (http://www.scholastic.com/harrypotter/home.asp).

Alfy (http://www.alfy.com) is the kind of site to make parents feel reassured: it's intended to be 'the web portal for kids' and has both its own content and links to child-friendly external Web sites. The content written specially for the site includes word and number games, retro games

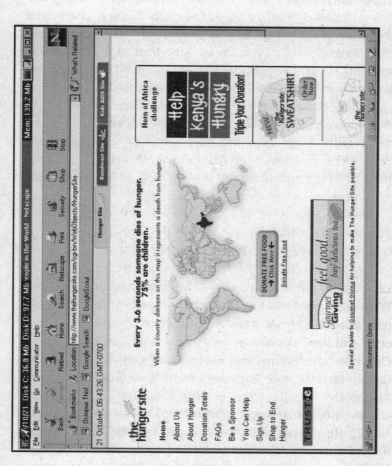

Figure 1. The Hunger Site.

such as Pac Man, a daily joke, riddles, news, stories, video clips and your own Alfy Web-based email. The home page has a Richard Scarry-style scene with cartoon characters doing different things; as you move your mouse over them the site reads out to you (in an American accent) what the area does, great for children who can't read yet. Click on the man in the spaceship and it takes you to space sites especially chosen for children's interest. There are warnings that indicate when children have strayed into the rest of the Web that say: 'You are now visiting a site outside of Alfy.' The problem with the site is that it's extremely graphic-heavy and therefore slow to load, at least the Flash version is.

Then there's Cadbury's children's site (http://www.yowie.co.uk), which has nothing to do with chocolate – for that you'll have to go to the company's main site (http://www.cadbury.co.uk) – but concentrates on teaching children about the natural world. Each environment (desert, waterways, wetlands, bushland, rainforest and woodland) has its own scene to explore. Hidden in the landscape are creatures that would live there. Find them, click and learn about their lives, what they eat and why they live in extreme conditions. The site requires the plug-in Shockwave (see **Plug-ins**).

Also fun for younger children is Dr Seuss's Seussville site (http://www.randomhouse.com/seussville/), where the idea is to entertain while teaching basic reading, writing, and maths skills. Purple Moon Place (http://www.purple-moon.com/cb/laslink/pm?stat+pm_place) is an outgrowth of a girls' games company now owned by Mattel and is aimed at girls without falling into stereotypes; girls are encouraged to collaborate on storytelling and the site's other features. Children who like *Star Wars* and its many outgrowths may also like The Force Net (http://www.theforce.net/), 'Your Daily Dose of *Star Wars*.' And the Virtual Petz site (http://www.petz.com) is hot with a lot of children.

On the other end, sites that adults probably won't like, but children probably will, try The Yuckiest site on the Internet (http://www.yucky.com), full of slightly gross games. Try whacking roaches with your mouse, or visit Worm World. There are two versions of the site, with or without Flash. Also in the adults-don't-look category is the South Park site (http://www.comedycentral.com/south-park/) and the many unofficial fan sites for the foul-mouthed cartoon show, where you can find songs, downloads, video clips and even whole shows, though you have to pay for these.

Of course, there are many sites on the Net that children can enjoy that aren't specifically aimed at children. In the end, your children will need to learn the same search techniques as everyone else and use them to find the sites that interest them (see **Search Engines).** Just like Pokémon cards or computer games, Web site and Internet facilities get passed from child to child by word of mouth. Any child can make his or her own Web page (see **Web Page, Make Your Own**), and you'll find that even homework-allergic children find themselves writing bits for each others' sites and spending hours with technical details they'd never touch if they had to learn about them in a school class.

Protecting your kids online

There is a great myth, promulgated by sensationalist stories in the media, that the Internet is massively unsafe for kids. It's not. Whatever damage may be done if a child comes across unpleasant material online is far less than can happen to them in the physical world. Nonetheless, it is possible for your child to run into trouble online by giving too much personal information to the wrong person or straying on to sites you'd rather he or she didn't see. There are ways you can protect against this.

The best safeguard you can have is a good, trusting relationship with your child. Ideally, your child should be able to come to you and ask about upsetting material s/he finds online, or tell you when an online relationship is beginning to spill over into the real world. Also, the more you yourself know about the Internet, the more accurately and helpfully you can answer your child's questions – something that looks horrible may in fact have a context that alters its apparent meaning. Also, the more you know the more you can suggest directions for your child's online use that you feel are appropriate to the child's age and development.

That said, some parents prefer to use filtering or blocking software – programs like Net Nanny, SafeSurf, SurfWatch, or CyberPatrol – which are supposed to block out inappropriate material. Be aware that these programs can be defeated by someone who is determined and technically knowledgeable, and also that they are secretive about their exact criteria for blocking sites, so they may include sites you wouldn't actually object to or that might even be useful for your child's homework. The Peacefire site (http://www.

peacefire.org), originally set up by an American high school student, goes into a lot of detail about each blocking program and its quirks. It's all worth reading before you make a decision on which program to buy and install. All these programs can be downloaded from their home pages. Some of these programs can be set to block a child from giving out personal information such as a home address and telephone number.

Parental filters are also built into online services such as CompuServe and AOL so that parents can feel comfortable letting their children use these services unattended. However – and this is a big however – one of the main features on AOL is real-time chat, and it's very difficult to control who your child might meet in those chat rooms or what the conversation will be like. Just as you tell your child not to accept gifts or rides from strangers, you need to tell your child not to give out personal details to or arrange meetings with people they meet online without talking to you about it first. Your children should also understand that if a conversation makes them uncomfortable they do not have to continue it. Most chat programs – ICQ, AOL's chat rooms, IRC – have ways you can log a conversation to read over later, and if the conversation is saved you can go through it with your child and discuss what made him or her uncomfortable and why.

Most search engines now also have a parental filter that will block offensive language and adult sites, and you can turn this on when you search or, often, set it permanently so it will always be used when someone searches from your machine.

In 1998, the US passed a law called the Child Online Protection Act, which limits what information sites may keep about children under 13. The upshot is you will see many US sites that will no longer allow a child under 13 to register without parental consent.

Finally, if you see illegal material – not offensive, but actually illegal, such as child pornography – you should report it to the Internet Watch Foundation (http://www.iwf.org.uk), a government-endorsed body that will inspect the material and, if it is actually illegal, report it to the police and direct UK-based ISPs to remove it from their servers. But the Internet is an international network, and the UK has no control over what may be hosted elsewhere in the world. The IWF also publishes a Safe Surfing Guide (http://www.iwf.org.uk/safe/index.htm), which you should read. However, keep some perspective: the IWF exists to highlight the dangers. On the vast majority of occasions the Internet is perfectly safe. However, like any other strange environment, you need to become familiar with it yourself before you can fully trust your judgement.

CHRISTMAS

Scoot is a good and useful UK directory all the time but at Christmas (http://christmas.scoot.co.uk/) it really comes into its own, with a Gift Finder, an advent calendar featuring Scoot's disaster-prone character Willie Make-it. Every day Willie is shown opening a present that somehow destroys him. On the same screen are links to shops and services relevant to Willie's present. Timing is usually one of the complicating factors in buying over the Internet to meet a deadline, so most of the big stores have included final dates for Christmas orders.

If your child wants to send email to Santa, the address is santa@northpole.com. The North Pole site itself (http://www.northpole.com) is full of Christmassy games, recipes, and chat.

CLIMBING

See under **Sports**.

CLOTHES

Clothes are supposed to be one of the few types of merchandise people are really willing to buy from mail-order catalogues in the UK. Everyone has different tastes in clothes, but if you like simple, sturdy, well-made stuff, two of the best catalogue retailers in the world have great Web sites: Land's End (http://www.landsend.co.uk and http://www.landsend.com) and LL Bean (http://www.llbean.com). Both have unlimited return policies – send something back at any time for any reason – and both have excellent customer service, great quality, consistent sizes and reasonable prices. I probably buy 90 per cent of my clothes from them.

Things get more complicated if your tastes are more exotic. Higher fashion clothes on the Net tend to be stocked by retailers with more graphics than sense. The departed Boo.com failed at least in part because it was horrible to use – you had to scroll sideways to look at items, and they were drawn, not photographed, so it was very difficult to discern their design or details like whether or not they had pockets. If you're used to the LL Bean and Land's End site, with their clean design, efficient search, real-time availability information, and good pictures, anything else is just too frustrating. Land's End's US site, a far more comprehensive and complex animal than its pale imitation UK one, lets you try clothes on an animated figure roughly proportioned to match your measurements, and one of the better uses of Java is that it lets you order men's shirts by picking fabrics, collar and cuff styles, and sizes from a series of charts, and then seeing how the finished shirt will look.

However. Eventually, the idea is that we will be able to send the results of a body scan off to a Web site and get back highly personalized clothes. Men can almost do this with Moda One to One (http://www.moda121.com), a site that sells custom-tailored Italian men's luxury suits and accessories at relatively reasonable prices. The site gives every customer a personal home page that stores customers' measurements and even provides a virtual mannequin on which to try out different combinations of suits, shirts, and ties. The site also gives fashion advice based on personal information you provide such as eye and hair colour and lifestyle.

Closer to home, back on the high-street fashion end, Marks and Spencer (http://www.marksandspencer.co.uk) has started selling clothes online, as well as flowers and gifts (though no food). It's a slow site, and gives little information about the items you're looking at beyond fabric content. A better site altogether is managed by Debenhams (http://www.debenhams.co.uk), which is much easier to use. If you want designer jeans at British prices, Diesel (http://www.diesel.co.uk) was one of the first to set up a site, and you can buy from it. The Gap site only sells inside the US, and Levis dropped its site in mid-2000.

Even people who are willing to buy clothes online baulk at shoes. Even so, there is a shoe portal (see **Yahoo! and Other Portals**) at ShoeWorld (http://www.shoeworld.co.uk). You have to be careful following the listings from this site, because half of them are American and they don't tell you which in advance. If what you want is athletic shoes, you will almost certainly have to either go offline or buy from the US at a probable shipping cost of about $30 – there just don't seem to be online athletic shoe retailers with any range of stock in the UK yet, at least not if your sport is tennis and you're female. Clarks (http://www.clarks.com), is even more frustrating, as it will happily show you pictures of its shoes, but refer you to a dealer if you want to buy any (in which case you may want to go back to LL Bean, which retails Clarks wallabees and desert boots). One of the exceptions to the British online shoe drought is Jones Bootmaker (http://www.jonesbootmaker.com), which lets you specify what you want (by sex, price and colour) and a huge range of shoes. But there again – and of course this is

the American influence speaking – there is so little information available. What does 'a very wearable height' mean
in terms of heels? What are 'fashion casual' shoes? Only an
expert knows for certain.

(See also **Fashion**).

COMICS

Like many things on the Net, comics are most easily
assessed if you're already an expert: the sites just assume
you know what you want and what you're buying. One of
the better sites is Page 45 (http://www.page45.couk.com),
which does make an effort to help by giving mini-reviews
of different writers and genres.

Other sites you might want to try include Books 'N'
Comics (http://www.booksncomics.co.uk/), which sports
Buffy the Vampire Slayer, *The Simpsons* and, of course,
the dreaded Pokémon on its primary listing, alongside
posters, graphic novels, comics, cards and figures. Comics
International (http://www.comics-international.com/Shops/
Comics_Shops_UK/comics_ shops_uk.html) has an exten-
sive list of comics shops worldwide, some online, most not.

For comics and cartoons actually online, of course you
can find Alex and Matt on the *Telegraph* site (http://www.
telegraph.co.uk), though you will have to register.

Of course, *the* outlet for cartoons in the US is *The New
Yorker*, and the magazine, which finally put its articles
online in early 2001 (http://www.newyorker.com), has set

up a site to capitalize on this. The Cartoon Bank (http://www. cartoonbank.com/) sells prints and reprints, licenses cartoons for commercial use, and even lets you send free cartoon eCards. Definitely worth a visit, if only just to browse. If you're feeling really rich, there's a site (http://www. markomics.com/list.html) that will sell you originals of some of these cartoons – but we're talking $2,600 for an original George Booth. Not that he isn't worth it.

Online strips

The Dilbert Zone (http://www.dilbert.com): today's comic strip depicting life in the bizarre world of the office cubicle, plus archives, online store, cursors and screensavers, and collaborative lists, for example, 'Top 273 biggest projects your boss assigned you but didn't tell you about.'

Lab Initio (http://www.linuxgrrls.org/~nick/): science-oriented weekly comic strip.

The Parking Lot Is Full (http://www.plif.com/): creatively bizarre cartoon series – somewhat the same feel as *The Far Side* – that began as a commentary on university life drawn by two students at the University of Waterloo in 1993 and continues now even though one of them lives in Korea and they collaborate electronically.

COMPUTERS

Possibly the least interesting thing on the Internet. Avoid.

For buying computers and/or parts online, the three online retailers that are generally the best regarded are Action (http://www.action.co.uk), MicroWarehouse (http://www.microwarehouse.co.uk), and DABS Direct (http://www.dabs.com). The Action site is a little cheaper than Micro-Warehouse; both helpfully indicate how many of an item they have in stock and/or when they would be able to ship so you can make an informed decision about whether or not to order. In personal experience, Action has delivered as promised with no trouble.

CONSUMER ISSUES

One of the biggest problems for newcomers to Web shopping is working out whom to trust. There are some standard guidelines – for example, you should look for the same affiliations online that guarantee businesses offline, such as ABTA or IATA bonding for travel agents. But beyond that, it's very difficult to judge the quality of a site's security or judge whether a business is going to be there a month from now when you need technical support (see also **Security**). For this reason, big names have an advantage online; you care less, for example, whether the computer supplier you buy from goes bust in six months if the computer you've bought is a Compaq or IBM and is backed up by a major company's warranty.

But only buying from the big names is a waste of a great opportunity: the Web is home to all kinds of niche and international businesses that you couldn't easily access before. One thing you can do when dealing with an unfamiliar name is try Epinions (http://www.epinions.com), which collects consumer opinions of products and services of all kinds. It is an American site, with no British analogue, but you can find opinions on almost anything.

Recognizing that people are taking greater risks in an unfamiliar setting, the Office of Fair Trading has set up a site (www.oft.gov.uk/html/shopping/index.html) specifically geared to offering online shoppers advice on choosing suppliers, conducting transactions and handling problems.

The site advises some common-sense guidelines: make sure you know where the company you're buying from is physically located; don't judge a company's bona fides by the flashiness of its Web site; ask around online (in, for example, discussion groups on a relevant topic – see **Argue**) for people's experiences in dealing with them. The most obvious piece of advice that they don't mention, however, is to assess the deal you're being offered using real-world perspective. If a market stall sells dirt-cheap Rolex watches, they are probably dodgy, so you wouldn't buy one. Apply the same rules to Web sites: if they look dubious, steer clear of them and go to a site with lots of dull small print that will guarantee your delivery and are as helpful as possible if things go wrong. For a really major purchase, try emailing the customer service line with a question to see how long it takes to get a response and whether that response actually answers your question. Alternatively, try a small purchase first and make sure you're happy with the service you receive (of course, this isn't always possible – you can't buy a bicycle to test a car dealer site).

Additional sites

National Association of Citizens Advice Bureaux (http://www.nacab.org.uk/): unfortunately, the CAB doesn't offer online advice, though you can look up your nearest office in its searcheable database. More interesting is the searchable collection of evidence reports, consultation submissions and legislative briefings that lay out the CAB's various social policies. Email them to volunteer for work.

Trading Standards Central (http://www.tradingstandards. gov.uk/): find your local office by typing in your postcode, look up the latest safety warnings and product recalls, and read all the advice leaflets. Good place to start if you're confused about your rights.

Trust UK (http://www.trustuk.org.uk): a government-endorsed non-profit organization whose logo appears on sites that you are supposed to be able to trust to protect your privacy, ensure your payments are secure, and deliver the goods or services you've ordered as agreed. This is, of course, not a complete solution, as many of the retailers you may want to buy from won't be located in the UK. Trust UK doesn't approve sites directly; instead, it authorizes other organizations (such as *Which?*) that in turn approve sites according to an ecommerce code of practice. The details of the code of practice are explained on the site.

Which? Online (http://www.which.net): much of the site is blocked off, requiring a subscription of £7.75 a month (after a 30-day free trial; you sign up online). However, each month the magazine publishes one free report on the site, and there's a nice daily news service that scans the twelve major national newspapers and posts brief snippets of all the consumer-oriented stories that appear. The site's shopping service and forums are members-only. For a consumer advocacy site, *Which?* doesn't practise what it ought to be preaching, as you can't read the terms and conditions before giving them all your personal details, and you have to actively cancel the free trial – by POST – if you decide you don't want to pay for a subscription. *Which?* also operates a logo scheme endorsing Web traders they believe are trustworthy.

COOKERY

It's hard to imagine what anyone could possibly want to cook that isn't in the Searchable Online Archive of Recipes (http://soar.berkeley.edu/recipes/). If you find anything, you can submit it for inclusion. We're talking a database that has not one but two recipes for spotted dick.

If you have a slightly more ghoulish turn of mind, of course you can try Bizarre Stuff (http://freeweb.pdq.net/headstrong/default.htm) – fun things to experiment with in the kitchen with a chemistry set. The Web site is remarkably slick, bearing in mind that it is run by Brian Carusella, who describes it as a 'warped semi-scientific cookbook of tricks, gimmicks and pointless experimentation'. Using the site is simple: you browse categories such as physics and optics, food ('mostly inedible') and electricity, to see what you can turn your hand to. The experiments range from the utterly useless (watching raisins dance in champagne) to interesting (making a Leyden jar) to making a motor. Other experiments can be learned in private and performed as party tricks, such as the burning sugar-cube trick and the illusion of having smoking fingers.

(See also **Food and Drink**.)

COPYRIGHT

The basic rule is: if you do not yourself own the copyright in a piece of intellectual property – song, movie, animation, graphic, text, software program, database – you shouldn't distribute it without the owner's permission. Certainly, you shouldn't distribute it for money.

Many people misunderstand copyright law and imagine that it's OK to distribute something as long as it has a copyright notice on it. Wrong! But their confusion is understandable, as the Internet is changing a lot of business models because of its reach and the ease of copying and distributing digital data (see **Finding and Reproducing Images** under **Art**).

Images pose a particular problem, because, as yet there is no standard licensing scheme to cover such uses, nor is there a standard licensing scheme to allow you to copy images off other Web pages for reproduction, either on the Web or in print. The exception, at least in common practice, is screen grabs of whole Web pages, which have, after all, been placed in public view. If the page is protected by a registration scheme, particularly if it's a subscription site, it's probably wise to ask permission. Copying parts of a page and using them in your own page – such as grabbing an image off someone else's page and using it intact or as a background graphic on your own page – is generally frowned on unless the page's owner has explicitly given permission either individually or in a stated policy on the page. Linking to a page, however, ought to require no explicit permission, as it's the concept on which the Web's design was based.

However, there have been cases in which the right to link was disputed. Usually, these have had to do with a technique called frames, which allows designers to create those top and left-hand menu bars that remain constant while the content in the centre changes. It is possible to fill that centre space with content from another site by linking, and this is the practice that fell foul of organizations such as *The Times*. The problem with linking that way is that the originating site's content is being displayed as if it were part of your site, affecting the originator's ability to collect advertising revenues and control how its content appears.

On top of that, the Internet is creating a lot of new forms of intellectual property, and no one is entirely sure what to do with them. For example: most online conferencing systems claim copyright in the compilation of messages that have been posted on the system, even though copyright in the individual messages resides with the author. But Usenet has no owner. Does a site like Deja News, which archives Usenet, have the right to claim copyright in its archives? What about the database of online biographies collected on a community site or the database of registered domain names?

Sites

Copyright FAQ (http://ahds.ac.uk/bkgd/copyrightfaq.html): basic guidelines for copying material on the Internet, with additional references and contact information for the main UK copyright organizations.

Papers by Pamela Samuelson (http://www.sims.berkeley.edu/~pam/papers.html): Samuelson, who won a MacArthur Foundation 'Genius' award for her work, has done more than anyone to look at what's happening to copyright as we move into the digital era.

CRAFTS

Of course, the primary craft on the Internet is computer programming (see **Geek** and **Hacking**). However, many other crafts are well represented online, and what follows is a short list of sites to get you started. If you don't find what you want here and have no success with a search (see **Search Engines**), for some crafts it can be fruitful to try the sites belonging to fantasy and role-playing societies, which often need to research and engage in old crafts in the process of re-enacting the lives of earlier eras (see **Fantasy and Role-playing Games**). The Society for Creative Anachronism (http://www.sca.org), for example, has a lot of information on mediaeval heraldry, illuminated scrollwork, and embroidery as part of its site.

For embroiderers, Aion Needlecrafts (http://www.aion-needlecrafts.co.uk/) has an impressive list of UK-based suppliers, many of whom sell supplies by mail or telephone order (but few of whom seem to sell online). There are also cross-stitch patterns and links to books and magazines on the subject. Particularly useful are the checklists, such as the one that gives RGB (red, blue, green) values for all of the DMC stranded cotton thread colours, allowing you to design a project on computer using a paint program and then match the colours precisely (or as precisely as computer monitors, unreliable beasts that they are, allow).

Jewellery makers seem to be thin on the ground online, at least so far, but PJ Minerals (http://www.beads.co.uk) sells a limited selection of its beads and jewellery supplies online. For the whole mail-order catalogue you have to post them £2 and your address. It's also always worth looking in the jewellery makers' list in the rec.arts.bodyart.piercing FAQ (see **FAQS**). One nice site, however, is the UK-based African Trade Beads (http://www.africantradebeads.com). The site is a little confusing at first, because the product listing at the left isn't linked to the actual products – you

have to click on the Index button to get to a second list,
which is linked (hint to the site's designers: eliminate the
intervening page!). The site primarily sells beads, as you'd
expect, but also rings, bracelets and necklaces, some of
them dating back fifty years or more. Metalworking itself
seems to be poorly covered, with the majority of sites on the
topic being advertisements for adult education classes.
However Google's Welding and Soldering directory page
(http: // directory.google.com / Top / Home / Do-It-Yourself /
Welding_and_Soldering/) links to a number of instructional
pages on how to work with metal. Particularly relevant may
be the Soldering Hints (http://www.bhi.co.uk/hints/solder.
htm) compiled from email messages posted to the Clocks
and Clockers lists.

Knitters may like to try the Knitting and Crochet Guild
(http://www.rgb.ndirect.co.uk/guild/); the site is unimpres-
sive so far, but there's a good listing of shows and workshops. Knitting and Crochet (http://www.needlecraftfair.
co.uk/knitting.htm) at Needlecraft Fair is a better place to
try for listings of suppliers, mostly offline.

There are, of course, knitters who are more technically
accomplished than Kaffe Fassett (http://www.kaffefassett.
com/), but Fassett changed the face of British knitwear
design with his bold experimentation with colours and
patterns. On the Web, his studio is wonderful to look at,
with his designs draped all over it, and while the site
doesn't sell anything itself, Fassett fans can find his latest
books and designs and where to buy them.

Bath Potters Supplies (http://www.bathpotters.demon.
co.uk) sells clays, colours and oxides, glazes, brushes, tools,

machines, and even flat-packed kilns online (instructions on the site), with delivery charges topping out at just over £58 for a tonne shipped more than sixty miles from Bath.

Celia Eddy's QuiltStory (http://www.quilt.co.uk/) focuses primarily on British quilting traditions; there are book reviews, events and workshops listings, a moderated message board, and how-to articles. The one thing that's missing is a really good list of sources of quilting supplies. You'll find those on the site belonging to the London Quilters (http://members.tripod.co.uk/London_Quilters/lq1.htm), which lists a number of UK-based online outlets for quilting supplies. It's also always worth trying Quilt Direct (http://www.quiltdirect.co.uk), which sells rotary cutters, specialist rulers, batting, books, and videos to consumers over the Web and retailers generally; its fabric selection is limited, though. Much more comprehensive links to suppliers, teachers, and information on different quilting techniques are available at the site belong to the US magazine *Quilt* (http://www.quiltmag.com), but the suppliers are American.

The World Wide Quilting Page (http://mail.kosmickitty.com/MainQuiltingPage.html) is a bit of a scruffy mess, but it has a good, up-to-date list of quilt shows around the world, including Europe (http://mail.kosmickitty.com/Shows/Europe.html) and a fine if traditional selection of quilting blocks, with cutting and piecing instructions, in a variety of sizes. Particularly helpful may be the section where users can post news about errors in books and magazines; check there first if the design you're trying to copy isn't working right.

At the Sewing Resource Guide (http://www.lilyabello.com/sewdir.htm) just about everything to do with sewing is covered. It's a directory rather than an information site itself, but what a directory: vintage clothing, patterns for clothes and even bears, button collections, pattern design software, textile care and restorations, fabric stores and information sites, and umpteen dozen FAQs on all types of sewing topics (fabric dying, needlework, thimbles). Any sewer could get lost in this site and not emerge for years.

Stained glass aficionados should probably start at Stained Glass News (http://www.stainedglassnews.co.uk/), which aims to be the comprehensive site for stained glass in the UK. The site isn't particularly well designed or handsome, but you'll find news on related topics (an international ring of stained glass grave robbers, what next?), as well as links to suppliers of the raw materials and notes on special offers, technical tips, and even a second-hand sales area for stained glass-making equipment.

CRICKET

See under **Sports**.

D

DARTS

See under **Sports**.

DEATH

According to the Death Clock (http://www.deathclock.
com), I have 1,021,915,228 seconds to live. What will I do
when it gets down to under a billion? The clock has three
settings: normal, pessimistic, and sadistic (mine was normal). A more individually targeted Death Clock – recast
more positively as 'What is your life expectancy?' – is at the
Long to Live site (http://www.longtolive.com/Death-
Clock.asp). You answer a few questions like the age to
which your grandparents lived, how much you exercise,
drink and smoke, and so on, and get back a projected
lifespan based on actuarial tables. (I like this site, as it
predicts I could live to be 98–100 if I visit my family more
often.) What's intriguing with this sort of site is that you can
experiment and see the effects on your projected life span of
changing how often you exercise or eat vegetables.

More practically, the Natural Death Centre (http://www.

naturaldeath.org.uk/) is intended to help those dying at home and their carers, the Death and Bereavement Index links to lists of hospices and bereavement societies as well as first aid and lifesaving advice, and Funeral Guide UK (http://www.funeralguide.bizland.com/) helps you find services near you. The British Humanist Association (http://www.humanism.org.uk) supplies secular funeral officiants.

Finally, if you have a ghoulish and slightly malicious turn of mind, you may like to enter your celebrity picks in the Dead Pool (http://www.stiffs.com).

DIARIES

On the net everyone can be Samuel Pepys. Online diaries are one of the great pastimes of the Web, either as straight diaries or as the curious phenomena known as Weblogs, or Blogs for short, which are a cross between a diary and a ship's log. In either case the diary's owner posts regular updates on whatever subject they wish – life experiences, new and nifty online discoveries, email exchanges with friends. A good one points you at strange treasures you might not have found otherwise that the owner has found while browsing. There are, by now, an immense number of these things. Start at the Weblogs (http://www.weblogs.com) site and try some samples. If you find one you like, follow the links from its site to other Blogs, as they link in circles of friends.

DICTIONARIES

You guessed it: Dictionary.com (http://www.dictionary.com). Word of the day, crossword puzzles, question-answering service, a translator and a thesaurus, too. For computer terms, it's also worth trying Webopedia (http://www.webopedia.com/) or the Free Online Dictionary of Computing (http://wombat.doc.ic.ac.uk/foldoc/contents.html). There are also dictionaries specializing in medicine (http://www.graylab.ac.uk/omd/), acronyms (http://www.AcronymFinder.com/), and a whole load more (http://www.refdesk.com/factdict.html).

Also try the excellent site How Things Work (www.howthingswork.com).

DINING OUT

Restaurants.co.uk (http://www.restaurants.co.uk) offers a comprehensive list of UK restaurants, searchable by area and keyword (restaurant name or type of food). The site also includes recipes, sources for catering supplies, and a facility for users to post reviews of their favourite restaurants. For those who like nothing but Indian food, Curry Fayre (http://www.curryfayre.co.uk/search.asp) lets you search for the nearest Indian takeaway. Within London, it's also worth trying the *Evening Standard*'s This is London (http://www.thisislondon.co.uk); click on Restaurants in the menu running down the left to get to listings of the hundred best London restaurants.

DIRECTORIES

Just as you need a phone book to find a telephone number you need a directory to find things on the net – because it's easy to update Web sites constantly, it's a much more efficient medium for everything from phone books and business guides to Net resources.

Domain names (http://www.betterwhois.com): look up who owns any name registered in .com, .net, or .org.

Electronic Yellow Pages (http://www.eyp.co.uk): just what it sounds like. Find businesses all over the UK.

Scoot (http://www.scoot.co.uk): company search, nationwide (and many other services).

E

EDUCATION

The BBC, in line with its charter, operates an online education service (http://www.bbc.co.uk/education/home/) which it's planning to beef up with a digital curriculum for all levels of education up to and including adult learning. The site has sections to help prepare for GCSEs, Standard Grades, and National Tests on just about every subject, including advice on exam skills and techniques, revision materials, and practice tests. The site makes good use of the interactivity of the Web – you can take a practice test, have it scored immediately, and head for the related study area. The revision area for *Macbeth*, for example, takes you step by step through the development of Lady Macbeth's character, popping up illustrative quotes as you move through the study questions. A set of highly active message boards lets students exchange help, advice, and yowls of frustration (the BBC, showing a sense of humour, has called the area 'Screech'). A really good service, and highly recommended.

For foreign, university-bound kids, the British Council runs the Education UK site (http://www.educationuk.org/eduuk.html), which offers an online guide to student life, links to all UK university prospectuses and colleges, and links to information on scholarships.

For the Open University (http://www.open.ac.uk), the traditional distance learning methods – TV, correspondence, brief residential periods – are still the most important. There are, however, a few courses that use online conferencing to supplement those techniques. For other universities, things are different, and there is now a long list of US-based online degree courses, which are catalogued at World Wide Learn (http://www.worldwidelearn.com/), some from very reputable universities such as Pennsylvania State. Particularly common are business degrees, which are typically taken by busy people later in life, when it's more difficult to schedule time away from family and existing work commitments. To assess an online degree course, before paying any money, check that the institution offering it is properly accredited, and ensure that it's what you want: studies to date have shown that online courses have a higher drop-out rate than classroom-based ones.

EMAIL

The Web gets the headlines, but for most people the most important thing the Internet gives them is email. Cheap and fast, email lets you stay in touch, daily, with far-flung family members and friends.

Writing email is easy. Once you've started your email software and chosen to write a new message, you fill in the recipient's address and a subject (the software should automatically fill in your reply address) and write the message.

Save it and log on to send it. In general, unless you're writing an official statement on behalf of your company, it is not necessary (or even desirable) to use formal salutations or style when writing email. At heart and in use, email is a casual form of conversation, a cross between a memo and a note rather than a letter or a telegram. Do not use all caps when writing email – it looks as though you're shouting and is difficult to read.

The most important thing about using email is remembering to check it. Unlike postal mail or telephone calls, in most cases, at least at home, email doesn't just arrive – you have to go and get it by dialling into your ISP and telling your email software to collect the mail. Once you start using email, you should make sure to collect email at least once every day or two. People who use email expect a quick response. If, for example, you list an item for sale on eBay with the listing due to expire in a week and you don't check your email for ten days, you may miss questions from potential bidders.

Fancy email

Email as sent over the Internet is plain text. In general, you should remember that basic principle, and avoid doing anything to your email to try to make it something else. You do not know what technology your correspondents use to read their email: sure, they might have the same software you do, but equally they might have something completely different. Plain text is the one format everyone can read. Turn off, for example, options that attach HTML (Web page) copies of your email to the message you've just typed in –

lots of people won't be able to read it, and those who can will gain nothing they wouldn't have gained anyway by reading the plain text.

That said, there are occasions when people need to send non-text files – if they're working together on a word-processed document, for example, or want to share a piece of music, a picture, or even a software program. These non-text files are known as binary files, and they must be converted to plain text before they can be carried across the Internet. Most email software does this automatically using a built-in utility program written for this purpose. The most common such utilities are UUencode and MIME, although you may occasionally see others. Most of the time, you shouldn't need to worry about this, as your email software will decode the attached file when it arrives. For security reasons – attached files sometimes carry viruses – you should ensure that your email software does not run these files automatically once they are decoded, and you should scan them for viruses before opening them. In general, you should not send attached files without checking first that they are welcome and that your recipient will be able to read the format you are sending. You should never assume that everyone uses the same word processor you do, for example, and you should bear in mind that for all you know, your correspondent is checking email on a mobile phone at vast expense in the middle of Athabasca.

If your email software supports it, you may want to set up groups of correspondents who have similar interests and to whom you send the same message. You might, for example, create a group of family members who receive periodic updates on your children's doings, or a group of fellow department members who need regular updates to the company meeting schedules and agendas. If you do set up such groups, ensure that you use blind carbon copy, a function that hides the list of correspondents from public view. The reason is partly to protect privacy and partly to make it easier for your correspondents to read the actual message. Displaying the entire list of recipients means someone else can copy the list and use it for their own purposes.

Mailing lists

Usenet is noisy and junk-ridden, and Web conferencing is slow. Public discussion via email provides an alternative: mailing lists can be moderated so that only authorized people can join the list and junk can be kept to a minimum, and everyone can receive the messages. Because they're so universally accessible, tens of thousands of mailing lists (http://www.liszt.com) exist to cover almost every imaginable topic.

Like Usenet, mailing lists have evolved some community standards which you should abide by if you want people to pay attention to your messages.

- Stick to plain text. Unless the list specifically allows it, do not post binary files or HTML.

- Quote selectively so the list members can see what you're responding to. Even if your email reader threads messages so they appear grouped together by subject, it can be very difficult to tell which message comments on which. Do not, however, quote lengthy screeds, adding little of your own. A repeated 35-line message with just 'I agree' appended to it is extremely annoying.

- Refrain from engaging in personal abuse.

- Abide by any rules of confidentiality that apply to the list. If they say you may not repeat anything from the list elsewhere, don't.

- Remember, conversely, that any rule of confidentiality can be broken, and avoid saying anything on the list you would be uncomfortable seeing repeated publicly. Many lists are archived and may be accessible much later by people you never imagined would read them.

- Save the welcome message you are sent when you join the list, which typically contains instructions for accessing the list archives and unsubscribing, as well as any rules that apply to posting to the list. If you later want to unsubscribe, follow the instructions in the welcome message to send your request to the list's owner. Unless you have a deep-seated need to look like a dork, do not send your unsubscribe request to the list itself.

(See also **Security**.)

EMOTICONS

Because text-only communication is stripped of the cues – tone of voice, gesture, body language – that smooth communication in the physical world, it's easy to misunderstand what people say online. Accordingly, online users have come up with standard combinations of ordinary characters that convey emotional nuances to make their meaning clearer. These are known as emoticons, and they become a very quick shorthand way of fleshing out what you're trying to say. (Of course, the most snobbish writers insist that good writing does away with the need for such frippery.) Here are a few of the most common ones you'll run across :) or :-) (the Smiley). Turn your head to the left, and you'll see it looks like a smile. You will sometimes see these turned the other way, for example, (:

Also common is:

: (or :-(Frown, expresses sadness or disappointment.

8-) or 8) Smiley wearing glasses.

ENTERTAINMENT LISTINGS

The first port of call in most cases is going to be Virgin Net (http://www.virgin.net), which has searchable movie, theatre, and other event listings all over the UK. Scoot (http://www.scoot.co.uk) also offers searchable nationwide cinema listings. The UK Gig Guide (http://www.gig-guide. org) is an extensive list of concert dates, primarily but not solely folk singers and bands. *Time Out* (http://www. timeout.com) has put its listings online for London and Dublin, as well as a range of other cities around the world (worth consulting if you're travelling).

For special events, consult the event's own Web site (these days, it usually has one). There's a gateway to all of Edinburgh's many festivals (http://www.go-edinburgh. co.uk/), for example. The Edinburgh Festival Fringe site (http://www.edfringe.com/) not only lists the annual programme, but has a nice match-making section for writers and performers who are looking for talents to complement their own.

ENVIRONMENT

Of course, everyone on the Internet is interested in preserving the environment: that's why they're using the Net instead of physically going places, right? You will find that just as there are plenty of conspiracy theories to go around (see **Truth**), there are plenty of sites promoting the idea that there's no such thing as global warming. Spend some time at the Global Warming site (http://www.globalwarm.com/), however, and the evidence gains in weight every day. The site is part of the WorldNews network, and is one of the more impressive members with a lot of British input: many of the headlined stories every day come from British newspapers. What the site is a little short of, however, is hard science – but it is a news site.

Use It Again (http://www.useitagain.org.uk) is aimed at helping people recycle and cut down on the amount of waste going into landfills in this country. Cut down on junk mail by registering with the Mail Preference Service (follow the links from http://www.dma.org.uk.), phone the Waste-line to find out whether there's a kerbside collection in your area, use recycled paper. UK Environment Week (http://www.ukenvironmentweek.org/index.htm) offers current news and links to a few more useful sites.

Friends of the Earth (http://www.foe.org.uk/), of course, has not let the Web go by. It and Greenpeace (http://www.greenpeace.org.uk) both operate sites with a lot of information about their various campaigns. Greenpeace's site includes a guide to consumer foods on the market showing which ones may have genetically modified ingredients.

EQUESTRIAN

See under **Sports**.

EXPATRIATES

The *Daily Telegraph* runs a site full of resources and nostalgia for British expatriates (http://www.globalnetwork.co.uk)

including news, sports, and advice for those living overseas. The Inland Revenue provides pages with specific tax advice for non residents (http://www.inlandrevenue.gov.uk/menus/non-residents.htm).

More enjoyably, one of the things expatriates miss most is familiar foods: good tea, digestive biscuits, even Marmite. Brits Abroad (http://www.britsabroad.co.uk) will ship all those nostalgia foods anywhere in the world. The prices – £3.40 for a box of Nestlé's Shreddies – don't include delivery (ineptly, the site gives no idea of delivery costs until you check out and give your personal details). But if you've been living in Churchill, Manitoba for 20 years without salad cream, this has got to look pretty good.

EXTRATERRESTRIAL INTELLIGENCE

If you want to help with the work of trying to find evidence of extraterrestrial intelligence, you can. SETI@Home (http://setiathome.ssl.berkeley.edu/) is a project to use individual computers all over the world to aid the search. You download a small bit of software to run unnoticeably in the background on your machine, using the spare computing power you don't even realize you have. The mastermind behind the project is a group of scientists at the University of California, who have been searching for aliens for many years and have recorded millions of signals from outer space. SETI uses computers to analyse all this data and look for louder-than-usual signals. Because there is so much data, it would take an unfeasibly large computer and a very long time to analyse it all. Therefore it has written a little program that analyses small chunks of the data that you download; when a block has been analysed, the software sends it back and gets another one. It's very simple to set up, fascinating to watch and probably the closest you'll get to life on Mars.

EZINES

There are probably tens of thousands of electronic newsletters published on a regular or semi-regular basis, most of them publicized by word of mouth. One of the best is Need to Know (Now), a sarcastic little round-up of British Net news (http://www.ntk.net). Also on Internet-related topics it's worth looking at the *Computer Underground Digest* (http://www.soci.niu.edu/~cudigest/), which goes back years and whose archives represent a comprehensive picture of the Net's development. *NetFuture* (http://www. netfuture.org/) is published by Stephen Talbott, author of *The Future Does Not Compute*. Finally, *Ansible* (http://www. ansible.org) is published by British science fiction writer Dave Langford, who has won many awards for *Ansible*.

F

FADS

Every so often, a craze sweeps the Internet and gets picked up by the mainstream media. The dancing baby on *Ally McBeal* (http://www.megababy.com), the phone booth in the Mojave Desert (http://www.deuceofclubs.com/moj/mojave.htm), 'I KISS YOU!!!!!!!!!' Mahir Cagri (http://members.nbci.com/primall/mahir/ and http://www.mahircentral.com), and the Hamster Dance (http://www.hamsterdance.com/original.html, make sure you have sound and animations turned on) and its legion of imitators are all examples. If you've heard about them but never knew what they were, now you do.

FANTASY AND ROLE-PLAYING GAMES

People who are trying to sell you new technology these days like to stress that it's interactive. They tell us, for example, that digital television is going to let us choose which camera feed to watch during a football match, which match to watch during a tennis tournament, and which of several possible endings to a movie we prefer.

Interactive, collaborative fiction, however, is unlikely to come in movie form – at least for a while – because the medium is too difficult to create. Instead, truly interactive fiction is to be found online in the oldest form of Internet communication: plain text. These online games are generally known as MUDs, for multi-user dungeons; a later variant, MOO, stands for multi-user object-oriented. Either way, think Dungeons and Dragons, only typed. Dungeons and Dragons itself, of course, also has a Web site (http://www.wizards.com/dnd/) with many interesting features and a heavy schedule of live chats.

Getting started in any of the virtual worlds isn't easy: the environment is confusing, the technology unfamiliar, the commands arcane, and the users all strangers. The best advice is: take it slow and have some patience. Read the help files, which are generally made available to you when you first log on. Almost all these systems have volunteer helpers, known variously as acolytes, wizards, oracles and even janitors, who will be willing to answer questions and help you find your feet. Generally, these things are easier if you already know someone on the system who is willing to answer stupid questions and come to your rescue if you get into trouble.

One warning: MUDs are one of the few parts of the Internet that people can become dangerously obsessive about, the other being chat. The mix of real-time interaction with other users, fantasy, and role-playing while remaining physically detached is a potent one. You have been warned.

Avaterra (http://www.avaterra.com), formerly known as

Worlds Away and developed in partnership between Fujitsu and CompuServe, is a graphical world in which characters interact via avatars – cartoon characters they choose from basic designs provided by the site. In Avaterra, characters walk from place to place and can build and decorate homes ('turfs') with objects they buy with in-world money ('tokens'). Characters get married, play games, write the history of the world, and have even been known to stage protests. Dreamscape, the main world of Avaterra, which dates all the way back to the early 1990s and its Fujitsu/CompuServe connection, costs $19.95 a month; the site operates as a social hub as well for $9.95 a month.

Additional sites

Lambda MOO (telnet://lambda.moo.mud.org:8888): you will need a Telnet client to get to Lambda, as it's all text-based. Lambda MOO is one of the best-known and oldest MOOs, and the life within its fantasy world has even been the subject of a whole book, Julian Dibbell's *My Tiny Life*. Lambda MOO is free.

Medievia (http://www.medievia.com): mediaeval-themed MUD, one of the older continuous MUDs on the Net. On arrival as a novice you pick one of four categories of character to be, and start learning your trade by killing the many 'bots' (software robots) that populate the city. As you gain experience and powers, you can join forces with other players in clans, and head off on multiplayer quests. Graphic violence in killing those bots – but it's only text. Medievia is free.

The Palace (http://www.palacetools.com): graphical virtual chat world in which people interact as little cartoon characters ('avatars'). Primarily oriented toward real-time chat. The Palace server is free, so many sites have been developed based on the technology, all different.

In addition to these virtual worlds, offline re-enactment societies usually run Web sites for their members as a way of staying in touch and providing an information resource. You can look up the Ermine Street Guard (http://www.esg.ndirect.co.uk/), dedicated to the Roman era; the Viking Experience (http://www.the-viking-experience.co.uk/); and the Society for Creative Anachronism (http://www.sca.org), dedicated to recreating the Middle Ages in the present as they ought to have been.

FAQS

On the Net FAQ universally stands for 'Frequently Asked Questions'. In fact, it's a slight misnomer, as what it actually refers to is files of answers to questions the file's keepers wish were asked less frequently.

FAQs came originally from Usenet in response to the annual influx of newcomers (every September, that year's freshman class got their Internet connections and created havoc until they learned the cultural norms). It's silly for a newsgroup's regulars to have to answer, sometimes on a daily basis, the same questions over and over again (sample, from rec.sport.tennis: 'How can I get Wimbledon tickets?').

So it was logical to compile a list of the most frequently asked questions, together with the relevant answers, and store them where anyone could get them. Thereafter, any of those questions would be met with the answer, sometimes the very rude answer, that the questioner should read the FAQ. By the mid 1990s, the term was so well-known that it was being universally adopted. Now everyone from banks posting consumer advice to software companies supplying help files is likely to call their information an FAQ.

Usenet FAQs (http://www.faqs.org) are still a tremendous source of information on a huge variety of subjects. Although Usenet has a reputation for noise and ill-informed opinion, FAQs tend to be assembled by the most knowledgeable participants of a newsgroup and revised over time so that errors get weeded out. It's worth searching these archives on almost any subject of interest.

Because FAQ has become such a common term, when you're looking for answers to questions on any topic, including commercial products and technical support, it's always a good gambit to enter the topic keywords plus the term FAQ into a search engine. There just may be an information file already out there that answers your question in detail, saving you the trouble of re-researching the wheel.

FASHION

Fashion in the real world is often associated with glossy photographs, starvation-victim women and rampant airbrushing. For that reason there's something seriously refreshing about Fashion UK, which has plenty of attitude and is also not pink, puffed up with excessive animations and graphics or full of irritating stereotypes. London-based, it includes click and buy fashion shoots, trends, streetstyle and young designer interviews. You'll find comprehensive photographic coverage of events like London Fashion Week, short news stories on current trends in fashion and beauty, and an impressive library of links to other sites, including designer labels from Jean Paul Gaultier to Ghost, online retailers, fashion magazines and cosmetic manufacturers. It's primarily aimed at women, but there are some items and links of interest to men.

Other popular sites include the less edgy and more ordinary *Vogue* site (http://www.vogue.co.uk) which includes content from the famous magazine as well as daily news, personalized email and, from the US site, a *Vogue*-cam that lets you watch the magazine's reception desk. It's not known if anyone's caught a Voguette coming to work in jeans and a T-shirt, but one can live in hope.

Hintmag (http://www.hintmag.com) features gossip, sexy shoots, hot designer features and an interactive message board. Fashion Wire Daily (http://www.fashionwiredaily.com) is a business-to-business newswire with fashion industry news, celebrity sightings, gossip and show reports, although the site is rather pink and requires you to register before you can read its features (the news is open access). Models.com (http://www.models.com) is everything you ever wanted to know about the modelling industry – or possibly more than that – along with instructional beauty and style features, gossip and interviews. There are plenty of photographs of famous models to keep you occupied if you don't feel like reading anything. Finally, Fashion Live (http://www.fashionlive.com) is a Paris-based high fashion Web site. Cool interactive visuals, trends, catwalk shows and fashion shoots.

(See also **Clothes**.)

FAX

You can use the Internet to send a fax anywhere in the world. The Phone Company (http://www.tpc.int/tpc_home.html) offers a fax service that depends on volunteers to work – you type your fax into the form on the site and hit the button. The site does not guarantee delivery, but it does count the entire UK as covered. The service is more credible than it sounds; co-founder Carl Malamud was the force behind the first Internet radio service (the Internet Multicasting Service) and some of the first experiments in getting government information online.

If you don't have a fax machine but do have email (as you now do, if you're reading this), you can use Digital Mail (http://www.digitalmail.com) to receive faxes – you get a fax number from Digital Mail's site, and anyone can send you a fax from any machine. You will receive it by email. The service is free, as Digital Mail gets a small payment from telephone connection charges. Demon offers a similar service to its subscribers (http://www.dfax.uk.demon.net/).

You can also send faxes to many UK businesses for free via Scoot, the directory service (see **Directories**). Search on the type of business and town, and if the business whose name you retrieve has a little fax icon next to it you can click on it, type in your message and Scoot will fax it for you – free.

FILMS

Some day, the Internet will be so pervasive and our access to it so fast that movies will be delivered to our TV sets over it.

Some day.

At the moment, you probably wouldn't want to wait the hours it would take to download an entire film, although users of Scour Exchange (http://www.scour.com) briefly experimented with exchanging movie files in a system somewhat similar to Napster's music system (see **Music**). But that part of Scour's site was shut down in response to complaints about copyright violations. At Scour, you can also watch commercial movie trailers – useful, if you're curious about movies that have yet to open in Britain.

In the meantime, most of the Internet's usefulness in relation to film is in finding information about movies or organizing groups to work on them. Fortunately, the Internet is very good for both of these activities.

The comprehensive resource for information about movies and anything relating to them – actors, screenwriters, photographs, soundtracks, plots – is the Internet Movies Database (http://www.imdb.co.uk). Set up originally by a couple of movie-loving students at Cardiff University in Wales in 1990 as a series of searchable **FAQs** (see entry) for the Usenet newsgroup rec.arts.movies, the IMDB was bought by Amazon.com in 1998. The IMDB is one of the best sites anywhere, and a perfect example of what the Internet can do that previous media couldn't. The database is constantly updated with new movies, often before their official release to the theatres. The site encourages users to add their own short reviews to existing comments (it also has official reviews from critic Leonard Maltin's published compendium). One of the best features is the ability to search on multiple actors' or crews' names so you can identify that unknown late-night movie by typing in the names of the two actors you recognize (you get to this option by clicking on 'More searches' under the main search field at the upper left of the screen). Because the IMDB is kept up-to-date with the American market, almost any movie you'd be likely to want to see or rent should be listed and reviewed by the time it gets to Britain. It also includes TV shows, though not as comprehensively.

DVD owners might also like to take a look at DVD Review, in particular its page (http://www.dvdreview.com/html/hidden_features.shtml) listing the hidden features in many DVDs – stuff you didn't know was there because the manufacturer didn't tell you.

Movie information and reviews
UK-wide cinema listings and short reviews: Virgin.net (http://www.virgin.net/movies/): type in a location or a

movie title, and get back a list of all the movies showing within striking distance, complete with cinema names and times.

Roger Ebert (http://www.suntimes.com/ebert): weekly movie review column, section answering questions from reader email, and extensive archives of reviews, interviews and festivals from the world's only Pulitzer Prize-winning movie critic.

Rotten Tomatoes (http://www.rottentomatoes.com): not all movies are good movies, we know that. This site offers round-ups of (mostly American and Canadian) reviews of newly released films.

Movie Mistakes (http://www.soton.ac.uk/-2.5jwes197/): As an undergraduate, Jon Sandys set up a Web site dedicated to movie mistakes; everything from the boom dangling into shot to serious anachronisms. Since then it has grown, thanks to the hundred of emails he receives daily from other eagle-eyed movie goers. Most of the films are listed alphabetically, but some are singled out for their errors.

Cannes Film Festival (http://www.festival-cannes.fr/): during the two weeks of the festival in May each year, Cannes' official site shows live video of press conferences and star appearances; details of all the films and the procedures for submissions are available year-round.

Sundance Festival (http://www.sundance.org): the independent film festival founded by Robert Redford runs writers' workshops and many other development programmes. Find out how to volunteer to help out during the festival – but you'd better have lodgings in Utah.

London Film Festival (http://www.lff.org.uk/index.php3): browse or search the entire programme and find out about the films on display; for some mysterious reason ticket prices are kept secret, and unfortunately there is no online booking (and why not, we'd like to know?).

DVD and video retailers

Blackstar (http://www.blackstar.co.uk/): well-regarded online seller of DVDs and videos.

DVD 4 View (http://www.dvd4view.com): nifty online DVD rental service. You pay £3.75 including postage and packing for seven nights; they send you the DVD in a cardboard mailer with a return mailer inside. Once you've rented from them three times, you can rent up to three titles at a time. Good range, great service.

DVD Box Office (http://www.dvdboxoffice.com): based in Canada, the prices on this retailer's site include postage, and they ship DVDs one at a time so they don't attract customs duty (this is perfectly legal). The downside is that they only handle region 1 discs, which European players aren't supposed to be able to play. But perhaps you own a hacked player . . .

DVD Zone 2 (http://www.dvdzone2.com): Netherlands-based retailer. Its prices don't look too good until you realize they're in Euros and include shipping; then they look great. Good range of titles including foreign and art films.

Sources for DVD players

One of the major mistakes the movie studios have made recently is to insist on regional coding for DVDs that turns what ought to be a single disc playable worldwide into a disc that only works on a particular region's players. North America is zone 1, Europe is zone 2. Because consumers hate this regime, a number of sites offer 'hacked' players that can play any region's discs. Watch out, though – the movie studios are moving on to round two, with so-called 'enhanced' regional coding that will block the multiregion players. But, doubtless, not for long . . .

Link Online (http://www.linkonline.co.uk): sells audio/visual equipment of all types including DVD players with multi-region hacks; will also modify a player if you send it to them.

Techtronics (http://www.techtronics.com): specializes in DVD players, modified or unmodified, and also sells multi-region kits for many players. Good prices, good service.

FOOD AND DRINK

Besides the usual grocery shopping sites, there are many specialized sites that offer the kind of food you might have thought doesn't exist any more if the only shop you ever have time to go to is a supermarket (see also **Groceries**).

Try Speciality Foods (http://www.speciality-foods.com): buy British, by region, from a selection of specialist retailers represented as a row of quaint buildings with clickable shop signs. Inside the shop, the areas are described as 'main aisle'. The row of shops annoyingly scrolls sideways (when will Web designers learn?) but you can search for a shop or product using an efficient search engine on the left of the screen. The range the site carries is impressive – smoked fish, Sussex dairy, fresh herbs.

A personal favourite is the much smaller Real Food Club (http://www.realfood.co.uk), which sells first and foremost excellent lamb, sausages and bacon from a small farmer in the Cotswolds who rears the animals under humane conditions and controls all aspects of production through the final curing and sausage-making. The site also sells specialist items sourced elsewhere, such as top-quality organic bread flours, imported Spanish olive oil and goat cheese, as well as seasonal items such as partridge, pheasant and pigeon. The Club began as a farmer selling his surplus to friends on the London-based electronic conferencing system CIX, and has grown from there simply because of the superb quality of the food he sells and the reasonable prices. Prospective customers need to bear in mind, however, that because it is a small operation items vary in availability; but (speaking from personal experience) they're worth the wait.

One other rather nice site is Inverawe (http://www. smoked-salmon.co.uk), a Scottish specialist in everything smoked. They do a mail order catalogue, but the site includes more information on the smoking process as well as recipes.

The traditional English retailers, such as Fortnum and Mason (http://www.fortnumandmason.com) of course will let you order traditional hampers online. If you want even fancier food, try Le Gourmet Français Online (http://

www.jayfruit.co.uk): black and white truffles, ostrich and emu pâté, quails stuffed with mushrooms, foie gras sold whole and half cooked (mi-cuit) in jars, an intelligently selected range of oils and preserves, and high cocoa-mass speciality cooking chocolate.

Also try Classic Gourmet (http://www.classicengland. co.uk/gourmets.htm): buy British! Handcrafted chocolates, hand-reared beef and poultry, Scottish hampers, you name it. This site lists dozens of small producers around the UK who sell online. 'Eat,' as the site says, 'your heart out'.

When it comes to organic food, Fresh Food (http://www. freshfood.co.uk) claims to be Britain's leading organic food shopping Web site. You click on the food heading you want – meat, fish, vegetables – and then make your selection from a long list of products. A giant fruit and vegetable box, for example, costs £39.95. You're allowed to specify two items you don't like and two you absolutely insist on, but over most of the box you have no control, as exactly what is supplied depends on the season. You get your order in roughly a week.

One of the better food processors' sites is the one belonging to Schwartz (http://www.schwartz.co.uk/), a nice straightforward design that lets you look up individual herbs and spices and find out, for example, that in mediaeval Europe it was believed that smelling basil would cause a scorpion to form in your brain. What's particularly nice is the receipe search engine – you tell it what food you've got and it will suggest something to cook with it. On the occasion we were down to only a chicken and an aubergine, for example, this site would have pointed us at Portuguese chicken with ratatouille or vegetable dahl, a lot more interesting than the rather more obvious roast and sauté method. Just don't smell the basil.

For tea, probably the best site is the homegrown Whittard of Chelsea (http://www.whittard.com), which carries some 150 teas and twenty different types of coffee on its site, along with instructions for making the perfect cup (at last, a set of instructions that notes how strong tea is if you make it according to the traditional recipe of one spoonful per person and another for the pot). If you feel like giving real money to the Post Office, you can also try the American Stash Tea (http://www.stashtea.com), which has a lengthy history section along with a virtual tour of a Darjeeling tea plantation.

Coffee drinkers who are willing to spend serious money on what is supposed to be the finest coffee, Jamaican Blue Mountain, can buy it from Fortnum and Mason, but there is actually a site (http://www.bluemountaincoffee.com) that sells it from the horse's mouth – or country. There's also an impressive selection at Coffee World (http://www.realcoffee.co.uk), which doesn't roast the beans until it fills your order (keep them in the freezer when they arrive). For more on coffee try consulting the – what else? – Coffee FAQ (http://www.coffeefaq.com/coffaq.htm) (see **FAQs**).

FOOTBALL

See under **Sports**.

G

GAMES

We all need a break from time to time, and the games included with computer operating systems can get pretty dull after a while. Amused (http://www.amused.com) is more or less along the lines of fun for the (somewhat) feeble-minded, but then if you're at work you don't want anything that will suck you in too far. The amusements range from little cartoons to games such as Dunk a Millionaire, or a Halloween message with a bug crawling all over your screen. And there are also pointless-but-fun interactive animations such as the Virtual Milkshake, which involves clicking on a button and watching the window of your browser jiggle around for a few seconds. The site requires Shockwave. The same people also run *Uproar* (http://www.uproar.com), a more complicated online games site where you can play bingo or an online version of the TV game family feud.

More complicated and a lot more intriguing is the Alien Fish Exchange (http://www.alifex.com), the first of a series of Web/WAP/interactive TV games from nGame, a Cambridge-based startup. The Web version is still in beta as I write this, but the game is addictive and fun, involving collecting thirty-seven varieties of very appealing alien fish. The site for the game includes message boards.

There are a huge number of other games online, from fantasy football leagues such as the one the *Telegraph* runs to online casinos such as the one at Galaxiworld (http://www.galaxiworld.com). The games pages at About.com (http://www.home.about.com/games/) are a good place to start exploring from, as is ZDNet's Gamespot (http://www.zdnet.com/gamespot/filters/).

GARDENING

The perfect gardening site for non-experts hasn't yet been invented. Stocked with all types of plants and aids, this site would let you enter a few specifics about your garden's location, direction and climate, along with a few preferences and maybe technical specifics like the type of soil, and give you back a list of plants to consider. To be fair, Crocus (http://www.crocus.co.uk) comes somewhat close, in that you can tell it you're 'keen but clueless' and want a low-maintenance garden, and it will come up with some recommendations. Apparently, I could be growing California lilacs, which would be fine with me. The site does rely a bit too much on icons you have to decode and teeny tiny print to click on, but it's quite handsome, with lots of good photographs. The site will even send you post-delivery email to ensure you're taking correct care of the plants you've bought.

Otherwise, if you're not an expert you'll have to do a lot of background research, as the better Web sites selling plants and gardening supplies tend to assume you have some idea what the different plants are.

Sending perishable plants through the post may seem a risky venture, but it's all in the packing. Even aquarium plants can arrive safely if handled correctly. So the Web can be a great place to find plants that aren't your standard run-of-the-garden-centre stock. This is one area where rural inhabitants ordinarily have an advantage: nurseries tend to be near them in obscure locations. Online nurseries place unusual plants and well-informed stockists within easy reach. One place to start is the compendious British Gardening On-Line site (http://www.oxalis.co.uk) where you will find links to all the relevant specialist sites.

Possibly the most richly stocked nursery in the UK is Cotswold Garden Flowers (http://www.cgf.net), run by the knowledgeable and opinionated (according to James Delingpole in his *Telegraph* column) Bob Brown. Just type in the initial letter of the plant you want and, unless he deems it unworthy, Bob will almost certainly stock it. He has, for example, at least thirty types of kniphofia, each given a score out of ten and accompanied by planting and care notes and, often, a clear photograph.

Other sites to try are Manor Nursery (http://www.gardenplants.co.uk), Four Seasons (http://www.fsperennials.co.uk), Martin Nest (http://www.martin-nest.demon.co.uk) (an alpine and auricula specialist) or Wales's Farmyard Nurseries (http://www.btinternet.com/farmyard.nurseries) run by the friendly Richard Bramley. Farmyard Nurseries has a good range of unusual herbaceous plants but what it does best, again according to Delingpole, are hellebores (beautifully illustrated and, states a *Telegraph* writer, one of the most extensive collections in the country), tricyrtis (the weird but wonderful toad lily) and schizostylis (the Autumn-flowering Kaffir lily).

The Thompson and Morgan site (http://www.thompson-morgan.com) not only has a massive range of seeds for sale but it also sells young plants. They also provide a section where their horticulturalists will answer your emailed queries.

The UK Gardening site (http://www.gardening-uk.com) is somewhat disappointing: even though it has a good-looking collection of links, many are out of date and the list is far from comprehensive. You would do better by going to Google (see **Search Engines**) and typing in the type of plant you're after followed by the words 'buy UK'. With any luck, that will get you a list of hits in which at least a few lead directly to online specialists in the types of plants you're looking for. The more specific the plant name you type in (*Ariocarpus* instead of cactus, for example), the more likely you are to get a direct hit.

The Rareplants site (http://rareplants.co.uk), run by a man named Paul Christian, claims to be the biggest and best bulb site on the Web. Besides being full of snazzy photographs of its wares, the site is extremely informative and lovingly maintained, and sells online every variety of bulb you could possibly desire, from tulips and fritillaries to lilies and orchids. Christian runs a winter list and a summer list, so timing is very important when you're ordering from him.

If what you want to do is talk about gardening – perhaps

to pick up advice from more experienced folks – a number of Usenet newsgroups cover the topic, including rec.gardens, rec.gardens.edible, and rec.gardens.ecosystem. It was those newsgroups that together came up with the Slug and Snail FAQ (http://www.powerup.com.au/~swimskins/slug_snail_FAQ.html). Some of the methods are a bit gruesome – spot 'n' squash, for example – but this is a perennial problem for almost every gardener.

Finally, one must not forget cacti. The pages at the Cactus Mall (http://www.cactus-mall.com) contain a comprehensive list of suppliers of cacti and succulents worldwide, including a number in the UK. From there, it's an easy matter to click through to sites like Chiltern Hills Cacti (http://www.chilternhillscacti.freeserve.co.uk) and others with comprehensive lists.

GEEK
(How to Become A)

Let's get one thing straight. Originally, geeks were sideshow circus people who bit the heads off chickens. (Remember that next time you insult one.) Then, in the late 1980s and early 1990s, they were sad, pathetic, painfully thin or very fat, young men who spent their whole lives at the computer screen and were incapable of exchanging plain English sentences in a social context. These days, the word 'geek' is almost a badge of honour: it means you have knowledge

beyond the norm about technology. It may even, so much
has popular mythology changed, mean that you are rich on
stock options from the company whose technology you
helped invent.

Of course, you yourself are not a geek. If you were, you
wouldn't be reading this book but writing the code to turn
it into a Web site. But you may know geeks and wish you
understood them, or you or your kid may wish to become
one, and the Web provides endless opportunities for all
these options.

The great geek pastime of the present day is creating
'open source' software. This is often referred to as 'free'
software, but what is free is not the software itself but the
right to access its inner workings and tinker with them. Or,
as free software guru Richard Stallman likes to put it, 'Think
free speech, not free beer.'

The best-known piece of open-source software is the
operating system generally known as Linux (Stallman pre-
fers to call it GNU/Linux, in recognition of the fact that
his GNU project wrote many of the routines that form part
of the operating system). Linux is functionally similar
to an operating system originally developed at AT&T in
the 1960s called UNIX, which is in widespread use on
many computers around the Internet. Because computer
software was not part of AT&T's charter after the 1984
breakup, the software was given away to academic insti-
tutions, which worked on it and improved it. Today, there
are a number of variants of UNIX, many of which are
commercially owned – for example, Sun Microsystems runs
its computers on a variant of UNIX known as Solaris, and

Microsoft, Apple, IBM and Hewlett-Packard all sell versions of UNIX.

A non-geek probably wouldn't want to run UNIX, even though Windows-like graphical interfaces are available to make it less intimidating. A non-geek might, however, want to run Linux because of the price: free. Even if you wind up paying a geek to set the system up for you and contribute technical support (one of the ways companies such as Red Hat and VA Linux make money out of the software), you can't beat the price of the actual software. For certain kinds of functions such as mail servers and file stores Linux works out much cheaper, more stable and more easily expandable than its commercial competitors. It also demands much less in the way of hardware overheads such as disk space and memory, and so it is slowly making its way into small businesses in those limited sorts of applications. The thing that scares non-geeks about Linux is the question of who to call to get technical support; in fact, there is a huge community of people working on the software worldwide, and because the software's code is open to modification Linux can be more easily modified to do exactly what you want than the closed-off, proprietary Windows.

Several hardware hacking projects of note have sprung up over the last few years. The Hack Furby (http://www.homestead.com/hackfurby/) effort aims to make toy Furbys controllable via an order TV remote. A project to hack Microsoft Barney (http://www.ics.uci.edu/~jpd/barney/) aims to make Barney talk on a wider range of subjects. And Lego Mindstorms (http://mindstorms.lego.com/) is supposed to make it possible for anyone to build something geeky and intriguing out of programmable bricks.

Additional sites

Free Software Foundation (http://www.gnu.org): the first free software project. Run by Richard Stallman, a former researcher at the artificial intelligence lab at the Massachusetts Institute of Technology, the FSF has as its most important project to create a full UNIX-like operating system known as GNU. Equally important is the FSF's 'copyleft' license, which has been widely imitated by other projects creating free, now often called open-source, software.

Freshmeat (http://www.freshmeat.org): tracks open-source projects in progress, and welcomes volunteers.

Linux (http://www.linux.org): download the operating system, read the news, volunteer to help work on a project.

Slashdot (http://www.slashdot.org): 'News for nerds. Stuff that matters.' The most important site for news, commentary and community discussion of everything related to software and programming, especially open-source software. If you want to look really geeky, write it '/.'.

GENEALOGY

The business of tracing ancestors is booming, if only because we live in so much more mobile a society than previous generations. Probably the most logical starting place for most people is UK & Ireland Genealogy (http://www.genuki.org.uk/). It's quick to load (being pretty much all text), has a collection of useful links to get you started, and a very good introductory tutorial on researching your family history. Barbara's Registration Web Page (http://www.dixons.clara.co.uk/Certificates/indexbd.htm) explains how to trace birth, death and marriage certificates.

Further afield, your best bet is probably to start with Cyndi's list (http://www.cyndislist.com/), which aims to be a comprehensive list of genealogy resources on the Net.

However, the genealogy sites recommend not overlooking books as an important source of information, and, if you're inexperienced in this field, you will probably get the best out of the Web resources if you read some background material first.

GIFTS

Flowers are a good match for the Web because being able to see a picture of what you're ordering is so obviously a better way to do things than guessing over the phone. One of the first places to look for flowers is the Interflora site (http://www.interflora.co.uk), which will deliver flowers anywhere in the UK and worldwide. The selection is somewhat limited, but the site makes recommendations for specific types of occasions, and you get the familiar Interflora service. The first successful online flower service, 1-800Flowers (http://

www.1800flowers.com), was named for the freephone area
code in the US and began life as a service on AOL. For US
deliveries it's still the best-designed and slickest service. It
will deliver flowers within the UK and be efficient about it,
but the selection is extremely limited and the pricing is in
dollars. The site also has a tendency to follow you with
unwanted promotional email.

It would be nice to report that there's a solid UK competitor that's just as good with a bigger range, but the fact is
that most of the UK online florists are very limited and not
nearly as well designed. Flowers Worldwide (http://www.
flowers-worldwide.co.uk), for example, delivers all over
the UK and worldwide, but its range is limited to a few
bouquets and baskets. Floritel (http://www.floritel.co.uk),
which partners with Yahoo!, offers much greater options,
including live green plants, but it's impossible to use – you
can't find the online catalogue to view the options and
prices. The only sensible way to use Floritel, therefore, is to
go in via Yahoo!'s shopping service (http://shopping.
yahoo.co.uk). Either click on Floritel's button as a featured
store or search Yahoo! shopping on flowers, and you'll
easily get access to all the nice Floritel pictures and options
in a much more understandable layout. Clearly there's a
major design error here; though they may have fixed it by
the time you read this. One can hope.

If you like a more hands-on approach so you can order
direct from the delivering florist and issue personal instructions, Wedding Florist UK (http://www.weddingflorist.
co.uk) offers a Find A Florist service. You enter a town
name and get back a page of the local florists with

complete contact information including a Web page, if any.

For chocolates ... well, you have dozens of choices as long as the recipient of your gift has no special needs (like a nut allergy). There is lots of good-quality chocolate available, but almost no site gives you any details about ingredients and you're often given little control over the exact contents beyond the box size, and usually the gift boxes themselves are equally silent on the matter. Thorntons (http://www.thorntons.co.uk) is an improvement, in that it offers a special diabetic assortment. If you're already familiar with their products, perhaps the lack of information on the Web site doesn't matter that much. But as a chocolate snob, it's unsatisfying. A good chocolate Web site should let you specify: only dark chocolate, no milk, no white (ugh), nut-free, whatever. So far, no one seems to do this. Probably the best choice is Chocolate Store (http://www. chocolatestore.com) which offers 'personalized' chocolates from a slick Amazon-knockoff interface, but this only means getting the recipient's name on the box. They do list the chocolate content, which is a step in the right direction, and the site is as easy to use as Amazon, which can't be anything but good. There's a fair range of goods here to choose from – Belgian truffles, Swiss truffles, and gift selections – but no way to eliminate milk and white chocolate.

ChocExpress (http://www.chocexpress.co.uk) has the idea that you can decide which kind of chocolate to buy according to who it's for, or what occasion it's for. So that's how you get to search the site. Unfortunately, even identifying yourself as a 'foodie' doesn't eliminate milk chocolate. In other words, they don't quite get it – but they do have an impressive range, and are a reasonable place to start for all but the most difficult recipients (check out their chocolate Christmas tree).

Of course, anything can be a gift: a bungee jump, a day of paintball, or a golf lesson. Buy a Gift (http://www.buyagift.co.uk) features all of these along with the more traditional flowers and chocolates. Shipping is included in the listed prices, and the site also runs charity events and posts pictures customers send in of their days out.

The Museum Shop (http://www.museumshop.com) is worth visiting: slow to load, but a great place to find interesting gift items from all those museum shops whose merchandise you otherwise only ever see once. You can browse the items by museum (Louvre, Prado, Cleveland Museum of Art), artist, or period. The giftfinder, however, is a nuisance, very slow, but it lets you target age, gender, and price. The selection of museum partners is good (Jewish Museum, V&A, British Museum); it's just a pity that despite the international range of the museums featured shipping is from the US – a minimum of $29.95 for international orders, with customs duty and VAT to come. Still, if your mother has always longed for that Roman necklace or glass pumpkin paperweight, it may be worth it.

GOLF

See under **Sports**.

GOSSIP

Gossip was travelling the world at Internet speed before the Internet was invented – remember the old line, 'A lie goes round the world while the truth is still getting its boots on.' For a long time, nearly everything on the Internet was gossip (though not celebrity gossip), and, even now, plenty of information you find out there is unreliable.

Items like the modem tax or the email tax (see **Hoaxes**) are examples of baseless Internet gossip. More reliable stories – such as, say, the news that Real Audio's Jukebox software was transmitting user data back to the home site – aren't exactly gossip, but they do fly around the Net and get exaggerated. In general, you should assume that the more shocking and outrageous the story, the more care you should take to ascertain whether it's true before passing it on. Some people like, for example, to post shockers just as a way of getting attention.

Celebrity gossip, of course, comes into its own on the Net. If you want to know whether Calista Flockhart of *Ally McBeal* is anorexic, or what really happened between Hugh Grant and Elizabeth Hurley, the Internet is certainly the place to find speculation about it. One thing that happens when you get enough people together in a single place is that eventually someone comes along who actually knows someone who knows someone who forgot something. On the alt.showbiz.gossip newsgroup, for example, it's not uncommon for people to turn up who went to school with someone famous; much more common, of course, is for a poster to have got an autograph or seen a star walking down the street in the distance.

There is a certain amount of malice in gossip at the best of times – if there weren't it wouldn't be gossip. Gwyneth Paltrow, for example, is frequently referred to on alt.showbiz.gossip as 'the pallid ectomorph' or, more simply, 'Fishstick'. (Celebrities devoid of a sense of humour probably should avoid reading the newsgroups devoted to them unless they participate regularly.)

Therefore, take heed of three pieces of advice. First: don't believe everything you read on the Internet; it may be sourced from one of the tabloids or made up by the poster of the message to make him/her sound knowledgeable and important. Second: remember that British libel laws are ferocious, and contrary to popular belief libel law does apply to the Internet. Third: if you're reading gossip, don't weigh in with a lengthy defence of the gossiped-about person ending with something along the lines of, 'I don't understand how everyone here can be so mean about her when she's really a nice person and I think she's wondeful.' On alt.showbiz.gossip we have a term for that, and it is YABWFTNOTNG (Yet Another Bozo Who Forgot The Name Of The News Group).

Additional sites

The Drudge Report (http://www.drudgereport.com): one-man band Matt Drudge has rarely been accused of finding his own gossip; instead, he headlines stories from other media outlets. His most prominent moment came when he leaked the details of a killed *Newsweek* story alleging an improper relationship between President Clinton and the intern we all now know as Monica Lewinsky. Drudge's site is simple, fast-loading and useful; besides his gossip headlines it has search engines for the news wires, links to every syndicated columnist in the US and most US and UK newspapers. Several of these, such as Amy Archerd and Liz Smith, are more traditional gossip columnists getting their stories the hard way – through contacts.

Mr Showbiz (http://www.mrshowbiz.com): US-oriented celebrity news and gossip sheet. Want to see pictures from the Oscars? This is one of the spots.

National Enquirer (http://www.nationalenquirer.com/): the US tabloid. You know, the one that told the truth in *Men in Black*.

Page Six (http://www.pagesix.com): the gossip page of the *New York Post*.

Usenet: alt.showbiz.gossip, alt.gossip.celebrities, alt.politics.gossip. The first of these is a personal stomping ground; feel the malice.

GOVERNMENT

Governments everywhere are thrilled by the Internet. They believe it's going to create a boom in the economy the way it has in Silicon Valley. Besides that, they see it as a way of streamlining government services and delivering them at far lower cost and greater convenience. Why, after all, shouldn't citizens be able to demand the same level of 24-hour service of their governments as they do of their telephone companies?

All of that – electronic delivery of benefits, schemes that let you change your address once and have it percolate out to all the necessary departments, immediate response – is some way in the future, if it ever happens. But the Internet has very definitely improved access to government information, at least for the people who have Internet access. Legislation that a few years ago would have cost £15 and a trip to HMSO to buy it is now readable for free online, and, contrary to what you might expect, that availability is actually increasing the sale of printed copies. Similarly, information you might spend hours on hold waiting for is readily available – if you know how to find it and can understand the language it's written in.

Obviously not all of the world's governments have worked out how to use the Internet to communicate with their citizens. But the US, the UK and the European Parliament are all doing a pretty good job on their Web sites – and these are the governments whose information UK people are most likely to need. For British government infor-

mation, start with the main Open Government site (http://
www.open.gov.uk). This site acts as a front end to all
government departments, listing them by subject and function. The site is well designed in the sense that it loads
quickly and pays attention to accessibility issues such as the
need for a plain text version. What is difficult, however, is
knowing which department you need for a specific topic:
the site assumes some familiarity with the structure of the
British government. There is a search engine, but it's somewhat rudimentary, throwing up lists of hits that can be
difficult to understand. In fact, you don't have to use the
Open Government site's search engine at all; a properly
constructed Google search should throw up links to the
correct page (see **Search Engines**).

The open Government site is, however, limited to executive stuff. For legislation, even if it's been proposed by one
of the departments, you have to look at Parliament's own
Web site (http://www. parliament.uk), where there is a full
listing of MPs and Lords, with links to their own pages, as
well as information about pending legislation and daily
proceedings. To find this information for, say, the House
of Commons, follow the link to the House of Commons
and then click on the link to publications (http://
www.publications.parliament.uk/pa/cm/cmpubns.htm).
One more click, on daily debates, and you're into Hansard
– the entire proceedings of Parliament. Also available are
standing committee debates on bills, indexes to House of
Commons debates and a mass of other legislative background. This is definitely access on a scale that has not been
available before.

Abroad, the European Parliament (http://www.europarl. eu.int/) has also done a good job of making its debates and legislation available, but, again, using its site requires you to know how the government works.

The US government sites (http://www.firstgov.gov) are just as complete, with a site for every department. Because legislation is in the public domain in the US, you will find many more mirror sites of legislation than in the UK, where legislation is under copyright to the Crown.

Sites

The official UK government site (http://www.open.gov.uk) is maintained by the Central Office of Information. It includes links to all central government departments, as well as government agencies and local authorities throughout the UK.

An alternative listing (http://www.namss.org.uk/lauth. htm) goes further than Open Government, including much of the same information in a somewhat simpler format. The local government list this site links to (http://www. gwydir.demon.co.uk/uklocalgov/) has a useful set of clickable maps linking to both local governments and unitary authorities for those who aren't sure which local authority applies to a particular location.

The Houses of Parliament (http://www.parliament.uk) have their own Web site, which branches into separate sites for the House of Commons and the House of Lords, each of which has links to individual MPs and Lords.

The Scottish Parliament (http://www.scottish.parliament. uk) has its own site.

Official Documents (http://www.official-documents.co.uk/) is a service in development from the HMSO, intended to make it much easier to locate official documents of all types without having to work out which site they might be on. Start here if you're looking for copies of legislation, the Budget, green papers, Hansard and so on.

GROCERIES

There are two kinds of people: those who can't understand why anyone would want to buy groceries online, and those who faint with gratitude at the thought. I belong to the latter category, so most of my grocery shopping (other than milk and produce, from around the corner) has been done online since Tesco first announced its trial service back in late 1996.

The first thing about online grocery shopping: do not expect it to be a perfect service. But if you think of it as a way of getting around the exhausting, repetitive tedium of slogging through traffic, crowded aisles and overlit, badly designed layouts to find a long list of heavy items you cart home every week, it can be quite successful. The leading grocery sites will typically let you save lists so you can set up a base group of items you order every time and then add to it.

Typically, the way these services work is that you browse categories of goods (somewhat like walking up an aisle) or search the entire store. When you find items you want, you click on them to add them to a shopping list or cart. Finally, you go over the list, making any adjustments you like, choose a two-hour delivery slot over the coming ten days or so (Sainsburys To You asks you to do this first, Tesco last), enter your credit card information and press the button. There is usually a delivery charge of about £5.

The problem everyone expects with buying groceries online is that they will get produce or meat they are unhappy with because they won't get to see and pick through the products themselves. This is really not the problem. Tescos, for example, allows you to add a note of instructions for each item, so if you prefer green bananas, exaggeratedly crisp apples and lean cuts of meat you can say this. The pickers who go through the shop assembling your order also know that poor quality merchandise will attract complaints, so they tend to do a pretty good job (except for occasional errors).

The big problem is the lack of information. The grocery sites are dealing with a huge number of constantly changing commodity items. The upshot is that, unlike ecommerce sites such as Amazon, which displays extensive information about most products they sell and has live, constantly updated information about availability, you can't read the label on a can on a grocery site for a list of ingredients or find out whether the item is in stock. The availability problem is due to the fact that orders for delivery are assembled at their nearest store from whatever's on the shelves, rather than from a centralized, computerized ware-house system. That's understandable, but if you're planning a menu you may not find out until the groceries are delivered that you're missing a key ingredient.

The first of these problems ought to be surmountable, especially since the commercial food processors must have this information available (to print the labels from), but it seems unlikely there will be any quick change. Tesco says it can supply lists of products suitable for people with certain types of allergies or other special dietary needs, but this isn't really an adequate substitute. It would matter less if it were easy to return or exchange items, but although the stores say they're perfectly willing to do this, it remains uncertain and awkward. It took Tesco three weeks to retrieve a mistakenly delivered bottle of food colouring.

Online grocery services
Asda @t Home (http://www.asda.co.uk)
The Food Ferry (http://www.foodferry.co.uk)
Iceland (http://www.iceland.co.uk)
Sainsburys To You (http://www.sainsburystoyou.com)
Tesco (http://www.tesco-direct.co.uk)
Waitrose (http://www.waitrose.co.uk)

H

HACKING

Despite the amount you read about hacking, most of the Net goes along untroubled most of the time. If you want to see archives of some of the more interesting Web site hacks, however, take a look at the site belonging to *2600: the Hacker Quarterly* (http://www.2600.com), which archives as many as it can get. Although *2600* is often treated as a dangerous publication, lots of the information it publishes is just geek oddities – pictures of phone booths worldwide, for example.

A more professional hacking/security business is the lopht (http://www.lopht.com, note the zero instead of a capital O, one way hackers avoid content filters), which publishes many articles on security holes and fixes.

(See also **Security**.)

HEALTH AND FITNESS

Doctors started complaining as early as 1998 that patients were coming into their offices and demanding treatments they'd read about on the Internet. While a little tact is a good idea – along with the recognition that some treatments you read about on the Internet are quackery and others are not, for one reason or another, available on the NHS – most doctors do agree that a better informed patient is a better patient.

The Internet is home to plenty of medical information, both simplified for the general public and the highly technical clinical information doctors read (see **Medicine**). Probably the most comprehensive site for consumers is Patient UK (http://www.patientuk.com), which links to all sorts of resources for just about every ailment you can think of. It's everything NHS Direct (http://www.nhsdirect.nhs.uk/) should be, although there is valuable information there, too, and also at the NHS Web site proper (www.nhs50.nhs.uk), which links to a number of very good consumer-oriented health sites.

A good range of information for couples dealing with pregnancy or the lack thereof is the Women's Health Information site (http://www.womens-health.co.uk), which also has an excellent page on finding quality medical information on the Internet (http://www.womens-health.co.uk/evidence. htm), with links to a number of related sites including Medline, a free medical journal search service.

The CancerHelp UK site (http://medweb.bham.ac.uk/ cancerhelp/indexg.html) is intended to help both cancer patients and those looking for advice on prevention. You can find information on how almost any cancer is diagnosed and treated – helpful stuff, particularly if you're wishing you had asked the right questions in a recent doctor's appointment. The site cannot, however, answer specific questions; it refers those seeking support to CancerBACUP (http://medweb.bham.ac.uk/cancerhelp/indexg.html), which provides information and support to cancer patients and their families.

Online chemists are thin on the ground in the UK, but Boots (http://www.boots.co.uk) has an online shop featuring both health and beauty items and a mother and baby section.

The US may be famously plagued with obesity, but it's equally home to health-conscious, fitness obsessives, and this is reflected online in the existence of probably thousands of sites dedicated to health and fitness. One of the better ones is Phys (http://www.phys.com), which as well as the normal online calculators that help you paranoiacally work out your body-mass index, waist-to-hip ratio, body-fat percentage and ideal weight, also offers workout guides, slideshow instructions for many exercises, a video showing the correct way to do a breast self-examination and even a guide to calculating the nutritional (or otherwise) value of restaurant meals. Phys would probably be the first to tell you that dieting alone isn't a healthy choice; take the fitness test, and then use one of the site's thirty-four calculators to see how many calories different sports burn up.

If you're trying to teach your child about the workings of the human body, one interesting site is Medtropolis's Virtual Body (http://www.medtropolis.com/VBody.asp), put together by the Columbia Healthcare Corporation, but you will need the Shockwave plug-in (see **Plug-ins**). The site consists of four main sections: the brain, the heart, the digestive system and the skeleton. Each section has animated graphics showing how things work, such as blood flowing through the heart. But there are also narrated tours of the body and games you can play, such as building a skeleton. Accompanying each section are hundreds of articles about health and fitness, written in an easily accessible magazine style. Advice flows on everything from why to avoid 'Celebrity Diets' to how to lower your cholesterol.

HELP

Of course, you don't need any more help than this book but, if you do, try Learn the Net (http://www.learnthenet.com/), or read the Big Dummy's Guide (http://www.hcc.hawaii.edu/bdgtti/bdgtti-1.02_2.html).

HISTORY

Timelines are very popular on the Web, in part because the format is so well suited to hyperlinks. The Timeline of British History (http://www.britannia.com/history/time1.html) is an example. Head, therefore, for Sourcebeat (http://history.searchbeat.com/), which has an immense collection of timelines and other links, particularly from American history, but also from just about everywhere else. You can probably investigate just about any subject in history from this starting point. Also attractive is the World History timeline (http://www.hyperhistory.com); click on bits of it to get more detail, maps and other addenda.

More entertaining historical features are to be had at the History Channel's site (http://thehistorychannel.co.uk), which complements the cable/satellite channel's programmes.

Specialized sites are too numerous to list, but two of the high spots are Argos (http://argos.evansville.edu/), which covers the ancient and mediaeval eras, and the Victorian Web (http://landow.stg.brown.edu/victorian/victov.html). Try the Chinese history timeline (http://www-chaos.umd.edu/history/time_line.html) as a starting place for dynasties and periods.

There is, of course, a great deal of Internet history on the Internet. Start with Hobbes's Internet Timeline (http://www.isoc.org/guest/zakon/Internet/History/HIT.html), and then head for *net.wars* (http://www.nyupress.nyu.edu), whose full text is online for free, and the sample chapters from its companion volume, *From Anarchy to Power: the Net Comes of Age.* These cover 1993–1997 and 1997–2000 respectively, and are an overview of the years in which the Internet changed from being an academic playground to a commercial mass medium.

HOAXES

Heard the one about the modem tax? Or the story about the kid who's dying of leukaemia and wants the world's biggest collection of email? Or the virus that will destroy your hard drive if you so much as open an email message bearing its name? Or the mobile number that, if dialled, gives other people free calls through your phone? This story was verified by IBM/the FBI/Microsoft just this morning, and they will pay two cents for every email message they receive! Forward it to all your friends!

Don't. Repeat: do *not* forward these messages. Even the one about the petition to help the Taliban women, worthy a cause though that is.

Many of these messages contain at least some germ of truth. The kid with leukaemia was a real child, but his original intent was to collect postcards, not email messages, and the publicity he got when he reached the *Guinness Book of World Records* got him treatment, funded by an anonymous donor. He's grown up now. Likewise, the story about the Taliban women and their plight is true, but the student who began the petition had her email address cancelled because her university's email server collapsed under the flood of messages.

When you get an email message of this type, *before* hitting the send button for your entire address book, no matter how immediately urgent the contents may be, *stop and think*. Then log on to one of the many hoax-tracking sites on the Net – Stiller Research's Hoax Page (http://www.stiller.com/hoaxes.htm), Urban Legends' Zeitgeist page (http://www.urbanlegends.com/ulz/index.html) or the 'How to Spot an Email Hoax' page (http://www.urbanlegends.about.com/science/urbanlegends/library/howto/hthoax.htm) – and take a minute to assess the message. There is nothing so urgent that a minute's delay is a problem. If you still want to forward it, call someone knowledgeable and check it with them.

Then don't do it.

There are, of course, other types of hoaxes that go around the Net – chain letters, get-rich-quick schemes, the scam where you're supposed to help someone in a third-world country move funds in return for a percentage. The basic rule there is: There Ain't No Such Thing As A Free Lunch (or TANSTAAFL, as it's known on the Net). If it looks too good to be true, it probably is. Keep an eye on the Internet Fraud Watch site (http://www.fraud.org) for news about the latest scams to beware.

HORSERACING

See under **Sports**.

HOTELS

If you're looking for a hotel online, you generally have three choices: search, use a general travel site like Expedia or Travelocity, or go straight to one of the major hotel chains' sites, such as Thistle (http://www.thistlehotels.co.uk). (See also **Search Engines** and **Travel**.)

Most of the major London hotels (http://www.london. hotels.co.uk/reservations/index.htm) have their own site, showing room availability in real time; the site takes online reservations for the Forte, Posthouse, Meridien, Travelodge and Heritage chains, as well as the Strand Palace and Regent Palace. Travelodge (http://www.travelodge.co.uk/) and Posthouse (http://www.posthouse-hotels.co.uk) also have their own online reservations sites covering the entire UK. If you know what hotel you'd like to stay at, picking one of the chains' sites is probably the easiest and most reliable way to go.

If you don't know what hotel you'd like to stay at, or if you're having no luck finding an available room, it's worth trying Late Rooms (http://www.laterooms.com), a site for last-minute bookings, somewhat better done than the badly executed LastMinute (see **Travel**). Handling only hotel reservations, Late Rooms is particularly strong on Britain, but also has listings from the US, most of Europe and even parts of Asia. Essentially, you pick a country and then tell the site the region or city you're interested in, the number of people, the date and the number of nights, and the site gives you back a list of available rooms and prices (a currency converter is available), with details about each hotel. You have to phone the hotel to make final arrangements (and, says one experienced user, when you do you sometimes get even better rates than those listed on the site), but the site goes a long way toward giving you an idea of where to start.

INSURANCE

It always sounds so good when you read about it in the newspapers: buying insurance online, and thereby cutting out the salesman and saving money. Somehow, it isn't as easy as that. For one thing, you generally have to give a raft of personal information just to get a quote, and if all you wanted to do was comparison shop it just doesn't seem worth it. Most of the usual suspects give quotes online. The AA (http://www.theaa.co.uk), for example, offers a 5 per cent Internet discount on home and car insurance; it submits the information you provide to a panel of insurers and finds you the best deal. Direct Line (http://www.directline.co.uk) offers its full range of services online, with a five per cent discount on home and travel insurance; you can even insure your pets against needing veterinary treatment. MoneyExtra (http://www.moneyextra.com/insurance/) also offers a comparison shopping service for travel and life insurance, with motor and household insurance to follow soon. Unlike the other sites, it runs a number of feature articles to help you make a more informed decision, looking closely at, for example, the high cost of medical insurance.

These sites routinely demand a lot of information, offputting if you have an exaggerated sense of privacy (see

Privacy). Does someone offering annual travel insurance really need your complete home address in order to tell you how much it's going to cost? You can't get away from the suspicion that a number of these sites are taking the opportunity to build larger-than-normal databases for marketing purposes. However, if you want to buy insurance by this route, in order to get a quote you will have no choice but to give the information they want; make sure the little opt-out (or sometimes opt-in) boxes are correctly checked (or unchecked) if you do not want follow-up junk mail or email.

Money extra (http://www.moneyextra.co.uk) and International Investor Interactive (http://www.iii.co.uk) both offer comparison tables for insurance rates, which are worth consulting before you buy.

INVESTING

There are two reasons why online share trading has taken off so quickly, and both of them are the dot-com boom. First of all, the people who trade the shares of these extremely volatile companies want quick, direct access to the market. Second of all, the growth of the Internet as a secure platform for electronic commerce is perfectly suited to trading shares, which are an information-heavy purchase with a physical manifestation that's no more difficult to ship than a piece of paper.

Choosing a broker

Three types of companies offer online share-trading facilities: start-ups set up for the purpose such as eTrade; traditional brokerages such as Donaldson Lufkin Jenrette (DLJ
Direct) or Charles Schwab Europe; and familiar banking
names such as the Halifax or Barclays. Costs and the exact
services they offer vary widely. Besides the obvious commission per trade (anything from £10 upwards), online
brokers may charge fees for annual maintenance, transfer-
ring share certificates, automatically reinvesting dividends,
and wiring deposits and withdrawing of funds. Most offer
in addition at least some information services about the
companies traded on the various exchanges, and they may
charge for higher-level access to these. Schwab, for example,
gives all account holders access to Reuters news services
including delayed quotes and current headlines; for an extra
£10 a month, Schwab investors get more comprehensive
access to Reuters' company information and analysts'
opinions.

The first thing to think about in choosing an online broker
is what type of trader you are. Buy-and-hold investors –
that is, people who are likely to hold shares for many years
– have very different needs from short-term traders. For a
buy-and-hold investor focusing on mature companies, for
example, paying a little more in commissions on trades may
be worth it if it means not paying annual fees. For a short-
term trader sticking with volatile new technology issues,
being able to check prices in real time and lock in a price
using limit orders before buying or selling may be the most
important issue. Short-term traders may also want to ensure

that the broker offers alternative means of access, such as telephone trading, in the event that the Web site crashes or the Internet clogs up at exactly the wrong moment. All of these costs and limitations make for a complex series of tradeoffs: DLJ Direct, for example, charges no annual maintenance fee, but charges £14.95 per trade, as opposed to Schwab Europe's £12.95 charge per trade, but added annual fee of £20; on the other hand Schwab offers 24-hour support.

Online brokers also vary in which stocks they handle. Stocktrade and eTrade, for example, will only deal in CREST-registered UK shares (although eTrade also operates US-based accounts for UK residents). Hargreaves Lansdown allows dealing in any LSE or AIM-registered shares, plus warrants if you've signed a special risk warning notice.

Another significant variation among brokers is how you pay for the shares you buy. Barclays, for example, debits the purchase amount directly from your bank or building society account; because of this, there's a £7,500 maximum on trades until your bank can supply a credit reference. Barclays will also put through sales for you without having the certificates in hand; you sign and transfer within five days of the trade. Brokers like eTrade, Schwab, or Hargreaves Lansdown expect you to deposit funds or share certificates before you place an order. There is no minimum balance for eTrade accounts or for Schwab Europe, but Schwab requires a minimum balance of $10,000 (in cash or securities) for a US-based account and Hargreaves Lansdown has a minimum of £1,000.

Most sites have facilities for getting a look at their trading screens and facilities before you commit funds, either

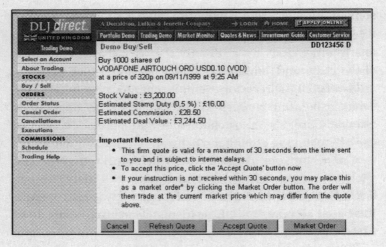

Figure 2. DLJ confirmation screen.

through an online demo (DLJ Direct) or by letting you set up an account online without depositing funds first (e-Trade). You should always try at least several of these out before definitely deciding on a broker. Ease of use is a big issue here: you do not want to make a mistake in a trade because you had trouble understanding the way the screen formatted quotes and data. Speed and the reliability of the prices quoted also counts. DLJ Direct's trading confirmation screen, for example, doesn't give you much in the way of frills, but it shows you what you're buying and how much it will cost in share price, commission and stamp duty, and guarantees the quote for 30 seconds.

One major issue that's difficult to check until it's too late is the quality of customer service. It's safe to assume that at some point every site is going to have a problem, whether it's a system crash, or a network clogging that expensively delays a trade, or some other crazy fluke that cuts off part of the Internet. Trades can go badly wrong in such cases.

Brokers that also act as underwriters for new issues may be attractive to those hoping to get in on IPOs (initial public offerings, the first sale of stock in a company to the public), as they may give qualified customers access to these. However, it's worth bearing in mind two rules. First, the only IPOs you can usually get in on are the ones you don't want. Second, most IPOs, even those that go through the roof on their first day of trading, are usually selling below their first-day close within a few weeks.

Putting through a trade is not difficult. In fact, it's arguable it should be harder (though of course not less clear – you don't want mistakes). Essentially, you click on a button to initiate the process and choose the stock and the number of shares you want to buy. Be careful about this, as you will be required to pay for shares when the settlement period is up, and if enough funds aren't in your account your broker can sell them to make up the shortfall. If you are trading on a service that allows you to do so, you will find fields that let you set limits on the price you're willing to pay or accept (if you're selling shares). You will generally be given a real-time quote, which may or may not be guaranteed as the price you will pay/get. Then you enter a password and click on a confirmation button to actually put through the trade. It may or may not go through instantly: if you've specified a price, it will be delayed until the broker can get that price, and of course it's perfectly possible for the

Internet or the broker's site to get backlogged, especially on very volatile market days. Most sites will email you a confirmation of the order, and you may also be able to view details of the completed transaction on the Web site in your account. You should also be able to get a postal confirmation. For obvious reasons, you should be very careful to keep your trading password secret: you will find it very difficult, if not impossible, to repudiate a trade that was put through using it.

Research

Besides the research offered by online brokers as a value-added service, it's important not to overlook the many independent information sites that have sprung up. These may be both more objective and more comprehensive.

Interactive Investor International (http://www.iii.co.uk) and Gomez (http://www.uk.gomez.com) both offer trading via gateways to several online brokers, along with a comparison service to help you choose. The primary purpose of both the Interactive Investor International and the Motley Fool's UK site, however, is really to provide background information on companies and investing. The Motley Fool is particularly strong on common-sense advice and analysis aimed at amateur investors, whereas Interactive Investor International tends to assume a higher level of knowledge. Both offer online discussion areas; these and other chat areas and bulletin boards can be an enormously useful source of information as they are often frequented by knowledgeable people, but they should be approached with caution. The Securities and Exchange Commission, which regulates the US stock markets, is prosecuting a number of Internet users who have heavily tipped shares to their own profit, and there is no reason to assume similar problems won't arise in the UK, where the Financial Services Authority has already said it intends to crack down on share-tipping on Web sites. It's wise to treat information gathered from these areas as if they were comments overheard in a bar, and consider the source very carefully. Then remember to apply the same caveats to the analysts and commentators who appear in the mass media.

Additional sites

Berkshire Hathaway (http://www.berkshirehathaway.com): the minimalist site belonging to Warren Buffett's company is home to Buffett's annual reports, themselves probably the best and clearest guide to sound investing strategies outside of his teacher Benjamin Graham's classic book, *The Intelligent Investor*. Worth reading, both for entertainment and for a reminder that investing does not have to be a form of gambling.

Money Extra (http://www.moneyextra.com): site comparing the overall costs of bank accounts, credit cards, mortgages and insurance. The site maintains weekly lists of rates across most of these categories, and lets you find the best rate for your needs. It's not comprehensive – a number of smaller banks don't pop up in the bank account comparison tables, for example, and you can't enter the details of the account you have now to compare against current offers. Still, it's a very useful service.

US trading

One possibility the Net opens up is letting non-US citizens trade US stocks directly without going through all the expensive layers of middlemen. This option is much cheaper, but has a few added difficulties. Increasingly, UK online brokers will handle US stocks for you, but this section is aimed at people who want to go direct to a US broker.

Not all US brokers accept accounts from British residents. Technically, UK regulations require US brokers to have a British presence if they market their services in the UK. Accordingly, you will find that some brokers require you to supply a US address if you want to open an account with them, and others will not open the account at all. Similarly, some mutual fund companies will not allow non-US citizens to invest. So check this point on each individual site first.

In general, US brokers offer more complete services at lower cost and far greater access to information than UK ones. Partly, this is a reflection of the overall ethos of the US market, whose regulator, the Securities and Exchange Commission, pushes heavily for increased openness. It is currently campaigning for all companies to Webcast their earnings conference calls with analysts.

US online commissions typically run from $8 to $30, there is no stamp duty, and few brokers charge annual management fees. However, there may be a minimum deposit required to open an account, and compare carefully how much brokers charge for extras such as phone access or registering shares in your name and sending paper certificates ($15 to $50 per issue). Also look at how much the broker charges for limit and stop orders that pin prices to

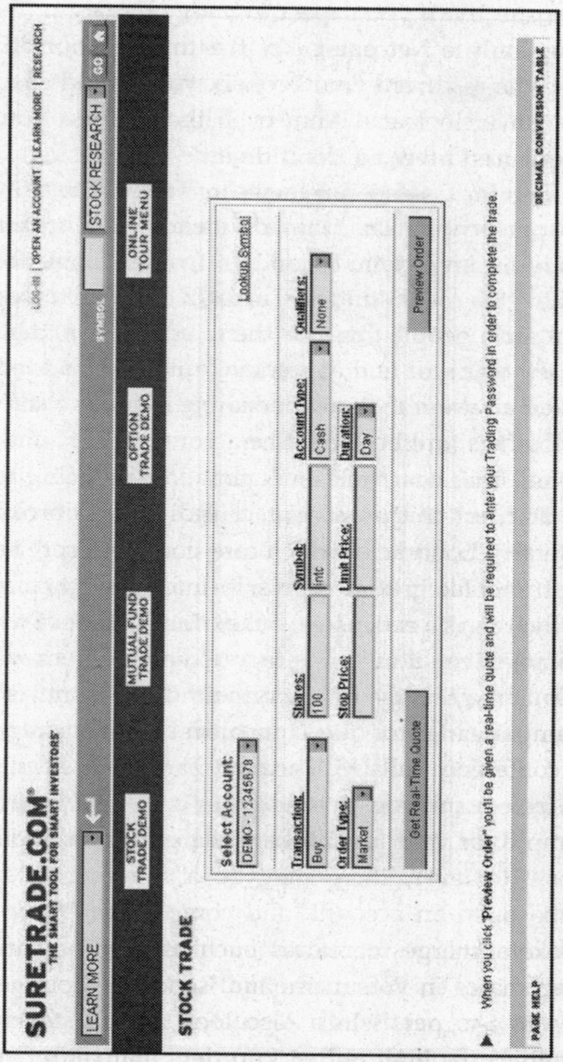

Figure 3. SureTrade trading scheme. Confirming trade requires second password.

levels you specify. If you expect to trade on margin (that is, putting up only a percentage of the money yourself and borrowing the rest from your broker), you should check on the cost of margin loans. And, even then, unless you're a very experienced investor, don't do it.

Don't forget taxes and currency conversion. The US with-holds 30 per cent in tax from dividends paid to foreign nationals (you can reclaim it), and you will be liable for UK capital gains tax on US trades. Currency rates are less of an issue than most people think, as the rates won't matter until you actually want to send or retrieve funds. The added risk is, however, a reason to limit US dealing to funds that won't be needed in the foreseeable future.

One final issue to check on is how you're going to get funds in and out of the account. Unless the US brokerage has an office in London, in which case it may accept Sterling cheques, it's unlikely to accept anything other than wired funds (which can be expensive) or US dollar cheques written on a US bank. Even if the brokerage accepts cheques written in pounds, it may refuse to let you withdraw money in any form other than a US cheque, a problem users have reported with DLJ Direct. As US cheques can cost substantial amounts in fees and take up to six weeks to clear in the UK, this is a point for short-term investors to check in advance.

Research
The amount of information available about US companies is simply amazing. The Securities and Exchange Commission (http://www.sec.gov), which regulates the US stock mar-kets, requires quarterly, rather than semi-annual, reporting,

and has been pushing for greater openness. The upshot is that just about every company has an investors information section on its Web site that includes at least the last few years of SEC filings, and many are opening their quarterly earnings conference calls and presentations, formerly only accessible to analysts, to the public via the Web.

Among free sites, Yahoo!'s financial area (http://finance.yahoo.com) is a good source for both stock quotes and for company profiles including notes on recent insider trades and ready access to historical charts of the share price as well as current numbers. The Quicken site (http://www.quicken.com) has an extremely useful stockfinder – you set a number of parameters such as dividend yield, growth rates, size of company, industry, and the site returns a list of matching stocks you can then research in more detail. Also, if you do have any trouble finding a company's official earnings reports, the SEC's own site has a complete, searchable database known as EDGAR (http://www.sec.gov/cgi-bin/srch-edgar) where you should be able to find them. At a pinch, of course, you just email or write to the company's investor relations person with your request; his or her name and contact information will certainly be on the site.

To get daily news and updates, the easiest way is to create a portfolio on a site such as the Motley Fool (http://www.fool.com) or CNBC (http://www.cnbc.com); you can watch the prices update on a 20-minute delay, and clicking on any of the symbols will give you that day's news for the company, as well as pointers to any articles appearing on the Fool or in its message boards.

There are, of course, many premium services that sell

analysts' reports and other information. Links to the ones covering the companies you're interested in should be displayed in the companies' profiles when you look them up on Quicken or Yahoo!. The best known is probably Standard and Poor, which operates a retail service (http://www.personalwealth.com) for about $10 a month or $100 a year giving access to its research. Multex Investor (http://www.multex.com) aims at professional investors.

Additional sites

CBS Marketwatch (http://www.marketwatch.com): seems to get the news up faster than CNBC; constantly updated.

The Industry Standard (http://www.thestandard.com): *the* magazine covering all aspects of the high-tech business. In the position *Wired* used to occupy as a must-read. All the magazine's content is on the Web site and freely searchable.

Red Herring (http://www.redherring.com): the California-based magazine covering new technology companies and the venture capital market. If you are interested in high-tech stocks then required reading to know what's coming next.

The Street.com (http://www.thestreet.com): US stock market analysis and commentary. Quite a bit of the site is free, but some is so-called premium content you must pay for. The 30-day free trial should be enough to tell you if the premium features are worth the money.

(See also **Quotes**.)

J

JOBS AND CAREERS

Magazines that rely on recruitment ads for their revenues have been among the first to suffer from the competition posed by the Web. Recruitment ads, more than anything else, are time-sensitive, and the ability to constantly update listings as jobs open up or are filled makes the process of looking for jobs much more efficient for both employers and employees. It's safe to say that by now you'd be unlikely to get a job in IT using traditional methods: if you aren't checking job openings on the Web and sending out resumés electronically, you're not going to be qualified. Other industries are likely to go the same way very quickly; online recruitment just offers too many advantages.

To give an idea of how much potential there is, in October 2000 the leading job sites boasted listings for hundreds of thousands of jobs. Monster, for example, claimed more than 12,000 job listings in the UK alone, with more than double that in Europe and a total of 440,000 worldwide; Topjobs said it had advertised 201,321 jobs in the previous month.

There are three types of recruitment sites. Basic job boards make no attempt at anything complicated; they are merely places to post jobs and CVs, with users doing their own matching. Monster, for example, maintains discussion boards and publishes features on subjects such as writing effective CVs, but the most complex feature tends to be email agents to notify you when new jobs in the database match your requirements and little is provided in the way of personal service. More complex sites try to do real recruitment like traditional agencies, matching people to jobs. There are many fewer of those – one example that specializes in IT professionals and jobs paying more than £50,000 a year is First Person Global (http://www.firstpersonglobal.com), which belongs to Harvey Nash. The third type is a Web front end to a traditional agency such as Russell Reynolds (http://www.russreyn.com/).

There are, of course, far more of the database-style sites that collect CVs and job listings than just these two. But as time goes on, expect to see these sites beefed up with additional features and services, partly because selling those services will make the companies money and partly because in the ultra-competitive Web environment adding features is the only way a site can continue to survive. A report from Forrester Research (read the press release at http://www.forrester.com/ER/Press/Release/0,1769,246,FF.html) predicts that the future of online recruitment is in what the company calls 'career networks' that will aggregate training, assessment and placement services. Forrester believes these career networks will capture 55 per cent of the $7.1 billion recruitment market by 2005.

In the meantime, though, we're stuck with the limitations of today's sites. At a site like the heavily advertised Monster, for example, you can search the job listings without creating an account on the site, but for anything else you need to register. The site lets you create an online CV and create 'agents' to spot jobs that match your requirements and email you when they're added to the database. Creating the online CV is a fairly painless, 15-minute operation. The site already has your contact details, so it enters those automatically. You add a descriptive title for the type of job you're looking for (so your CV will pop up in searches) and an outline of your goals, along with all the other background typically included. The site guides you through step by step. It's a bit of a nuisance that you can't simply post your existing CV, which is probably on your computer already in electronic form, but of course you can copy and paste existing text into the boxes in the online form.

The good thing about these sites is that you can post your CV on all of them – it's not like a headhunting agency that wants exclusivity. For the sites themselves, this is a bad thing, of course, as it militates against the development of ongoing relationships with their customers, the kind of thing that is necessary to turn them into profitable businesses with good long-term prospects. For recruiters and job-hunters, it also means a lot more searching and checking; even so, it's still more convenient to check six Web sites than to trudge to six separate agency offices.

One thing that's much easier online is checking up on your prospective employer and learning enough about the company to look smart and well-informed at the interview. Start by taking a look at the company's Web site (if you don't know the address, use the tips in the section on **Search Engines** to find it). With any luck, the site will include a potted history of the company, the names and backgrounds of the company directors, and information on the company's products and services. If the company is a public one, you'll also be able to look at investor information such as financial reports, earnings projections, analysts' research, and a history of the stock price (useful if part of the compensation you're being offered is in the form of stock or options). You can also search the Web for oustanding controversy and/or legal actions against the company and some idea of how it stacks up against its competitors. You may even be able to find out what its ex-employees think of it, all useful information, and compare notes with other workers in the same types of jobs and locations to get a feel for typical salaries and benefits.

Recruitment sites

CV Services (http://www.cvservices.net): advice on writing CVs.

Jobsite (www.jobsite.co.uk): like all these sites, Jobsite lets you post a CV and send it to recruitment agencies, and get emailed notification of relevant jobs (users report this is very effective for producing calls from prospective employers). The site also offers industry headlines and job advice.

Jobworld (http://www.jobworld.co.uk or http://www.newmonday.co.uk): site lets you search training courses as well as jobs available; plus there's the usual facility for posting a CV.

The London Professional Recruitment Guide (http://www.recruitment500.com/): ranks recruitment services in a variety of fields. Primarily aimed at employers.

Monster (http://www.monster.co.uk): search the database, set up a profile and wait for email as new jobs are added that match the specifications you've set.

Top Jobs (http://www.topjobs.co.uk): more of the same, and lots of it.

JOKES

There's no denying it: a lot of the jokes on the Net (and there are a lot of jokes on the Net) are geek jokes. Jokes.com (http://www.jokes.com) tries to be different with absurd news and an emailed joke every day; you can send electronic postcards to friends or, if you are a parent, preset the cleanliness level in the jokes your children get. Lots of the jokes are pretty lame ('A blonde opened a hair salon next to a graveyard and named it Curl Up and Dye'), but you do at least get to vote on how bad you think they are. Connoisseurs of anthropology humour might also like the chronicles of the Nacirema people (http://www.beadsland.com/nacirema/) of North America and their strange worship rituals.

But this is tame stuff. Real Netheads prefer the Onion (http://www.theonion.com), whose book of archived stories became a surprise bestseller in 2000. Irreverent ('God Wondering Whatever Happened to That Planet Where He Made All Those Monkeys'), caustic ('Bush Horrified to Learn Presidential Salary'), snide (its celebrity interviews page is called 'Justify Your Existence') and often crude, the Onion

('America's Finest News Source') is one of the most consistently funny things on the Net. Suck (http://www.suck.com) is a highly sarcastic daily commentary on a current event; it's less funny that it was, but always worth looking at.

A couple of perennial personal favourites. The Web, you may be surprised to learn, can take your picture; see the Magic Cyber Camera (http://www.geocities.com/Heartland/Acres/3072/camera2.html). And Digicrime (http://www.digicrime.com): hackers for hire. Show it to an unsuspecting geek with unsaved data, and watch him have a heart attack.

JUNK (EMAIL AND OTHER)

One of the nice things about the earliest days of the Net was that there was no junk. Or very little: the occasional chain-letter posting ('Make Money Fast!') and one or two more, and that was it. All that changed in 1994, when a pair of lawyers named Laurence Canter and Martha Siegel posted the first widespread online ad (to more than 10,000 Usenet newsgroups); they were pilloried on the Net, but the damage was done. These days, advertising on the Web is common, Usenet is drenched in spam, and junk email harasses everyone. Technically, junk email is correctly known as UCE (for Unsolicited Commercial Email) or UBE (for Unsolicited Bulk Email). Many people refer to it as spam, but this term technically only applies to advertisements posted in bulk to Usenet. If you complain to your

ISP, use UCE or UBE – you'll get a little more respect for using the correct term.

Dealing with junk email

Few Internet users can keep a sense of perspective about junk email. Even though it's less wasteful of resources than postal junk mail and far less intrusive than junk phone calls, junk email feels like a massive invasion of a personal space, perhaps because of the intimate setting in which computers are generally used. You probably can't eliminate junk email entirely, but you can do quite a lot to minimize its impact.

There are really three types of junk email. First is out-and-out junk – get-rich-quick schemes, ads for CD-ROMs of email addresses to be used for more bulk mailings, so-called credit repair services and chain letters. Second is marketing email for traders in legitimate items who don't care whom they annoy; these ads for products like laser toner cartridges, satellite descramblers and other products often come from non-UK retailers and are of no use to UK residents. Third is email follow-ups from Web sites you've visited, shopped at or registered with. Each of these categories require a different strategy.

Taking the third type first, if you shop at a Web site there's little you can do about their having your email address (see **Privacy**). They need it to send you order confirmations and alert you to any problems that may arise with your order. You can, however, use a separate email address for online purchases, perhaps one from a free Web email service, ignoring it except when you actually have a transaction in progress. Most of these companies will provide a Web address you can go to in order to get your name off the mailing list. These you can use safely. At a pinch – remember these companies do want your business – forward the offending message to postmaster@<the site's address> with a polite note pointing out that you've asked not to receive these messages and asking for help getting off the lists. These days, sadly, a number of sites don't realize that it's a standard requirement for each domain to have a valid postmaster address that is staffed by a human on continuous call; for the majority that do, the postmaster generally will help you.

To keep from getting these messages in the first place, always peruse registration and ordering forms carefully, looking for the box to check to indicate that you do not want emailed promotional offers or newsletters. The one exception you might want to make if you care about privacy is for changes to a site's privacy policy: you do want to know if they make changes in how they intend to handle the personal data they accumulate about you as a customer.

For Web sites you just want to check out but that require registration in order for you to do so, there is a simple solution: give the minimum of information on the form. Estimates are that about a quarter of online users lie on these forms. A number of sites get around this possibility by insisting on emailing you a password (that way you have to give a genuine address). This is the time a lot of people use a special address, either a spare ID (on, for example, AOL or Demon, which allow multiple user IDs per account) or a throwaway address on one of the free services. Bear in mind, however, that for some sites the data you provide on the registration form is one of the things that helps them survive financially: advertising sponsorship depends on the demographic data they can point to when setting rates. Even so, it's arguable that you shouldn't have to supply your name, address and phone number just to find out what a site has to offer – it's as if a shop posted a guard at the entrance demanding that information before they let you look around.

Badly targeted marketing email for commodity products like laser toner cartridges and so on are harder to deal with. For one thing, the companies sending them often don't care that they've annoyed people. Bulk email is incredibly cheap compared to any other form of marketing, so for companies who don't have a long-standing reputation to protect there is little motivation to stop using it. In the interests of the Net at large, do not buy from companies that operate irresponsible email policies; dealing with junk email is a huge burden on many companies and ISPs and it's better not to encourage the perpetrators. It's generally held that it's a bad idea to use the 'remove' address a lot of these messages include at the bottom, however, as responding to that address verifies that your email address works, leaving it open to resale to yet other bulk emailers. A dignified silence is the best gambit.

If these messages (and their brethren, as the first type of email includes ads for porn sites) come from known ISPs, such as AOL, Hotmail or Excite, you can complain to those ISPs by forwarding the entire message, header included, to abuse@<the ISP's domain name>. For Hotmail, for example, that would be abuse@hotmail.com. You will most likely get an autoresponse message back acknowledging receipt of your complaint and giving additional information about the ISP's acceptable use policies. Often, the message will tell you the junk emailer's account has been cancelled. Don't get too excited about this, however, as many of the companies that advertise by this method know their accounts won't last long, and use the free services as throwaway accounts. Almost as often, the message will tell you that although the message appeared to come from their system it was in fact a forgery. Those who want to pursue junk emailers and spammers to the ends of the earth to make them cry for forgiveness, should look at the Stop Spam site (http://www.stopspam.org) for an explanation of how to read email headers and trace a message's true origins (http://www.stopspam.org/email/headers/headers.html).

The first line of defence is your ISP or your company's network administrator. Because junk email places a heavy burden on ISPs' systems, many make the effort to block junk directed at their users; Web services such as Bigfoot (http://www.bigfoot.com) offer this as one of their selling points. Blocking isn't a perfect solution, as filters are crude bludgeons and you can't block all bulk email without blocking the emailing lists people have subscribed to. In addition, some users take offense and see the practice as censorship. Nonetheless, it can help, in part because ISPs operate some sophisticated schemes for identifying junk.

The second line of defence is your email software. Good email software is designed so that users can build their own filters to block out unwanted communications. It can be difficult, if only because the source of the messages is so unpredictable. Most people can't afford to, say, block all of AOL or Hotmail (both common sources of spam because it's so easy to set up a new account). In the software I use, Ameol, I have rules set that block out messages based on common phrases like 'call now for your free' or 'stuffing envelopes at home'. The only way to build up an effective set of rules is to go through a bunch of junk email carefully looking for common factors. And then you will have to repeat the exercise in six months or a year, as the junk emailers become more sophisticated.

(See also **Privacy**.)

Additional sites

Twelve Simple Things You Can Do to Save the Internet (http://www.rahul.net/falk/whatToDo.html).

Campaign Against Unsolicited Commercial Email (http://www.cauce.org).

Usenet: news.admin.net-abuse

K

KNOWLEDGE

Find out what the Knowledge required of London taxi drivers really is (http://www.taxiknowledge.co.uk/index4.html). There's a practice test . . .

L

LEGAL

Law, like medicine, is one of those subjects where you have to start somewhere and learn as you go. The place to start for legal information seems to be Law on the Web (http://www.lawontheweb.co.uk/intro.htm), which aims to make the law more accessible to ordinary individuals. Read the advice, consult the directory to find a lawyer, browse the links and then – strange as it sounds – have fun catching up on the latest happenings on *Ally McBeal* and read some lawyer jokes.

One of the better specialist British legal sites is the Penal Lexicon (http://www.penlex.org.uk/), which covers absolutely everything to do with the prison service – statistics, the workings of the justice system, annual reports and so on. Most of the material is drawn from public sources such as Hansard, reports from the various government agencies and the like, but putting it all together would be – has been – a lengthy job. An invaluable resource for anyone interested in the state of criminal justice in the UK or who knows a prisoner.

LIBRARY

The Library and Information Service at the University of Exeter (http://www.ex.ac.uk/library/wwwlibs.html) indexes an impressive number of online libraries and catalogues around the UK. Particularly impressive are the lists of higher education and research libraries and public libraries. From the UK Public Libraries on the Web page (http://dspace.dial.pipex.com/town/square/ac940/weblibs.html), you can find any UK library that has an online presence, find out what its services and opening hours are and, in many cases, access the card catalogue online. While that might seem kind of silly at first – after all, you still have to go in and get the book – online access can save you time by letting you reserve the book so it's ready for collection when you get there. Better than that, you can renew books online.

For browsing the world's libraries, a good place to start is the WWW Virtual Library (http://www.mth.uea.ac.uk/VL/Overview.html), which uses a Yahoo!-like directory structure to move you quickly through libraries by subject (see **Yahoo! and Other Portals**). A few clicks can take you to resources on almost any subject.

More traditionally, there is the British Library (http://www.bl.uk): a guide to the library's many collections and exhibits, though most of these have to be visited in person. The site also offers a service called Inside, which delivers articles from 20,000 research journals by fax or electronically in PDF (Acrobat) format; users pay annual fees starting at £500 for a password to allow them to access the service, plus a copyright fee per article (typically £4.50 for electronic delivery).

Libraries are one institution whose role is expected to change dramatically because of the Internet. What, after all, is the purpose of libraries in a world where everything is online? Do we need buildings to act as repositories? 'The End of Information and the Future of Libraries' by Phil Agre (http://www.libr.org/PL/12–13_Agre.html) is a good place to start exploring the debates about these issues.

Additional sites

The Internet Archive (http://www.archive.org): project to archive the Internet. On average a Web page only stays up for 70 days, so there's a lot to store. Access to the collections is by special arrangement.

The Internet Public Library (http://www.ipl.org/): hosted at the School of Information at the University of Michigan, the Internet Public Library is an experiment to see what librarians and the Internet can contribute to each other. The site offers links to electronic texts, special exhibits, magazines, newspapers and help with Web searching. In late 2000, for example, the site had on display a collection of four hundred photographs of lighthouses and a research project on killer whales.

The Library of Congress (http://www.loc.gov): the US's copyright library has everything from an extensive online catalogue of every book ever published in the US (useful for looking up out-of-print titles) and online exhibitions to everything you ever wanted to know about American copyright law.

LITERARY

Everyone is going to have a different idea of what's a good literary site online. These are some personal favourites.

Arts & Letters Daily (http://www.cybereditions.com): elegantly designed page of links to online publications all over the Internet, with long columns of four-line article summaries headed Articles of Note, New Books and Essays and Opinions, plus permanent links to online newspapers, (mostly American) columnists, search engines and a few amusing sites.

Feed (http://www.feedmag.com): one of the older and better online magazines, running features and essays.

Salon (http://www.salon.com): what *The New Yorker* online would be if it were based in San Francisco, a little more high-tech in orientation and online since 1995. A personal favourite, but it has to be – I've written for them.

Slate (http://www.slate.com): Microsoft-funded, but edited by Michael Kinsley, who wrote for every high-quality US magazine for years before moving to Seattle. *Slate* is better than you expect – though *Salon* is probably what it should have been.

LIVE EVENTS

You can actually have live events on the Internet, though the effect is usually spoiled by these events' being archived for replay afterwards. Talk City (http://www.talkcity.com) does archive the live chats it runs with celebrity (and not-so-celebrity) guests, but being there at least gives you a chance to be one of the people asking the questions. Check the site's schedule to find out who's coming up that might interest you.

Live concerts are less common, even though the Rolling Stones (http://www.stones.com) were one of the first to broadcast a few songs live. More frequent are live Webcasts of earnings conference calls by major companies – to find those, you should browse the investors information section of the site of the company you're interested in and note the date of the next earnings release. Then it's a matter of checking back nearer the time and looking for instructions.

M

MAPS

Streetmap (http://www.streetmap.co.uk/) solves the problem of how to find things in a strange town. Enter a London postcode, or the name of a place in the UK, and get back a local map.

MATHS

'Mathematics is not only real, but it is the only reality,' said Martin Gardner, former mathematical games columnist for *Scientific American*, in 1994. Gardner's explanation of why forms part of the archive of mathematical quotations at Furman University (http://math.furman.edu/~mwoodard/mqs/mquot.shtml).

At least some of the history Gardner wishes were more widely taught is to be found at the MacTutor History of Mathematics Archive (http://www-groups.dcs.st-and.ac.uk/~history/) which is hosted by the School of Mathematics and Statistics at the University of St Andrews, and it includes many fascinating features on different branches and periods of mathematics, as well as several thousand biographies of important mathematicians going all the way back to Ahmes (1680–1620 BC).

Finally, for some current, entertaining mathematics features, try +Plus (http://pass.maths.org.uk/index.html), a Web mathematics magazine sponsored by Cambridge University.

MEDIA

Of course you'll find a comprehensive listing of online newspapers and magazines in the UK at Yahoo! (see **Yahoo! and Other Portals**). But Media UK (http://www.mediauk.com) has newspaper, TV, radio and magazine directories, newsfeeds, journalists' resources and discussion forums. The site's owner, James Cridland, makes a supreme effort to make the site as comprehensive as possible, and it's a great effort.

For resources for PR and marketing professionals, try PR Source (http://www.prsource.co.uk). For press guides, try Hollis (http://www.hollis-pr.co.uk), publisher of both the Hollis directories and Willings Press Guide. For an aggregator of press releases, try PR Newswire's Newsdesk (http://www.newsdesk.co.uk), which is also the UK contact site for Profnet, a service for journalists that circulates requests for expert academic commentary to university PR people.

It's also worth checking out NetMedia (http://www.net-media.co.uk/), which runs annual conferences on new media as well as the Online Journalism awards. It's always worth looking at the sites of the award winners, and besides that there are the results of a survey carried out by Net Media in conjunction with City University of print and broadcast journalists to explore how they use the Internet in gathering news.

On Usenet, the relevant newsgroups are uk.media and alt.journalism. Finally, there's the Fleet Street Forum (http://www.fleetstreet.org.uk), the online journalists' discussion group I helped found in 1995. Anyone can post, and you can read the site using either a Web-based interface or a Usenet newsreader following the instructions on the front page.

MEDICINE

The child of thirty years ago played with the Visible Man and Visible Woman, ultra-modern, clear, plastic models with removable organs, as a way of learning human anatomy (later supplemented with Isaac Asimov's book *The Human Body*). Today's child learns about human anatomy by exploring the data available from the Visible Human Project across the Web using one of several viewers designed for the purpose. There's a two-dimension viewer at the University of Adelaide (http://www.dhpc.adelaide.edu.au/projects/vishuman2/), which lets you view either the man or woman, slice by slice, from a variety of angles (you'll need Java). The National Institutes of Health publishes a list (http://www.nlm.nih.gov/research/visible/

applications.html) of the various projects around the Net to let people view the Visible Human data. Though avoid the 3D version at the University of Syracuse; the idea of a 3D virtual reality view sounds good, but even over a high-speed connection like ADSL you will need a gigaload of patience, as anything to do with VRML is just unbelievably slow. The Cross-section viewer at Loyola University (http://www.meddean.luc.edu/lumen/MedEd/GrossAnatomy/cross_section/index.html) is a lot more accessible, though a little spooky as accessing the cross-section of your choice involves clicking on a photo of a live human.

The British Medical Association (http://www.bma.org.uk) provides little information for the public; its site is primarily aimed at its doctor members and students. However, Free Medical Journals.com (http://www.freemedical journals.com/) aims to open up access to medical journal literature to the public. Unfortunately, the site doesn't offer a search facility across all those journals; you have to have some idea what you're looking for. WebMedLit (http://webmedlit.silverplatter.com/), however, scans the premier medical Web sites daily, extracting citations, abstracts and full-text articles. The site lets you search all this material or browse it organized into ten categories. Several more high-end databases are searchable if you follow links from Medscape (http://www.medscape.com/Home/Search/Search.html), which also includes (thankfully) a link to an online medical dictionary.

Outside the UK, the World Health Organization (http://www.who.int), the National Institutes of Health (http://www.nih.gov) and the Centers for Disease Control (http://www.cdc.

gov) all publish useful public-interest information on international issues and emerging diseases.

Also worth looking at is Quackwatch (http://www.quackwatch.com), which goes into some detail in explaining the hows and whys of the scientific method by which treatments need to be assessed, both online and offline. Before you start spending good money on that alternative therapy that sounds so much more comforting and less scary than the doctor's recommendation, take a look at what this site has to say about the therapy you're interested in.

(See also **Health and Fitness**.)

MISTAKES

Read it and panic. The Human Error Website (http://panko.cba.hawaii.edu/HumanErr/) aims to chart as comprehensively as possible the ways in which humans make cognitive mistakes. You know those financial experts? They all use spreadsheets. This site explains why not to trust them. Then there's a nice piece on the unreliability of human testimony, 'The Truth in Judging: Testimony ("Fifty Bare-Arsed Highlanders")' (http://carmen.murdoch.edu.au/~zariski/testimon.html). And a not-too-technical paper on chronocenteredness and the perfection of hindsight, 'Twenty-Five/Twenty-Five or, Hindsight Is Always Somewhat "Perfect" (But Perhaps We Can Invent the Future!)', by Charles Urbanowicz at California State University (http: //www.csuchico.edu/~curban/Jan'98_Millennium_Paper.html).

MOBILE USERS

This section covers what you need to do to ensure that you'll be able to get on to the Internet while you're away from home; for instructions on accessing a corporate local area network across the Internet you'll need to talk to your company's network administrator.

The first question is whether you need Internet access from your own or your company's laptop or whether you just need to be able to check email and perhaps a couple of Web pages while you're away. In the latter case, life should be fairly simple. In most parts of Europe and even the more remote parts of the world public access via Internet cafés (there are hundreds in the UK alone) is widespread enough to keep you going pretty consistently. If you use one of the free Web-based email services, such as Hotmail or Yahoo!, that's all you need.

The one place you may have trouble is the US, where the tendency is to expect people to have access at home and at work and therefore not to need public terminals. It's perfectly possible, for example, to spend hours unable to find a public access Internet terminal in the heart of San Francisco's new media district. At a pinch, try the local library, and also try the widespread chain of copy shops known as Kinkos (see http://www.kinkos.com for locations).

Things are a little more complicated if what you want is access to an email account hosted by your regular ISP. In this case, you need to check with your ISP how to access your account when you're not actually dialled directly into

the service. Most ISPs use a standard type of email server
known as POP3 (for Post Office Protocol 3). In many cases,
you'll be able to access your email via the Web. In others,
your ISP may instruct you how to access your email using
an Internet facility known as Telnet. Telnet, which lets you
operate a remote computer as though you were sitting at a
terminal connected directly to it, is an older Internet function; it's text-based and pre-dates the Web. Versions of
Windows from 95 onwards all include a Telnet client, and it
seems to be universally available on the machines in Internet
cafés, though you may have to hunt through the Start menu
for it. (To bring up the Start menu, hit CTRL-ESC simul-
taneously.) AOL, which uses a proprietary email system,
now allows users to access their email via the Web. Just go
to AOL's Web site (http://www.aol.co.uk) and enter your
screen name and password to read, manage and reply to
your email.

The most complicated situation is the one where you're
travelling with a laptop and need dial-up access. The first
task is to ensure that all the software you will need is
installed correctly on the laptop. That includes: a copy of
whatever email software you use and a Web browser. If you
regularly use other Internet software, such as IRC, ICQ or
AOL Instant Messenger, or a Telnet, MUD, or FTP client,
you should install copies of those, too. You will also find
life easier if you can copy across your bookmark file from
the Web browser on your desktop machine – Netscape users
should search for the file BOOKMARK.HTM on their
hard drives. It should also be possible to copy across the
address book for your email software; it's just a matter of

finding out the name of the file and copying it to the appropriate directory on your laptop. Copying these files will go a long way toward making using the Internet on your laptop exactly the same as you're used to on your desktop.

The next item on the list is to configure your dial-up software (in Windows this is known as Dial-Up Networking) so you can reach the ISP you'll be using from the location you'll be in. Within the UK, your biggest problem will be finding a phone jack: just about every ISP now has a non-geographic local access number that you can dial from anywhere in the country for the same price. All you need to do, therefore, is ensure that the number is entered in your laptop's settings.

Outside the UK, things get a little more difficult. For one thing, those local access numbers generally don't work from outside the UK, so you will need to find one that does. Start by checking whether your ISP has dial-up numbers outside the UK, preferably local numbers where you'll be. Many do, either because they themselves have world-wide local access (CompuServe, AOL) or because they have agreements with other ISPs (CIX, Pipex with an additional charge). Demon, which has operations in the Netherlands and the UK, has dial-up access in just those two countries. In some European countries, you may be able to sign up with free services similar to those available in the UK (Freeserve), but it's safer not to count on it.

If your ISP doesn't have local dial-up access in the area you're travelling to, chances are the least expensive and most reliable option is to sign up with CompuServe or AOL.

CompuServe in particular has been in the business of providing worldwide access for well over a decade. Before you leave, set up the account and ensure it's working, and retrieve the numbers you're going to need from CompuServe's access numbers page on its Web site (http://www.compuserve.com/content/phone/phone.asp?floc=nvbr). If you're truly cautious or access is going to be absolutely crucial, try the number you're going to be using from the UK to make sure you can connect to it without trouble (and while technical support in your own language is easily reachable).

One last modem chore: you should check that the modem will work in the country you're going to without alteration. Years of travelling around Europe and in the US have failed to give me any problem, but there are genuine differences in dialling and other tones, and you may still want to check with the manufacturer. Some companies, notably Psion, provide software with their modems that lets you switch the country they're set for; if you make sure the software is installed on your laptop you should be ready for all eventualities.

Knowing you've got dial-up numbers and modem software sorted out, however, is only part of the preparations you'll need to make. How are you going to plug your modem into the phone line? British telephone jacks are distinctly non-standard. In the US, Ireland and parts of the rest of the world, phone plugs are small, square, transparent plastic affairs known as RJ-11s. Many British modems come with converters, if only because the manufacturers supply US-style cables with their modems and throw in a converter plug to the British design with modems sold in the UK. Other countries, notably Switzerland, have plugs no one else uses. So the next step is to check what phone plugs you'll need (http://kropla.com/phones.htm) and source any necessary adaptors. The usual supplier is Tele-Adapt; it's not cheap, but it does stock every one of the forty telephone plugs in use worldwide. (This is the point where you should realize what a miracle the Internet truly is: in the space of less than a decade, by consensus, the entire computer industry converted to a single set of protocols that allowed every computer in the world to talk to every other computer.)

Tele-Adapt is also the source of last resort to solve your next problem: mains adaptor plugs. The first thing you should check, however, is that your laptop's power supply is auto-sensing; if it is, it will say something like '110–240V 50–60Hz' on the bottom and/or in the specifications in the owner's manual. Almost all power supplies today are auto-sensing, but if by any chance yours is not you will need to find out the voltage in use in the country you're travelling to and buy either a converter or, if one is available, the power supply made for your laptop in that country (which will come with a local power cord, saving you the trouble of sourcing the correct plug).

Assuming your power supply is auto-sensing, all you need is a plug that fits the electrical sockets in the country you're travelling to. If you are going to the US or within Europe, the necessary converter plugs are readily available in most airports and sometimes even in High Street shops like Boots. If you're going further afield, Tele-Adapt is, again, the most convenient source; they'll usually sell you a pack for the country you're going to that includes both phone plug and AC adaptor. Tele-Adapt also sells spare batteries and power extender cords for most laptop models so you can plug in on the plane.

Additional sites

Internet Café Guide (http://www.netcafeguide.com/frames. html): awful-looking site, but it does the trick, with a regularly updated, searchable list of cafés. The list isn't comprehensive – there's at least one café missing, in Rhethimno, Crete – but it's certainly enough to make a very good start. People with a long itinerary may prefer to buy the printed book, at $14.95.

Steve Kropla's Help for World Travelers (http://www. kropla.com): guides to electrical systems and phone plugs, world television standards, international dialling codes and other highly useful travel links, everything from how to pack to be a carry-on only traveller to the full list of airport codes.

Tele-Adapt (http://www.teleadapt.co.uk): comprehensive source of information and equipment to let you plug in and dial up anywhere in the world.

MOTOR RACING

See under **Sports**.

MOVING HOUSE

Moving house is one of the biggest upheavals most people will ever experience – and there's very little training for it other than having done it before. Making a move go smoothly is possible if you think through everything in advance and organize it properly. A number of sites exist on the Net to help you do this. The Mortgage Store, of course, focuses primarily on mortgage issues in its section on moving (http://www.mortgagestore.ie/your_mortgage/movinghouse/index.shtml). Your New Home (http://www.yournewhome.co.uk/2000/home.cfm_) is overly Flash-laden and cute, but it does attempt to cover all the bases, from looking at properties to getting through the actual move. The site's extensive checklist is designed to help set a timetable for the move and ensure that you don't forget anything important.

Simply Move (http://www.simplymove.co.uk) takes all this one step further, and will take your new address and contact government departments, utilities and other suppliers on your behalf to help you change address. To get the best of this site, you must register, but doing so lets you keep checklists and dates online, making it easier to keep things together if you're trying to coordinate a move both at home and at work.

It's also worth looking at *Loot* (http://www.loot.com), which alongside its property listings offers help finding good deals on conveyancing, surveys, finance and related services.

(See also **Property**.)

MUSEUMS

The first museum project on the Web, now called the Web Museum (http://www.ibiblio.org/wm/net/) was the brainchild of an individual who wanted to put some of the great paintings online, where everyone could see them. He called it the WebLouvre, until the famous museum objected. His collection of famous paintings, medieval illuminations such as the *Très Riches Heures du Duc de Berry*, and much more is still one of the obvious places to start, not least because you can even host the collection yourself – it's been mirrored all over the world and is one of the most readily accessible of Net resources.

By now, of course, just about all of the world's great names have online collections. For the UK, one place to start is Cornucopia (http://www.cornucopia.org.uk/home.html), which lists UK museums by region and type of collection, as well as whose work is in them – look up Jane Austen, for example, to find out where to see her memorabilia. The picture gallery contains some samples. The site is somewhat unfinished, but it is impressive nonetheless.

Museums Around the World (http://www.icom.org/vlmp/world.html) attempts to do something similar on a global scale. It's not comprehensive, as it's limited to museums that have at least some online presence. There are all sorts of unexpected museums listed here, from the UK's own Papplewick Pumping Station, dedicated to Victorian architecture, to the beautifully illustrated Museum of Art in Macau's Mexican art collection. While nothing can take the place of physical presence, browsing these many collections is a great way to prepare for visiting them; and it's even better for those who dislike spending long hours traipsing through the buildings themselves.

More specific sites worth visiting include Oxford University's Bodleian Library, which besides its online catalogues and other information, has placed images of its extensive collection of illuminated manuscripts online (http://www. bodley.ox.ac.uk/dept/scwmss/wmss/medieval/browse. htm). Each manuscript gets a page with thumbnails (that is, small images) and brief descriptions; links load larger sized copies you can examine in more detail. It's a stunning collection, and well worth a visit.

Also impressive is the Perseus Project (http://www. perseus.tufts.edu/), a digital library of resources for studying the ancient world. The Perseus Project, unlike many online museums, is not just a collection of pictures – you'll find Latin texts and commentaries, for example. But there is also an extensive catalogue of art and architecture, and images are available of many of these.

Putting museum collections online has also opened the way to giving the public a view of items that are so precious or easily damaged that they've simply been locked away. One example is the Vatican (http://www.vatican.va) collection of 'secret' archives – manuscripts and ancient books.

If all this is just a bit too worthy, try the Museum of Bad Art (http://www.glyphs.com/moba/), dedicated to works of art that probably shouldn't have been opened to the public.

MUSIC

Buying music online is easy: go to one of the CD retailers listed below, search for the artist, song, soundtrack or classical album you're interested in, play a clip, and click to buy. But the real action now is in digitized music – you don't need a CD to play music on your computer – and fans all over the world have begun trading music files. The record companies hate it, but in fact this is the future of the music business, which is being remade by the Internet while we watch.

To play music on your computer, you need: a sound board (almost all computers now come with one of these installed as standard), speakers (ditto), a cable to hook the computer to the speakers (ditto), and a media player, so-called, that can handle the format the music is in. The most popular format in late 2000 was MP3, but there are many others in common use including Real Audio, Liquid Audio and Windows Media. Some of these players will have been included as plug-ins with your Web browser or accessory programs with your operating system (usually Windows). Don't worry about it either way; you will generally be told when you try to access a file online if you haven't got the right player and offered a link to a page you can download it from.

To download music onto your computer, it's a big advantage to have an advanced connection to the Internet such as ADSL or cable. The speed makes downloads painless, and the always-on nature means that if something does take a long time you aren't sitting there counting phone bill pennies. You will also need disk space: even highly compressed MP3 files, which take up roughly one-tenth of the space of the same music in audio CD format, typically are 3Mb to 6Mb. That can add up fast.

The best-known music service on the Internet is Napster (http://www.napster.com), largely because the lawsuits against it have been so well publicized. It is not the only service, but it is the one that most clearly points to what the future of the music business will probably look like. To a user, Napster looks like a giant database of music files that's searchable on scraps of artists' names, song titles or even the name of the movie you heard the song in. That database, however, doesn't exactly exist; it's assembled out of the files on individual users' hard drives, and changes constantly as users log in and log out.

When you install the Napster software, you specify which directories you're willing to share, and connect to its server. Once connected, you use the Search window to find music you're interested in, and choose from the list that pops up. By convention, MP3 files are named with the artist's name, the song's title and the extension MP3. There may also be a movie or TV show name. The theme from the TV show *Friends*, for example, might have the name 'The Rembrandts – I'll Be There For You (Friends theme).mp3'.

Following this convention is what makes the searches work. The list of hits you get back can be quite a jumble, as pieces of song titles and artists' names are rarely unique. From the list, you click on the songs you want to download and hit the button. Once the download is complete, you can right-click on the file to play it via the Napster client's internal player (the controls for the player itself are on the Library screen). The system is very simple to use, and enormous fun: you find yourself looking up all kinds of half-remembered bits and pieces, in the process discovering all kinds of music you either never heard of or had forgotten about. Even classical music and, more importantly, out-of-print recordings turn up on Napster, though it may take you some time and repeated effort to find them. Court rulings in March 2001 required Napster to begin blocking copyrighted material, so some of your favourite artists may be missing.

Other music services work differently – for one thing, most of them are traditional Web sites rather than special-ized client software – but the gist is the same: search, select, click, play.

As of late 2000, Napster was actually a series of servers that weren't connected to each other, meaning that if you couldn't find something you wanted it sometimes made sense to disconnect and reconnect, as you'd be likely to wind up on a different server with a different group of users (and consequently a different selection of music). The company planned, however, to connect all these disparate servers, and if this happens the service will be able to offer continuous access to a single, truly giant, global database. Napster was also under severe threat from the Recording Industry Association of America, and while its future is uncertain as I write this, there are already similar efforts that will be even harder to control waiting in the wings. Gnutella (http://gnutella.wego.com) puts users' machines directly in contact with each other to share all kinds of files, not just music, and the Open Napster project (http://www.opennap.org) is creating the potential for users to set up their own Napster-compatible servers. Finally, Napigator (http://www.napigator.com) allows you to use your Napster software but choose a different server, one not under RIAA threat.

There are, of course, many other music services. CD retailers such as American discounter CDNow.com have facilities to let you play snippets of songs from the track listings for the CDs they sell. Sites dedicated to independent artists such as MP3.com offer free downloads in a variety of formats. And Gnutella offers file-sharing without the centralized database in Napster's design. Even outside these services, you can search for the music you're interested in by typing the artist's name or a song title plus the term MP3 into any search engine.

The big flaw in all this is **Copyright** (see entry). Technically, it is illegal to make copies of music files and distribute them, even for no profit and for personal use. However, the practice is now so widespread – by the middle of 2000 Napster was estimating that it had 20 million users worldwide – that it is probably not stoppable no matter how much the record companies wish it were. In late 2000, both MP3.com and Napster were in court fighting lawsuits filed against them by the recording companies and by the Recording Industry Association of America. The general assessment, however, was that no matter what the eventual judgements were downloading music is here to stay. When this many people are breaking the law, it will be the law that changes – along with the business model by which musicians and record companies get paid.

How to make an MP3

We will assume for the purposes of this explanation that you actually own the copyright to the CD whose songs you want to turn into MP3s. There are essentially two steps: first, 'rip' the song off the CD, and, second, convert it to MP3. Songs on CDs are actually just data files in a format known as WAV. In this format, they are huge files – probably 50 to 60Mb for a single song – which is the reason the sound quality is so good. However, because the file structure is different for an audio CD than it is on your computer's hard drive, you have to extract the WAV file before you can convert it to MP3. For this, you need a CD ripper and enough storage space to hold the whole file while your computer is operating on it. The second step requires an MP3 encoder, and is a much slower process.

There are many programs available on the Net that handle these functions, and which one you use is largely a matter of personal preference. Audiograbber (http://www.audiograbber.com) is available in both free and commercial versions ($25); the only difference between them is that the free version will only rip half a CD's tracks, chosen randomly, whereas the commercial one will do any or all of a CD. If you put an MP3 encoder such as Blade Encoder (http://bladeenc.mp3.no/ or download it from the Audio-Grabber download page) in the same directory, Audio-Grabber will use it as a plug-in and you can do the whole CD-to-MP3 conversion with one mouse click. Also built into

AudioGrabber is a neat feature: it connects to the the CD Database (http://www.cddb.com) and automatically downloads the artist and track information for commercial CDs. If you're encoding MP3s from commercial CDs for personal use, this means not having to type in names for the tracks as these will be generated automatically. For the curious, CDDB, which has been renamed Gracenote, works with supported software CD players (http://www.cddb.com/players.html) to recognize CDs by reading the lengths of the tracks on the disc; this data is unique frequently enough to enable it to match the CD correctly from its database. If you have a CD the CDDB doesn't recognize, you can change that by typing in the artist and track information and uploading it.

Music sites
Digital Tradition (http://www.mudcat.org/) – repository of lyrics for more than 8,000 traditional folk songs.

Gnutella (http://gnutella.wego.com/) – thoroughly distributed file-sharing service that runs on users' PCs without a central database and allows individuals to trade MP3 music files by linking directly to each other. More for do-it-yourselfer übergeeks than Napster or MP3.com, but equally can't be as easily shut down by angry authorities.

MP3.com (http://www.mp3.com) – site featuring free music mostly from unsigned bands and independent artists. Site also sells CDs and other merchandise. If it can resolve the relevant legal disputes, MP3.com intends to reopen its database of commercial CD tracks ('My MP3.com') converted to

MP3s (you need to be able to put a CD in your computer's drive to access its tracks). As of late 2000, MP3.com had agreements in place with four of the five major record companies (Sony, BMG, EMI and Warner), but was still in court with the fifth, Universal Music Group. Software needed: MP3 player, MP3.com, 'Beam-It' software for the My MP3.com service.

Online music retailers (recordings and sheet music)

Amazon UK (http://www.amazon.co.uk): primarily known for selling books online, Amazon UK also sells CDs and videos. With the demise of Boxman in October 2000, Amazon automatically became one of the most important online suppliers of music.

CDNow (http://www.cdnow.com): American-based seller of CDs and videos, worth mentioning because it was the first, and its customer service and prices – even with shipping, duty and VAT added – are still superb. Comprehensive track listings for just about all the titles they sell, with clips to play from many of the cuts.

Ginger (http://www.gingershop.com): Virgin Radio's retailing arm, selling CDs (via Amazon), concert tickets, and other entertainment-related merchandise such as videos and DVDs and even domain names. Not comprehensive, but a good site if you like bright colours; probably the facility for buying tickets is the most compelling feature.

HMV (http://www.hmv.co.uk): not the easiest site to navigate, but the range available is impressive, the shipping

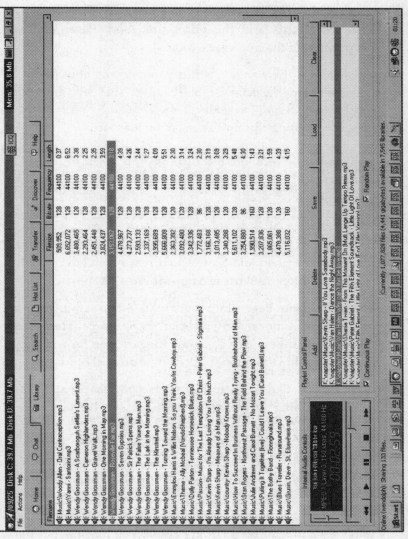

Figure 4. Napster in action.

starts at £1 per CD and goes down rapidly from there (2 CDs cost £1.40), and the prices are good. Nice, lengthy biographies of the musicians, too.

Musicians' Exchange (http://musicians.about.com/musicperform/musicians/mbody.htm): site by and for musicians, offering job listings, sheet music, concert schedules, songwriting tips and even contract advice.

Tower Records (http://uk.towerrecords.com): somewhat slow but otherwise navigable and good about telling you whether an item is in stock or not, Tower Records' most unusual feature is its used CDs section, which features a wide range of titles at roughly £6.50 or so each. The one drawback to the site is that pricing is in dollars, although the prices are good and there's a currency converter readily available. Shipping starts at $2.95 for one CD.

The UK Piano Page (http://www.uk-piano.org/): find a piano tuner, remover, or technician in your area. Then look up where to buy one or someone to teach you how to play at the Virtual Piano Shop (http://www.pianoshop.co.uk/).

Sheet Music Online (http://nfo.net/.LNX/lsheetmu.html): extensive listing of online sources for sheet music, free, printed and sold, even downloadable. Just a pity the site doesn't have a search function that would let you work out which publisher/site sold the specific piece of music you're looking for. The Music Room (http://www.musicroom. com), based in the UK, is supposed to be a one-stop shop for sheet music online – pay, download and print. Also sells CDs and features a UK gig guide. You may have better luck finding a broader range of titles at substantially lower prices at the US-based Sheet Music Plus (http://www. sheetmusicplus.com).

UK Online Record Shops (http://www.moremusic.co.uk/ links/uk_shops.htm): more or less comprehensive listing of UK online record dealers, with links to all the sites listed. The site's design is a bit messy, and it puts up an irritating pop-up window trying to get you to subscribe to its ezine. But it even lists sources for folk music and vinyl. A terrific resource.

World Wide Wax (http://www.worldwidewax.com): looking for that old vinyl? World Wide Wax has an extensive listing of classic vinyl from several record collections it's selling off. Based in the US, accepts credit cards. Even if you don't want to buy anything, you may enjoy just looking at the cover art. There are plenty more sites like this one. A comprehensive list of individuals and companies trading or selling vinyl on the Web is on Yahoo! (http://uk.dir. yahoo.com/Business_and_Economy/Shopping_and_Services/ Music/CDs__Records__and_Taxpes/Vinyl/).

N

NEIGHBOURHOOD

Where do you live? Or rather, what is where you live really like? The Web site Up My Street (http://www.upmystreet.com) will tell you if you enter your postcode: local housing prices compared to national averages, where to find the nearest advice centre or 24-hour takeaway. You'll even find your MP's email address and the local crime rate. There's also a profile of the type of people who live in your street: I am, apparently, an ACORN type 19, although I don't recognize myself in the description, except for the note that my neighbourhood is more likely than the national average to go shopping on foot. Well, that's certainly true – except for all the shopping I do online, which is most of it.

But this is the kind of thing that proves how wrong people are to focus on the Internet as a worldwide medium. Really old-time Netheads tend to stress that the most important power of the medium is to strengthen and deepen the ties within one's own community. Online communities that have their roots in a single area – London's CIX, San Francisco's The WELL, all those back-bedroom bulletin board systems – tend to be the strongest ones. Do your community a favour: get it a Web page and a message board. Share the rubbish collection schedules, the complaints about the tube station, the experience with the schools.

NETIQUETTE

Briefly:

- Keep messages short and to the point.

- Eschew fripperies such as attached files and HTML unless you know for sure that they are welcomed by your correspondent. If you want to forward a Web page, use the Text option.

- Limit your end-of-message signature to four lines or less.

- Avoiding quoting long screeds from other people's messages and adding only a few words at the bottom. Quote just enough so the recipient understands what you're talking about in case he/she hasn't seen the original message, and make your comments substantive.

- Do not forward email you receive to your entire address book just because the email message contains a sentence telling you to do so, even if the message says the information it contains is endorsed by a major company such as IBM, Microsoft, or AOL.

- Do not engage in personal attacks and/or abuse, even if same are directed at you.

- Do not expect the rest of the Net to do your homework for you.

The word netiquette is formed from Net + etiquette, and refers to a series of behavioural conventions that formed in the early days of the Net and are still more or less applicable now. While these norms may seem arbitrary and even arrogant to newcomers, they have as much reason behind them as real-world rules like not chewing with your mouth open.

The dinner-table comparison is actually pretty apt. Most table manners are designed with the intent of keeping you from interfering with your companion's enjoyment of the meal. You don't put your elbows on the table because you might knock something over; you don't chew with your mouth open so you don't disgust your fellow diner. Thinking of Netiquette as not interfering with someone else's enjoyment or use of the Net makes a lot of the rules seem logical. Keep messages short and to the point, because long, fuzzy ones take longer to download and read, and make responding more difficult. Keep your Web site streamlined and accessible to the sight-impaired (by using text alternatives for images and avoiding navigation aids that require special plug-ins and high-speed connections to function barely acceptably). Avoid personal attacks and abuse. Don't post umpteen copies of the same advertising message. And so on.

Netiquette began as a 1992 posting by then Usenet god Gene Spafford in an attempt to encourage minimally acceptable standards of behaviour for Usenet, the global bulletin boards that in a very real sense form the town square of the

Internet. Entitled 'Emily Postnews Answers Your Questions on Netiquette', the posting was half satire, half serious. You can read it still at Emily Post news (http://www.mathcs.richmond.edu/~barnett/cs100/Emily_Postnews.html).

Essentially, the basis of courtesy online is to assume that the person you're corresponding with, whether that's by sending them a Web page on request or exchanging email, is doing so with some difficulty. Assume connections are slow and expensive and that economy of language and transmission are therefore necessary. No one's asking you to write telegrams, but if, for example, you have a choice between sending a bit of text as lines pasted into an email message or an attached, formatted Word document, go for the few lines of text.

The old Usenet conventions are also just about as applicable in today's Web discussion boards as they were in the old days. If it's the kind of system where messages are displayed one at a time (as many Web boards are) or where messages may not arrive in the order in which they're sent (as in many electronic mailing lists and on Usenet), quote selectively from the message you're answering so people know which points you're responding to. Keep the quotes as short as you can and ensure that the comments you add are actually of value. Good: quoting the five lines that are relevant to your argument and then explaining why you agree or disagree. Bad: quoting all of a 50-line message and adding only 'Me, too.' (If you do this, people will accuse you of being from AOL, which is Netspeak for calling you an idiot; AOL's software for some reason encourages this kind of thing.)

The standard advice is to read the discussion group you're interested in for a couple of weeks before jumping in and posting. It's a good idea. Also a good idea is to find out whether the group has what's known as an FAQ (for Frequently Asked Questions), so that when you do post you don't commit the cardinal sin of being the 1,437,568th person that week to ask a question the group has answered even more times. The FAQ will typically also include information about the group's purpose in life, along with notes about what constitutes appropriate postings. For alt.showbiz. gossip, for example, the rule is you can say anything about anyone as long as it's malicious; the FAQ (or more properly, the Anti-FAQ, as that's what they call it) will explain this to you and also gloss the frequently seen abbreviation YABWFTNOTNG, which stands for 'Yet Another Bozo Who Forgot the Name of the Newsgroup'. The FAQ will typically also explain the in-jokes that form in any group of people that communicate regularly over a period of time, saving you a lot of time and incomprehension (see **FAQs**).

The Net helps those who help themselves. This means that if, for example, you join a discussion group on a particular topic because you have to research it for work or school and you want help, you can't expect the members of the group to do your homework for you. It's fine to ask for help; but you will get a lot more assistance if you have taken reasonable efforts on your own first and say what those are. A posting like, 'Hi. My teacher says I have to write a paper about one of the planets. What is Venus like?' is unlikely to get many answers. A posting that says, 'Hi. I'm writing a paper about the planet Mars, and I've looked up the basics about the planet and I know its atmosphere is made up of 95 per cent carbon dioxide, 7 per cent nitrogen, and 1.6 per cent argon, but I've been unable to find out when the first fly-by took place. Does anyone know?' will probably produce a link to a site where the answer can be found. (Even though in fact you could find this out quite easily by typing 'mars first flyby jpl' into the best search engine, Google; one of the top links takes you to the Space FAQ, part 8, which tells you it was in 1965. By the way, you'd find the atmospheric composition by typing in 'mars atmosphere composition'.)

One thing that isn't covered by Netiquette, but qualifies as good advice, is to remember that you should take everything you read with a grain of salt. Over time, as you become familiar with a group and its style, you will become much better at telling when people are joking and identifying the posters whose views are unlikely to be well-founded. It is perfectly acceptable to email a regular privately and ask what they make of something you don't understand.

NEWS

Everyone has their own favourite selection of news sites, often starting with the online version of their favourite newspaper. The *Telegraph*'s site (http://www.telegraph.co.uk) carries a selection of stories from the newspaper and lets you page back through related stories for anything you've missed on a given topic. Registration is required to read the articles or access the archives, but it's free. The list below attempts to catalogue some of the better sites for breaking news – unsurprisingly, many of them are run by TV companies, who are already out there collecting material for immediate broadcast.

Business
Bloomberg (http://www.bloomberg.com): publishes a selection of business headlines from several countries on a 24-hour basis. UK technology business news (http://www.bloomberg.com/uk/technews.html) covers the most volatile part of the market.

Financial Times (http://www.ft.com): just about everything that's in the paper, plus company profiles and updating market indices.

General
BBC (http://www.bbc.co.uk/news): no doubt about it, the BBC has the resources to put together probably the best official British news site.

CNN Europe (http://www.cnneurope.com).

Teletext (http://www.teletext.co.uk): on the Web, as well as on TV.

Computers and Internet related
C I Net (http://www.cnet.com).

The Industry Standard (http://www.thestandard.com/europe).

Nando (http://www.nando.net): it may seem odd that a news service based in Raleigh, North Carolina, could be an important competitor, but there's a huge technology enclave down there.

Newsbytes (http://www.newsbytes.com): the oldest computer-related wire service.

The Register (http://www.theregister.co.uk): useful, sarcastic and quick UK-based news service covering all the main areas. Probably most people in the tech industries check this site several times a day.

Wired News (http://www.wired.com): now part of the Lycos network, the original home of the digital revolution. High-tech culture, politics and business.

(See also **Yahoo! and other Portals** for how to find a list of all the British newspapers with Web sites.)

O

OLYMPICS

See under **Sports**.

ORDINATION

The Universal Life Church (http://www.ulc.org) will ordain anyone that asks, without question of faith. The ULC has been around since at least the 1970s, and ULC ministers can legally perform weddings and other ministerial tasks, at least in the US. For $5 the Church will send you a certificate of ordination, and it's happy to sell you other congregational supplies, including anointing oil, incense, tax guides and church organization documents.

(If you have a genuine vocation see **Religion**.)

OUTDOORS

Unless you're going to be like that guy who cycled across the US with a laptop and a mobile phone strapped to his handlebars, chances are the Internet will be an indoor pastime for you.

However, the National Cycle Network (http://www.sustrans.org.uk) is a Millennium Commission project, the second largest after the Millennium Dome and a lot more successful. The Network includes 5,000 miles of routes for cyclists as well as new routes for walkers and wheelchairs. Almost half the network is entirely traffic-free; the site tells you how to get on the network, with detailed maps you can print out or buy from the site's shop, along with highlights and helpful cycling information. The Internet is great for this kind of project, which involves gathering together information from over 400 local authorities as well as landowners and businesses. Also take a look at the sites owned by the Cyclists' Touring Club (http://www.ctc.org.uk) and the London Cycling Campaign (http://www.lcc.org.uk), which both feature routes and relevant news.

For ramblers, the Countryside Commission (http://www.countryside.gov.uk/) has done a similar job, with links to the National Trails of Britain Web sites. The trails are split into sections and packed with information, including history of the area, places to visit nearby, facts and figures, wildlife to look out for, and contacts such as tourist information and the highway authorities. Especially useful is the inclusion of exactly the right Ordnance Survey maps you might need for both Landranger and Pathfinder scales. But if you are familiar with the area and don't need a map, there are also recommendations for more poetic books by authors inspired by the landscape.

Like most subjects, fishing has a lot of American sites,

including the Utah-based Anglersfly (http://www.anglersfly.com/), which claims to be the world's most complete fly shop. For equipment for any outdoor pursuit, it's also almost always worth looking at LL Bean (http://www.llbean.com). The New York-based Urban Angler (http://www.urban-angler.com) adds a useful service to its online store: weekly reports on fishing conditions, mainly covering the greater New York area but occasionally including popular destinations around the world. Glasgow's Angling Store (http://www.fishingmegastore.com) supplies equipment for all types of fishing. Finally, UK and European sites (http://www.fishing-catalog.com/links/ukandeuropeansites.html) is a guide to fishing sites all over the UK and Europe.

P

PAYMENTS

The predominant method of payment on the Net is credit cards. Increasingly, some UK sites also accept Switch cards, but in general you should avoid using these. For one thing, Switch cards lack the liability protection that limits the amount you have to pay to £50 if your credit card is stolen. For another, where sending an ecommerce site your credit card number grants it access to your credit balance, sending your Switch card number grants it access to your actual money – and without the preset spending limits credit cards have. While it's tempting and convenient to use Switch cards online, therefore, the best recommendation is, don't, unless there's a very, very good reason. You would be better off putting a cheque in the post.

One of the Holy Grails that has never quite materialized on the Web is micropayments. Content providers long for a simple way of charging us all a few pence to read an article or download a song. Credit cards are too expensive for transactions under £5, and consumers tend to resist schemes that require them to deposit money in an account to pay for services in advance. It's generally held that the absence of micropayments is seriously holding back the Web's development.

Yet no one has quite cracked it. One attempt is Beenz (http://www.beenz.com), which awards points (called beenz) similar to those you get on supermarket loyalty cards. These come from the site's various partners – retailers, content providers – and you use them up on other partner sites. The idea is that eventually beenz will become pervasive.

More useful for the moment are services such as Paypal (http://www.paypal.com) and Billpoint (http://www. billpoint.com). These essentially allow online buyers to consolidate payments, which are then charged to your credit card. Smaller retailers find it convenient and cheap to use Paypal compared to setting up their own credit card authorization. Billpoint, which is built into eBay, similarly allows quick credit card payments to individuals – once the price is agreed, they send you an invoice and you authorize its payment via the credit card you have set up. Be aware that this is dangerous, however: it makes it just too easy to spend money.

In almost every case, if you want to pay for an ecommerce purchase by calling in your credit card instead of entering the details online, you are allowed to do so. And, of course, if you want to pay by cheque, you can do that, too, but be prepared for delays while the cheque clears and be aware that you will not have the same level of protection available to you if the sale goes wrong as you would if you paid by credit card.

PEOPLE

One of the great joys of the Internet is being able to find out what happened to all those people you went to school with decades ago. To find people, try the online directory Scoot (http://www.scoot.co.uk), which has a people search (see **Directories**). It's a reciprocal service: you have to join in order to be able to look someone up.

BT has put the entire national database of phone numbers (http://www.phonenetuk.bt.com:8080/) on the Web; follow the instructions on the site to search. Unlike the telephone version, the online search is free. Besides, you don't have to fight with operators who persist in asking you the exact address of the person you're looking for. After all, if you knew the exact address you'd probably have the phone number.

If the person's name is somewhat unusual, you can, of course, type it into a **Search Engine** (see entry); if it's a common one you may still be able to get results if you add to the search terms the names of known close relatives or the person's hobbies.

PERSONAL FINANCE

Before you do anything else, go look at the Bill Gates Personal Wealth Clock (http://www.webho.com/WealthClockIntl), which updates in real time. As of 20 October 2000, Bill Gates owned $12.0604 for every person in the world, give or take the birth rate. Just some perspective.

Like buying cars or buying shares, personal finance is an area of life that is information-intensive and in which consumers operate at a disadvantage because they're so easily exploited by professionals. Many sites have sprung up to help consumers manage their own finances, and, typically, these offer not just advice but interactive calculators and direct comparison shopping for insurance, mortgages and banking services. Chances are not all of these sites will last, but for the moment you can take your pick of good-quality, free services to help you manage your affairs. There is a lot of overlap – they all pretty much offer you calculators to help you work out the real cost of loans and mortgages as well as comparison tables of rates for bank accounts, ISAs and credit cards – so ultimately which site you gravitate toward will be a matter of personal taste and ease of navigation.

Additional sites

*FT*YourMoney (http://www.ftyourmoney.com): news, advice, comparison shopping tools for everything from bank accounts to pensions, and many other helpful features. The quality you'd expect from the *FT*.

Interactive Investor International (http://www.iii.co.uk). Although the site's primary focus is on investing, the site also offers comparison shopping for many related products, including up-to-date tables of mortgage rates and bank fees, even common rates for traded endowments. It is phasing in direct sales of insurance. You will have to register to gain access to most of the site's features.

MoneyExtra (http://www.moneyextra.com): recently bought by Bristol and West (a subsidiary of the Bank of Ireland), MoneyExtra nonetheless claims to be independent. The site intends to expand from financial advice and transactions into a fully fledged personal face-to-face and contact centre based service. Members also get discounts on holidays and medical insurance bought through the site.

Motley Fool (http://www.fool.co.uk): focuses primarily on investing, but has some good no-nonsense advice features on tax and other pesky personal finance problems.

This is Money (http://www.thisismoney.co.uk): the personal finance site belonging to Associated Newspapers, publisher of the *Evening Standard*. A bit sparse, but some useful features.

(See also **Banking, Investment, Personal Finance, Security**.)

PERSONALIZING THE WEB

Most heavy Web users long for some way to automate the business of browsing their most frequently visited sites, either to save themselves time, or to save on the phone bills, or simply to ensure they don't miss an important resource (see also **Browsing Tips**). A few years ago, there was a vogue for offline Web browsers. Products like Web

Whacker let you pick a site, specify how deep you wanted to go in terms of links, and set it going to download everything on to your hard drive for faster and cheaper perusal offline.

Some of this software is still around. As unmetered, high-speed Internet access slowly becomes a reality, the offline features of such software become less important, except in the wireless arena. Take a look, for example, at Avantgo, which has deals with a number of content providers, including the Web magazine Salon.com and the BBC. You pick the sites you want and it downloads them for you formatted for your WAP phone, Palm Pilot or Windows CE device, ready to pass to the device at the next synchronization.

These are, however, only limited solutions. The Web has become much more complex in the last few years, and the average Web user is likely to be in the habit of visiting a lot more sites: cinema listings, weather, bank accounts, ecommerce orders in progress, news headlines. Large portals like Yahoo!, Freeserve or MSN have tried to come to grips with this by letting users create personalized pages that give access to email and discussion boards as well as stock quotes and news. But these sites typically work with only a tiny number of content providers that they have pre-selected as partners. For the average heavy Web user, these aren't particularly satisfying, as the sites you're in the habit of using are not on their lists.

At least some of the answer may lie in current experiments in creating metabrowsers, similar to personalized home pages but capable of much more. What these essentially do is allow you to create a home page out of content you select from around the Web so it can be displayed quickly and easily at one location.

Quickbrowse is probably the simplest. You enter a set of URLs, and it gives you back a page with all the content from those addresses in a long screed. It's not elegant, it's not aesthetic and it doesn't filter out ads or big graphics. But it is useful, especially given its email option: you can schedule the site to send you the content from those pages by email at regular intervals. For a travelling user with limited Web access, this would be a real convenience.

Onepage gives you somewhat more sophisticated layout options, based on a number of existing templates. You are supposed to be able to add any window you like to your layout, either a URL you type in from the Web at large or one of their preselected content windows, but typed-in URLs produced error messages. Non-US Onepage users will also have to work a little harder for their pages, as standard functions like the weather report assume you are based in a place with a five-digit zip code.

Octopus is a lot more complicated. Essentially, you build up the page you want out of elements such as URLs, text, graphics and so on, more like using a desktop publishing program. Of all the services mentioned here, this one is the most difficult to work out how to use. While the pages you can build this way are much more sophisticated, because it depends heavily on Java actually using the service is very slow (as measured on an AMD K6 with 128Mb of RAM running Netscape over an ADSL connection). It does, however, stick an extra button on your browser that lets you grab any URL you like for placement on your page.

Where these run on the companies' own servers across the Web, DoDots gives you software to download. Thereafter, you create 'Dots' out of Internet content you select, with it all winding up in small windows on your own desktop in the layout of your choice. Like Octopus, Dots runs rather slowly. As a service, it's less satisfying than it might be: it depends on packaged pieces of content on your desktop and seems not to have enough advantages over an ordinary Web browser (after all, there's nothing unusual about having umpteen browser windows open).

Moreover, which bills itself as 'the world's largest collection of Webfeeds', lets you put together a custom page of headlines at its site or – and this is nifty – add five headlines free from any of their feeds to your own site. Moreover also has a feature called Newsblogger that makes it easy to add articles with comments to daily Weblogs. For Moreover, the free service is at least partly a way of advertising its main business, which is supplying customized newsfeeds to corporates.

Yodlee is probably the most sophisticated of the lot, in that it allows you one-stop access to all your online accounts – bank, credit card, ecommerce site. There is, of course, at least some security risk, in that Yodlee stores for you all your user IDs and passwords in order to do this. For a lot of people, however, for whom the alternative is to write down all the varied IDs (another risk), it's got to be a great convenience.

There is, at some point, probably going to be a huge copyright battle over at least a few of these sites. Cherry-picking the exact content you want is great for users, but anathema to commercial content providers who want those users to have to pay in time watching advertising. None of these services are quite ideal yet – although Quickbrowse's emailed versions and Onepage's one-click access are powerful features – but they point the way to a much more personalized Web, something that's going to be increasingly desirable.

Sites

Avantgo (http://www.avantgo.com)

Dots (http://www.dodots.com)

Octopus (http://www.octopus.com)

Onepage (http://www.onepage.com)

Quickbrowse (http://www.quickbrowse.com)

Web Whacker (http://www.webwhacker.com): now primarily marketed as a tool for parents and teachers to control what material kids may access, but the software still does the main job of downloading an entire site so you can read it offline, without phone bills ticking up and with the pages loading almost instantly.

(See also **Bookmarks**.)

PETS

Online pet stores have not done well: at the end of 2000 the
two biggest both went bust. It's a shame because Pets.com
had a lot of good information for pet owners, even if you
didn't want to buy dog food from them. Nonetheless, a
number of pet sites still exist, and it's a good thing, because
if you own anything more exotic than a dog or cat it isn't
always easy to find good information on how to take care
of it. One of the better advice sites is the luridly coloured,
UK-based Pets on the Brain (http://www.petsonthebrain.
com), which has an extensive veterinary section: the vet
diary, consisting of vets' stories from around the country –
sort of James Herriott without the glamour. Both sites run
online shops, though ordering pet supplies from the US is
probably pointless unless there's some vital item you can't
get here.

For less common pets, the listings at About's Exotic Pets
page (http://www.exoticpets.about.com) should help get
you started. Although their idea of exotic isn't all that
unusual: salamanders might be exotic, but surely not rabbits
and gerbils.

Also worth looking at is *Animal Planet*, the programme
showing regularly on the Discovery Channel, which runs a
'Yelp line' (http://animal.discovery.com/yelpline/yelpline.
html), an advice helpline for perplexed owners.

Animail (http://www.animail.co.uk) is a UK-based
retailer of pet-related items with yet another stupid, noisy
Flash introduction, but the site sells more than two thousand

pet products for dogs, cats and what it calls 'small pets', which is their term for miscellanea like goldfish and ferrets. The site will give you a nervous twitch from the flickering graphics and cartoon animals, but it does have a good range of stock including Science Diet-style cat foods and speciality items too embarrassing for non-pet owners to talk about.

Finally, the UK Pets Directory (http://www.ukpets. co.uk/) lists over 15,000 kennels, catteries, pet shops and services. If you're looking for someone to officiate at your cat's funeral, this is the place to find them.

Fish

Aquaria have always been popular on the Internet, if only because there's a certain amount of similarity between staring at a screensaver and watching fish swim around inside a glass box. There is even a hidden command in Netscape that brings up the company 'fishcam' – a Webcam pointed at a large fish tank. Just hit CTRL-ALT-F from inside Netscape to see it.

It's worth going into some detail about fish, if only because the level of knowledge you find in many aquarium stores is so poor. (There are, of course, many exceptions to this.)

Fishkeeping is a geeky sort of pastime; doing it right involves learning a fair amount of technical background and being willing to fiddle with small bits of machinery. So the Internet is a phenomenal resource for anything to do with aquarium fish. It is always advisable to look up any unfamiliar fish on the Net before buying, to ensure that you can provide the right conditions.

The first resource is the group of FAQs compiled by the members of the rec.aquaria Usenet newsgroups. These are invaluable. The Beginning Fishkeeping FAQ, for example, covers the basics of nitrogen cycling in well-written and understandable detail, and makes some solid recommendations for good and bad first fish (don't get goldfish until you've had some experience). Other FAQs in the series cover aquarium plants, saltwater and brackish aquaria, common fish diseases and treatments, breeding, books and mailorder sources, and live food. (See **FAQs**.)

Once you've digested all that, you should be able to get ongoing help with your fish either from the various information sites and/or their discussion boards and, most especially, from the Usenet rec.aquaria newsgroups. Although you will get conflicting advice from the newsgroups, typically you'll be talking to a large group of fishkeepers, some of whom are very experienced. At 8 p.m. when you've just discovered your fish is sick, it's likely to be your quickest source of helpful advice.

Sites

Aquaria Central (http://www.aquariacentral.com): US-based online aquarium shop. The information part of the site is excellent, with a searchable or browsable database with background information and care requirements for more than 700 types of commonly available aquarium fish: freshwater, brackish, marine, coldwater. Photo gallery, discussion groups and features covering more general topics. Although the ecommerce part of the site is fairly useless to UK residents, it's a great site for researching your fish before buying.

Aquatics Direct (http://www.aquatics-direct.com): UK-based mail order catalogue supplier of tanks, filters and media, plants, tests, food and decor. A useful and efficient service (and there aren't many online competitors), but watch out for silly animations on the front page and very tiny type on the catalogue pages. Good prices for consumable items such as filter media as compared to aquarium shops. Site includes a fish sale/swapping board.

Goldfish Care (http://puregold.aquaria.net): authoritative site on how to buy and care for goldfish, fancy and otherwise, covering basics, diseases, treatments and living conditions for these popular but somewhat delicate fish.

The Krib (http://www.thekrib.com): archives of Usenet postings, the rec.aquaria FAQs, and over 38Gb of well-organized information on fishkeeping topics. The oldest aquarium site, set up in 1994.

Amos the Puffer Fish (http://www.achrn.demon.co.uk/amos.html): who says you can't have a relationship with a fish? Amos's life story (he lives in the UK) and myriad photos. Even if you're not planning to keep a giant mbu puffer, the site gives a good idea of what's involved in long-term fishkeeping. Good advice on how to move fish and their tanks, and links to other puffer information.

Virtual pets

Virtual pets take the idea of an imaginary friend to new heights: virtual cats and dogs live in animated form on your computer desktop, where they grow and breed just like . . .

well, just like the real thing. Except that you have to sign an adoption certificate promising to take good care of them. These pets are intended for people who find Tamagotchis too demanding. Virtual Life's Catz and Dogz (http://www. petz.com) are said to be so addictive that kids (Kidz?) who are otherwise not fascinated by computers will still insist on playing with them and, of course, upgrading their breedz whenever a new version of the software comes out. Whole online communities have been built up around all this, where people trade petz and stage shows.

Of course, this isn't all. The Web plays home to a number of artificial intelligence projects intended to produce more and more believable virtual characters of all types, and also to a large community of slightly deranged folks who are trying to add to the capabilities of electronically enhanced toys like Microsoft Barney and the Furby to make the toys do things their manufacturers never intended.

PHOTO ALBUMS

Wish there were a convenient way to show the grandparents pictures of the grandkids? Photopoint (http://www. photopoint.com) and My Family (http://www.myfamily. com) both have well-designed services to let you create an online photo album and restrict access to just your close friends and relatives. If you use a digital camera, you can take pictures at the wedding and put them up almost in real time, so missing guests can still participate in the occasion at least a bit. The portal Lycos (see **Yahoo! and Other Portals**) offers this sort of function, with the added feature of letting users quickly upload and share video snippets. One caveat to be aware of if you want to use these sites: both Photopoint and My Family are assiduous about sending out reminder and promotional email, even after you've asked them not to. Unless you dislike someone *very* much, do not give My Family their email address.

PLUG-INS

A plug-in is a bit of software that, literally, plugs into a Web browser and gives it extra capabilities (because of open standards, you can use the same plug-ins no matter which browser you use). Common plug-ins include the reader for PDF files (Acrobat), players for animation software such as Flash and Shockwave, and music players such as Real Audio and Winamp. In general, if you land on a page that has features requiring a particular plug-in you will be offered a link to a page where you can download it. It's up to you to decide whether you want to read that page enough to get the software; if you do, you will generally find installation instructions on the download page.

Details of exactly how to install the software vary, but in general you will download the file and run it, and it will automatically install, modifying your Web browser so that any time you start to access a file of that particular type this plug-in will be called up to display it. It's a process that's very similar to what Windows itself does in associating file types and particular pieces of software, so that when you double-click on a text file, Notepad loads and displays it.

The complete list of plug-ins (http://home.netscape.com/plugins/) numbers in the hundreds and includes some very useful items – files for playing virtual reality software across the Web, viewing special types of images, playing presentations. The list below is of the most commonly used plug-ins, noting what they do and where to get them. Note that these bits of software are constantly being updated and files created for the software may require features from newer versions. Therefore, although you've downloaded them once (or got them bundled with your Web browser) as time goes on you may find that some files of the right type fail to display correctly; if that happens, chances are you need to update the software.

One final note: when you download these plug-ins you are typically asked for your name and email address. Read the forms carefully before proceeding to download, as they often include a box or two indicating your willingness to receive promotional email for the site and/or its commercial partners. Usually these are opt-out (that is, the default is to receive the email), so check carefully before proceeding to download. You are not generally given the option not to provide an email address; but this is the sort of situation where a throwaway address can be very useful (see **Junk**). If you download the plug-ins from Netscape's page you will be required to create a Netcenter ID; I usually avoid this by going to the plug-in's own home page, where the amount of information they want is less.

Additional sites

Acrobat Reader (http://www.adobe.com/support/downloads
/main.html and look down the list for Acrobat Reader
and your operating system): reader for PDF format, in
common use on the Web for documents whose original
formatting and/or graphics need to be preserved, such as
corporate annual reports and research papers. Available
for Windows, Mac and UNIX. If you already have Acrobat
and you get errors when you're trying to read a PDF file,
chances are what's happened is that the file has been
made with a newer version than the one you have. Look
for and download an update, if one is available. Acrobat
Reader is free; the Acrobat software itself, which includes
the ability to create PDF files, costs a couple of hundred
dollars.

Flash (http://www.macromedia.com/software/downloads/
and pick Flash Player or Flash and Shockwave Players from
the list of available downloads): it's arguable that the world
does not need animations and cute sounds to dress up Web
sites, but you may find yourself in the awkward position of
having no choice about using a particular site that persists
in the delusion that Flash and/or Shockwave is necessary in
life. Proprietary software from Macromedia.

Liquid Audio (http://www.liquidaudio.com): bills itself as
a CD-quality player for the Internet. Allows you to stream
or download music and burn it to a CD (if you have the
right CD writer). Unlike most such players, Liquid Audio
includes facilities for buying songs and CDs.

Net2Phone (http://www.net2phone.com): call from your PC to any phone, anywhere in the world, for a few cents a minute. You need to fund your account before you can start making international calls (that is, calls anywhere but within the US). The same site offers Net2Fax, a facility for sending faxes via the Internet. Time lag, Internet access costs and voice quality (especially over dial-up) will probably limit the usefulness of Net2Phone to non-UK calling, but at the price it may be worth a try.

Quicktime (http://www.apple.com/quicktime/): video player created by Apple but available for not only Mac but Windows. All kinds of stuff is available in Quicktime, from commercial movie trailers and music videos to short movies and Japanese animations.

Real Player (http://www.real.com): probably the most common streaming (that is, live, rather than stored and played later) audio and video format (RA or RAM). Typically there is a chargeable version that has the best and newest features, and a free version that lags behind. Real also makes a Jukebox, which plays MP3s, creates CDs and is compatible with the leading portable (physical) MP3 players. Real Jukebox and its parent company, Real Networks, got a fair bit of awkward publicity in early 2000 when the player was revealed to have been transmitting data about its users' tastes back to the parent site behind the scenes. The player now should ask you if you are willing for your data to be collected.

Winamp (http://www.winamp.com): *the* MP3 player; also plays CDs and other formats. Free for 14 days, then pay $10

to register. Possible to customize with a variety of 'skins' –
that is, covering images that change the look and feel, but
not the functioning, of the player.

POLITICS

Of the three main political parties, the Liberal Democrats
were the first to make really good use of the online world,
in part because then leader Paddy Ashdown is a not-so-
secret **Geek** (see entry). By now, all the main parties have
Web sites: Labour (http://www.labour.org.uk), Lib Dems
(http://www.libdems.org.uk) and Conservatives (http://
www.conservatives.com). (Interestingly the Conservatives
are in .com instead of the more populist and nationalist .org.
uk.) For politics on the Net, these are good places to start.
For an independent site, try the British Politics Pages (http:/
/www.ukpol.co.uk), which maintains mailing lists as well as
offering political news and a section covering specific issues.

But the Net is the ideal medium for special-interest
groups, so if you're interested in a specific issue you're more
likely to want to find a site dedicated to it. One example is
the anti-Euro Business for Sterling (http://www.bfors.com),
which aims to foster a proper debate about the issues
surrounding the single currency. Fairly, the site's links section leads to the pro-Euro campaign, as well as dozens of
other useful Web sites. While you are there, click on the
People button to see the list of council members in Business
for Sterling; it reads like *Who's Who*.

Politics *about* the Internet has always been the most popular sector of politics online, and there are many Internet activist groups espousing one or another of the main planks of Internet freedom. In Britain, in recent years the most important has been the Regulation of Investigatory Powers Act, which regulates law enforcement access to encrypted data (précis: encrypted data could be anything from your credit card details to your patient records at your GP's surgery). Several sites cover this in detail, including Stand (http://www.stand.org.uk) and the RIP pages at the Foundation for Information Policy Research (http://www.fipr.org/rip).

Freedom of speech – if you want to get someone mad at you on the Internet the quickest way is to tell them they can't say something – is well covered at the Global Internet Liberty Campaign (http://www.gilc.org), which takes an international view. Ironically, the Campaign Against Censorship of the Internet in Britain got kicked off the Net by its British ISP after a legal decision covered on the site left ISPs nervous about their online liability; the main anti-censorship site is the US's Electronic Frontier Foundation's blue-ribbon campaign (http://www.eff.org/blueribbon. html).

PORNOGRAPHY

One of the great myths about the Internet is that all you have to do is log on and a stream of obscene images will immediately take over your computer, like turning on a television. In fact, it's perfectly possible to use the Internet extensively for years at a time without ever seeing an image that would embarrass you in front of your kids. But there's no denying, of course, that pornography is there for the finding if it is intentionally sought out. The following is information you should be aware of.

Although there are Web sites that advertise free porn, invariably these sites are offering a temporary free trial of a subscription service. In those cases, it is typically necessary to enter a credit card number in order to gain access, so to avoid charges ensure that the trial is cancelled. The pay-for-porn Web sites (which is the most common type) generally put only relatively small images on their front page, intended to hook visitors into paying for the service. The credit card requirement isn't entirely a matter of greed; even though a child can borrow a parent's card, being able to type in a valid credit card number gives the service some reason it can claim to believe that the visitor is over eighteen.

However, even these thumbnails (as small copies of larger images are known) can be very explicit, much more so than the front covers of the magazines you find on the top shelf at the newsagent's. There isn't much you can do about this: the Internet isn't controlled by any single regulatory authority and what shocks people in this country may be perfectly legal and acceptable elsewhere.

Be aware, however, that there are categories of pornography that are actually illegal, not just to create but to own copies of, whether these are printed on paper or stored as computer files. Primarily, this means child pornography.

But under British law child pornography has a rather broad definition, including not only pornography created by abusing real children but pornography using digitized or altered images made to look like children and even full-grown adults with immature bodies. Downloading and keeping any such material on either your computer at work (where the discovery of such a hoard would get you fired) or at home is obviously an offence. The rock singer Gary Glitter's cache of such images was revealed when he took his computer into PC World for repair and the staff saw it and called the police.

Browsing pornography online leaves traces on any computer as Web browsers use a local directory (folder), known as a cache, to store the pages and files they are pointed at to make it faster to move back and forth among the pages. What many people don't realize is that the files aren't automatically deleted when the browser is closed. Instead, the browser continues adding files until the size of the cache (in disk storage space) has reached the limit set from within the browser. At that point, it begins to clear the oldest files as it needs to make room for new ones. But until they're deleted to make space, the files stay on the hard drive. The result is that someone who wants to know what kinds of sites have been browsed can take a look through the files in the cache and get a pretty accurate idea. So if you're a parent and are concerned about what your child has been viewing, you can look through those files. A similar situation applies to the history files browsers keep, which is simply a list of URLs that have been visited in the last month (or however many days you have set in your browser options). To view the list, in Netscape hit CTRL-H and in Internet Explorer click on the History button.

PRIVACY

There are two contradictory myths about privacy and the Internet. One is that the instant you go online everybody can tell everything about you, from the details of your bank account to the colour socks you put on this morning. The other is that no one you know is going to read anything you post in an online discussion area, so it's perfectly safe to log into that Web forum and divulge your inner-most secrets to a multitude of anonymous strangers.

Both are wrong, but the fact that these conflicting images both prevail serves to illuminate the confusion and contradictory emotions with which many people think about the Net.

There are two halves to the first problem. The one of the most immediate concern is security for confidential information such as patient data and credit card details. This is discussed elsewhere (see **Security**). The other is the privacy issue inherent in the ability of Web sites to track what you do online.

Both Web sites and ISPs keep logs of customer activity. Even if you don't fill in a registration form, Web sites can gather quite a lot of information about you and your computer system as you browse to them. A typical Web site can, for example, tell what ISP number you're coming from, what type of computer you have, the size of your monitor, the time zone you're logging in from, which browser you're running, which security features are enabled, which plug-ins you have installed and what site you came from. (For a demonstration of all this, see http://privacy.net/ anonymizer/.) Web sites can also track which of their own pages you've visited and in what order, and obviously anyone you buy goods or services from will have records of those purchases. In addition, to 'remember' who you are and what you were doing, Web sites store strings of gibberish known as 'cookies' on your hard drive. People get very upset about cookies sometimes, but they're not the biggest problem, as you can always delete them and then set your browser to refuse them in future (although the upshot will be you won't be able to use many, many sites).

All this data enables sites to offer you a more personalized service. Information about your likes and dislikes, for example, allows third-party services like the advertising agency DoubleClick to supply at least somewhat targeted banner ads. It also allows the site itself to suggest additional services or products you might be interested in.

One of the more sophisticated versions of this is software that Amazon.com bought called Alexa. Using information about the purchases customers have made, the software makes recommendations based on the tastes of other people who have made similar purchases to yours. Experience varies regarding how good this software is. Some people say the recommendations are so good they're spooky; others find the recommendations relatively useless, as their customer records are confused by gifts they've bought for other people, plus of course the software is inherently ignorant about the existing contents of your home.

Bear in mind that when you use sites located outside Europe the familiar rules about data protection do not necessarily apply. The US in particular has no legislation in place governing what sites can or cannot do with the data. In mid-2000 the Federal Trade Commission sued the then recently defunct Toysmart.com to block it from selling its accumulated customer data as an asset in the bankruptcy sale. Unfortunately, however, the move backfired. To protect themselves in case of a bankruptcy or sale, other ecommerce sites began altering their policies so that customer data could be regarded as a saleable asset, even though those same sites had promised faithfully that the data would be kept private permanently. Many sites promise not to send you junk email; the trick is making sure their definition of junk matches yours.

To avoid a lot of this, you can start your browsing session from the Anonymizer (http://www.anonymizer.com), which acts as a middleman sitting between you and the site you're looking at and hides your information from the site.

No matter how safe and private you feel in an online area, it is always safest to assume that the possibility exists that what you say will be archived or copied by someone, no matter what promise the members have made to keep everything said there confidential. As long as a copy exists, there is no guarantee that it won't surface one day to haunt you.

People are a lot more identifiable than we often think. There is absolutely nothing wrong with discussing your alcoholism, the details of the fraud you perpetrated at work, or the problems your teenage daughter is having with bulimia in an online forum that is intended for the purpose. Just don't think your words will be erased as soon as you've typed them and pressed the 'submit' button. Many sites keep archives of old messages, and while you may know everyone who has access to the site now, you have no way of controlling who may be able to access the archives in the future. Usenet is a good case in point. Many people think of it as ephemeral because most ISPs only store the last couple of weeks' worth of messages. However, the Deja News (http://www.deja.com) site stores years of back Usenet archives, making it possible to locate messages whose authors have forgotten the contents, written perhaps when they were students. On Usenet, you can prevent your messages from being stored in the official archive sites by adding the line 'X-no-archive=yes' to the top of your postings, but that won't stop individuals from keeping copies. Even messages that have no official archives may be stored on someone's hard disk, retrievable if someone thinks to ask.

Additional sites

Data Protection Registrar (http://www.dataprotection.gov.uk): the horse's mouth when it comes to data protection legislation in the UK.

AdSubtract (http://www.adsubtract.com): software you download and install that blocks Internet advertising and prevents sites from picking up personal data – you can grant permission on an individual basis. Also blocks all those immensely annoying pop-up windows. Your computer's performance might slow down a bit, but it's worth it.

Privacy International (http://www.privacy.org): the leading privacy campaign organization in Britain.

PROPERTY

Buy or sell a house online? You've got to be joking.

Not necessarily. Obviously you will want to view the house in person – or at least send someone you trust. But property is one of the most intelligent things to put online, as if you're moving to a new area it can be very difficult to stay in touch with estate agents or to eliminate obviously wrong properties that they nonetheless persist in showing you. Researching the field online means you can get a good idea of prices and of the kind of available housing, as well as pick up local information about schools, social life and other facilities before you ever set foot in the estate agent's office. With any luck, the online research you do should save you time by eliminating obvious dead ends.

The major estate agency chains all have Web sites now that list all or part of their current stock. You may find it easier, however, to use one of the many independent sites – start by checking out Yahoo!'s list (http://uk. dir.yahoo.com/Regional/Countries/United_Kingdom/ Business_and_Economy/Property/Listings/) – that lets you search a geographical area by price, number of bedrooms and other requirements, and has listings from a variety of estate agents. If you want more information, the site will direct you to the appropriate agent's office. You should also try a more general search on Google or one of the other engines using something like 'house Cambridge UK sale' to find local estate agents or houses sold directly by their owners that might not pop up any other way. (You will probably also get a list of hits about the surrounding area, which is helpful, too.) (See **Search Engines**.)

You also might want to take a look at Up My Street (http://www.upmystreet.com), which will give you a demographic overview of the area you're moving into (see **Neighbourhood**) – if everyone on the street you're looking at reads the *Sun*, is this the place for you?

Buying and selling direct

Intrepid do-it-yourselfers who want to sell their homes directly and use a Web site to do it have a much easier and cheaper time than the old days where they'd have had to buy newspaper ads. If you decide to go this route, there are several sites that can help you get the news out to a wider range of people. Try 4 Sale By Owner (http://www.4salebyowner.co.uk) which lets you list your home for free, and provides search services and discussion areas for DIY sellers (although parts of the site are curiously blank). It also provides a link to Scoot to help find relevant professionals, such as surveyors. Easier (http://www.easier.co.uk) performs a similar job; however, to view listings or add your own home to them you must register. It's also worth looking at *Loot* (http://www.loot.com), which at last count had more than 12,000 property listings; its resources include help finding good deals on conveyancing, surveys, finance and other moving services.

(See also **Moving House**.)

Q

Q&A

Ask Me, just ask me, I dare you (http://www.askme.com).
Actually, Ask Me is your chance to ask a whole lot of other
people – real people, answering real questions. This is a
twist on the longer-standing Ask Jeeves, known just as Ask
(http://www.ask.co.uk) in the UK. Instead of doing all that
complicated search stuff (see **Search Engines**), you type in
a natural language question, something like 'Who is Wendy
Grossman?' and get back results from both Ask's own
database and a number of the Web's other search engines.
The thing is: Jeeves or no Jeeves, it just doesn't work very
well. But it can be very entertaining to watch the questions
other people are asking as they scroll past in real time –
kind of like browsing the dictionary serendipitously without
the heavy lifting.

Also on the Web these days is the *Guardian*'s long-running
Notes and Queries column (http://www.guardianunlimited.
co.uk/notesandqueries/), which publishes questions that
readers answer. The site lets you send a query, browse (but
not search) a selection of past columns, and submit answers
to outstanding questions. Some of those unanswered questions (why put candles on a birthday cake?) might make a
great place to start honing your Web research skills.

Probably most people in the UK haven't heard of the Straight Dope, the weekly column of questions and answers that kicked off the fad for such things. Bylined Cecil Adams, the columns originate at the alternative weekly *The Chicago Reader*, and are picked up by many other such weeklies around the US. The column has so far spawned five books, all redolent with Adams's biting insults and smart answers to readers' questions. Now, the Web site (http://www.straightdope.com) offers a daily question, message boards, and a full, searchable archive of what Adams modestly describes as 'containing all worthwhile human knowledge'. *And* he's funny. Go for it.

QUEEN

The Royal Web site (http://www.royal.gov.uk), created in 1997 by a team at the Central Office of Information, chronicles the life and times of the present Queen as well as other members of her immediate family and includes a monthly magazine called *Royal Insight*. This is the place to get the final word on succession, the Crown Jewels, and a host of other related subjects.

For a slightly irreverent Australian view of the Queen (she is, after all, their monarch, too), try Her Majesty's Unofficial Web Site (http://www.zip.com.au/~rocket/queen.htm).

QUICK START

Follow the instructions supplied you by your Internet service provicer and log on to the Internet and start your Web browser. If you have trouble doing this, try the **Trouble(shooting)** section or call your ISP's technical support desk. Once you're logged in and you have your Web browser open, in Netscape or Internet Explorer, you enter the address you want to go to by typing CTRL-O or ALT-F for the File menu and then O to open a page. This gives you a little box into which you type in an Internet address. Try typing in telegraph.co.uk and going to the Connected section. Follow the link and that will take you to the Web page for this book.

To access one of the links, move your mouse so the cursor is positioned over the link and left-click. You should be taken to the page. Happy browsing!

QUIZZES

There's something about Internet quizzes: you fill them out when no one is looking in the privacy of your own home, and there's no crumpled page covered with pencil marks afterwards to give you away.

The Internet is home to all sorts of quizzes, from the *Guardian*'s news quiz (http://www.newsunlimited.co.uk/quiz/) to quiz games such as CoolQuiz (http://www.

coolquiz.com) and Jamba (http://www.jamba.co.uk, requires Shockwave), as well as reputable surveys of Internet use (http://www.cc.gatech.edu/gvu/user_surveys/).

Most important: find out if you're a geek (http://www. geekquiz.com). If you find yourself checking email on the way back to bed after raiding the refrigerator in the middle of the night, you're in real trouble.

QUOTATIONS (LITERARY)

Start at the Quotations page (http://www.quotationspage. com). You'll also find the familiar *Bartlett's Quotations* (http://www.bartleby.com/99/) online in a searchable format.

QUOTES (STOCK MARKET)

Unless you're willing to pay, the quotes you find online will be delayed by about 20 minutes. This isn't bad – you have to be a professional trader to need instant updates, and if you are you'll already be paying for the service. The one exception is the quotes offered by your online broker right before you make a trade. Those have to be real-time so you can see how much you'll be paying.

Sites

Financial Times (http://www.ft.com): the daily newspaper plus much more, including company profiles, current quotes and market updates.

London Stock Exchange (http://www.londonstockexchange.com): everything you ever wanted to know about the British stock exchanges and the companies that trade on them.

After Hours Trading (http://www.afterhourstrading.com): watch directly for yourself the price fluctuations of pre-market and post-market US trading in NASDAQ stocks instead of waiting for CNBC to deliver an update. Requires Java.

Bloomberg (http://www.bloomberg.com/uk): a cut-down edition for the Web of the financial news service used by almost every media outlet.

Tornado Insider (http://www.tornado-insider.com): pan-European 'New Economy' site tracking companies at all stages from start-up to publicly traded monolith. With quotes from all European exchanges.

Oanda (http://www.oanda.com): *the* foreign exchange site. Daily rates, historical database, links to relevant articles, custom-built cross-rate tables, converters, business traveller's survival kit, news, and even a WAP service. Sadly, the service delivering foreign currency or traveller's cheques to a home address is only available to US residents.

Phonesoft (http://www.phone-soft.com/cyber-world/makeframe.php3?framename=0467i.htm): list of where to get quotes for most national or international exchanges.

The Motley Fool (http://www.fool.co.uk and http://www.fool.com): create a portfolio and watch the prices update. The UK site offers quotes from the LSE and AIM; the US site covers NYSE, NASDAQ and AMEX.

(See also **Investing**.)

R

RADIO

Now everyone can be a ham operator, listening to stations from Poland or Paraguay. Radio is a great broadcast medium to carry over the Web. For one thing, you can play it in the background while you browse. For another, we're tolerant of imperfections in radio from all those years of listening to the signal drop out in the car.

To listen to radio over the Internet, you need a computer with a sound board and speakers (or headphones); an Internet connection; a Web browser (for finding stations); and the right client software for the station you want to listen to, which will typically be Real Player (see **Plug-ins**). Radio broadcasts over the Web are streamed – that is, they are played live without storing the file on your hard drive – so you won't need much disk space. All you have to do to listen in is find a station and click on the link to the broadcast, whether it's live or stored from an earlier transmission. Real Player will start up, load chunks of data into its memory buffer so that if the data stream gets momentarily disturbed your feed will continue uninterrupted, and within a minute or so you're listening to WVBR-FM, the student-owned and operated radio station from Cornell University in Ithaca, NY. Or whatever. London's Virgin

Radio says it's quite popular among North American listeners, who like the relatively low quantity of ads and the different format.

The only question is how to find the radio broadcast of your dreams. You could start at the Internet Radio List (http://www.internetradiolist.com), which lists stations by country, language and type of music; you can also search for stations by name, country, language or keyword. An even more comprehensive list is maintained by the Massachusetts Institute of Technology (http://wmbr.mit.edu/stations/), which indexes over 9,000 electronic radio stations primarily searchable by location; its European list (http://wmbr.mit.edu/stations/w-eu.html) is more than 1,000 stations long and it even lists 65 online stations in Africa. Finally, the list at Best of the Net (http://www.goan.com/radio.html) is more selective and hence perhaps a bit more manageable; Best of the Net also lists Web TV stations (see **TV**).

Or, if you don't like any of those, create your own radio station: Imagine Radio (http://www.imagineradio.com) lets you choose your own playlists and uses intelligent software to add songs similar to ones it already knows you like.

RELIGION

The best online site for Anglicans (http://www.anglicans.org) isn't run by the Church of England, which took years to produce a report concluding that the Internet might be valuable; it's run by Brian Reid, one of the original instigators of the alt Usenet hierarchy and a programmer at Digital Equipment Corporation. The site, which was set up as long ago as 1994, is thoughtful and well designed, with essays, Bible quotations and study resources, all updated weekly (appropriately enough, on Sundays).

Catholics may like the Catholic World News site (http://www.cwnews.com/), which is just what it sounds like, or the Catholic Church in England and Wales (http://www.tasc.ac.uk/cc/index.htm). Jewishnet (http://jewishnet.net/) aims to be a global resource, and the *Jewish Chronicle* runs a site with archives and discussions for readers (you have to register for this one).

Atheists may prefer the Biblical Contradictions (http://www.atheists.org/church/contradictions.html) page, which looks at internal inconsistencies within the Bible.

On the Net itself, however, the primary religions are PCs, Macs and Linux. We recommend avoiding these sensitive subjects in mixed company.

RESEARCH

Britannica Online (http://www.britannica.com): watching the venerable and ultra-respected *Encyclopædia Britannica* come to grips with the electronic era has been a fascinating case study in change. From the well-known massive set of volumes costing thousands of pounds, *Britannica*'s first electronic effort was a much-too-expensive CD, then a much cheaper CD and finally this online version, completely free. The site gives access to all 44 million words of the mammoth encyclopedia, and the home page is filled with current news (see its 2000 Olympics archive), views and links. Every search produces four sets of results: the encyclopedia entry, a set of links to the best Web sites on the subject, as chosen and reviewed by the *Encyclopædia Britannica* staff, references to magazine articles on the subject and a list of relevant books. Useful for researchers of all ages and free.

For everything else try a search (see **Search Engines**).

ROWING

See under **Sports**.

RUGBY

See under **Sports**.

S

SCHEDULES

How many computers do you use in how many locations? If the answer is more than two, online scheduling may be for you. Storing your schedule and contact book online means you can access the data from anywhere you happen to be. Customized email alerts remind you of scheduled appointments. The best of these even synch with popular PC packages, so that you never need to enter data more than once. You will need to check out the sites below carefully before making a final decision as to which site will work best for you. Choose the password to protect your data carefully! Most are free.

Sites

Any Day (http://www.anyday.com): lets you publish a calendar and add news, weather and sports results.

MSN Calendar (http://calendar.msn.com/calendar.html): imports data from Yahoo!, Palm, Outlook and Windows CE; includes a mobile version for viewing from phones.

Schedule Online (http://www.scheduleonline.com): allows cooperative scheduling with colleagues or family and friends.

Visto (http://www.visto.com): email, group calendaring and 15Mb of file storage.

Yahoo! (http://calendar.yahoo.com): synchs with Outlook and Palm Pilot, and ties into other parts of Yahoo! such as chat, pager and email services.

SCIENCE

Among popular science sites, it's always worth looking at the slow-to-load Discovery Channel Europe (http://www. discoveryeurope.com), which ran an excellent special section for the 1999 eclipse and has ongoing sections such as Animal Planet that are both good fun and educational. It's intriguing to learn, for example, in a feature on speed comparisons between humans and animals, that twenty competitors on their way to the Sydney Olympics raced against emus at the London Zoo before departing. Also good fun is the site belonging to the similarly named but unrelated US magazine *Discover* (http://www.discover. com), which has a set of links to other equally entertaining popular science sites.

To most people, 'science' means astronomy and sometimes medicine. These are, after all, the sciences that get written up in the papers, astronomy because all those pictures make for great-looking pages and medicine because people are endlessly fascinated with anything that might prolong their lives even just a little bit. The upshot is that

all kinds of other sciences get forgotten: geology, archae-
ology, chemistry, biology, physics and even computer
science.

Things are different on the Internet, where academic
departments aimed to share resources for mutual benefit
and where the earliest users were academics – the Internet's
backbone was originally built to let universities all over the
US share five regional supercomputing centres. So if you
look you'll find massive coverage of scientific disciplines
such as pharmacology that you never hear about in the
mainstream press.

Going into detail on such a wide range of expert subjects
is beyond the scope of this book, though a good range of
current science news is available from either *Science News*
(http://www.sciencenews.com) or the more comprehensive
World Scientist (http://www.worldscientist.com). For more
specialized coverage, the best way to find out what's going
on in a specific scientific discipline is probably to look for
discussion groups on the subject. Start with Usenet's
sci.hierarchy, which has a newsgroup on most major subjects and many smaller ones; if that fails, use the search
functions at Deja (http://www.deja.com) to search for relevant newsgroups in other hierarchies. If the newsgroups
you find are too overrun with idiots who are loud, confident
and wrong, or are cluttered with spam and junk postings
but not much meat (which does happen sometimes), you
will have to look elsewhere. Try, for example, eGroups,
which serves as a home for a number of discussion groups
on serious topics (see **Argue**); as one example, the Evolutionary Psychology list is hosted there, and manages to

cover this extremely contentious area in a civilized manner. Also look at Liszt (http://www.liszt.com), which is a comprehensive directory of more than 90,000 electronic mailing lists. These tend to be more serious and focused than Usenet, as many of them were started in part because Usenet had become too noisy.

Of course, the topics that get a lot of play on the Internet are often the ones that are most controversial; people who can't get what they believe is a fair hearing by the scientific establishment are happier taking their case direct to the public. Subjects like nanotechnology (http://www.foresight. org), for example, have extremely visible adherents online, even though it's uncertain whether the central idea – that it should be possible to design bacteria that will build any device we want for us – will ever bear fruit.

One thing that is important to understand, however, is the way the Internet is changing the world of science publishing. Traditionally, a research paper could take years to see publication in an academic journal, being submitted, peer-reviewed and perhaps revised; during that time the research probably remained unseen by anyone who wasn't directly connected with the work or the publication. Now, scientists are unlikely to want to wait that long, even though they still want the endorsement of their work and the prestige implied by official publication. It has become commonplace for draft versions of academic research papers to appear on the Net, speeding up access to the research even though it's understood that the final draft may contain important revisions. This is, of course, a change that cuts both ways. While it does give scientists faster access to important research, it also creates the conditions for another 'cold fusion'-type incident, where the absence of peer review allowed a wild claim mass publicity.

In any event, the point about science is that it is not, as many people think, a source of simple answers. Science is far more often a set of questions. But more important, science is a process for establishing truth; its most essential cornerstone is the scientific method, which requires research results to be replicable by independent researchers before being accepted as part of the knowledge base. For examples of why this is important, see the Junk Science site (http://www.junkscience.com). More fun science is at Science Hobbyist (http://www.amasci.com/), with meditations on traffic patterns and sample experiments you can try at home and at the Exploratorium (http://www.exploratorium.edu/), which points Webcams at its live exhibits and trys making a bubble bomb out of a zip-lock bag, vinegar and some bicarbonate of soda.

It's easy to forget that the US, too, has public broadcasting. Boston's WGBH, part of the Public Broadcasting Service, co-produces a number of science programmes with the BBC. *A Science Odyssey* isn't one of them – but even though the programme itself is American and you may never see it, the Web site (www.pbs.org/wgbh/aso) has nearly as much to see as a multimedia CD-Rom. Compare, for example, the state of scientific knowledge in 1900, when the Milky Way galaxy was the known universe, Newton's laws explained the physical world and matter was made of atoms, with today, when there are millions of galaxies, many sets of laws to try to explain the physical world and atoms are made up of subatomic particles. Overall, the site makes all its topics approachable, and a moving timeline shows a living room changing its electrical appliances over the years, with the inventions explained along the way. The site also features a game show called 'That's my theory' in which you try to work out which of three possibilities is the real Einstein, Freud or pioneering computer Eniac. Parts of the site require Shockwave.

The Web sites belonging to the American Association for the Advancement of Science (http://www.aaas.org) and the British Association for the Advancement of Science (http://www.britassoc.org.uk) are both sadly disappointing, the American one because most of the useful published material is off-limits to non-members, the British one because its links are primarily to other professional organizations. Scroll down its links page, however, to the PUS listings – PUS standing for 'Public Understanding of Science' – and you find some good sites if you take the time to look at them. The Pub Understanding of Science page (http://www.alegba.demon.co.uk/beermats.html) has a clever collection of scientific conundrums (what percentage of cells in the human body are actually not human?*) designed to fit on beermats.

Also take a look at AlphaGalileo (http://www.alphagalileo.com). Primarily aimed at journalists, Alpha-Galileo is a rolling press release service for European scientific discoveries and announcements of all types – postings on genetic surveys, new insights into the makeup of the

* The answer is 90 per cent.

Milky Way and marriage trends in Sweden. Anyone can read the press releases, but to gain full access to Alpha-Galileo you need to register in one of three categories: journalist, contributor (press officer and scientist) or visitor (everyone else). Journalists gain access to embargoed information and contact details for contributors, but have to supply either an employer's name or, if they're freelance, a reference. Only contributors, who go through a similar procedure, may post material to the site.

Finally, if you or someone close to you is interested in becoming a science writer, a brochure on the topic is available at the site belonging to the Association of British Science Writers (http://www.absw.org.uk/careers.htm), an organization that boasts some of Britain's best-known science writers and broadcasters as members.

No collection of science sites is complete without humour. Try the Annals of Improbable Research (http://www.improb.com), sponsors of the annual Ig Nobel awards. AIR is famous for highlighting wacky bits of genuine scientific research that sound too bizarre to be true – but are.

SEARCH ENGINES

Unlike TV, the Internet isn't a broadcasting medium. In practice, this means that when you turn on your computer and log on the information doesn't just flow over your screen: you have to go out and get it. In most cases, you won't know where to find what you want, so you will have to search for it. The most important services on the Net, therefore, are the search engines, which send little pieces of 'robot' software out to scour the Net and build indexes. When you use a search engine, this is what you search.

Quick tips on searches

- If you're searching for information about a particular product, try typing the manufacturer's name, the make, and the model number into Google (http:// www.google.com). Model numbers are almost always unique from manufacturer to manufacturer, and you should get back a list of very tightly targeted hits.

- In the main search engines, throw in as many unusual words as you can that are likely to appear in the final document – this will help eliminate irrelevant junk. Don't just type in 'Frasier' if you're trying to find out what breed Martin Crane's dog is; type in 'Frasier TV Eddie dog breed' (the second hit on Google's list tells you that he's a Jack Russell terrier).

- If your search returns no hits, check the correct spelling of the terms you used. In the last example, Google was smart enough to recognize Eddy or Eddie, but the difference between Frasier and Frazier would have killed the search's effectiveness.

- Read the help files of the specific search engine you're using to learn the most effective strategies. They're all different.

- Forget all the other general search engines you may have heard of (Altavista, Excite, Lycos) and go straight to Google (http://www.google.com).

Google searches

Google is faster, slicker, less cluttered with junk and produces the best and most accurate hits. It's even entertaining: despite the site's prominent lack of any graphics to slow down its interface, in honour of special events it decorates its logo – a bullseye on one of the days of the Olympics, fireworks for Bastille Day and a green hat and shamrock for St Patrick's Day. You can customize the number of hits the site displays and the number of languages it searches in by clicking on the 'Language, Display, and Filtering Options' link. There is an Advanced Search on Google (just click the link) which will let you constrain searches so that you can, for example, exclude Christmas dinner recipes when you're looking for pages about Turkey. However, in my experience, if you are clever about your search terms you won't need this advanced option.

The way Google works is different enough from other search engines for its technology to be patent-pending. Most search engines rely on keywords and indexing; Google does this, too, but claims its system can be more easily upgraded to handle larger amounts of data. In addition it uses an algorithm known as PageRank, developed at Stanford University, which takes into account the linking structure of the Web and the number of pages linking to a page to determine its relevance to a given search. The upshot is that a Google search produces far fewer broken links and is much faster and more accurate than anything else. Because Google also has a clean, uncluttered interface that loads quickly and limits ads to a one-phrase link with no graphics, it is blindingly fast.

The best strategy for conducting a really accurate Google search is to enter as many unusual words into the search box as you know will have to be in the document you want. Google assumes you want hits that contain all the words you enter. Let's say, for example, that you want to find a song you heard in the 1996 movie *Twister*, and all you remember is a bit where 'Shine on, shine on' is blaring out of the loudspeaker on top of one of the trucks. You have no idea who recorded it, what the rest of the song's lyrics are like, or whether it was written specifically for the movie.

There are a number of ways you could attack this search. One would be to start at the Internet Movies Database (http://www.imdb.com), look up *Twister* and click on the button (on the left, under 'Fun Stuff') to display its sound-track listing. From there, you could go to a CD retailer like CDNow (http://www.cdnow.com) and search on the individual titles to play clips. Or, if you've set up Napster (see **Music**), you could download each song on the list and play each song one by one until you found it. You can do the same search much faster using Google as long as you enter enough search terms. 'Twister soundtrack', for example, isn't going to get you any further than the Internet Movies Database did in identifying the specific song, and 'Shine on' by itself is hopeless.

But try 'shine +on twister soundtrack lyrics 1996'. One of the first few hits should direct you to something like, 'Best

Of Vol. 1 ©1996. 1, Eruption. 2, Ain ... Humans Being'
(from the *Twister* soundtrack). And that's it: Van Halen's
Best of, Volume I, with the lyrics of the song 'Humans
Being' showing 'Shine on, shine on' as the chorus and noting
that the song appeared in the movie. Plug that into Napster
or CDNow, and you're there. (Since you're asking, when I
originally did this search, I did it the first way. It took about
four hours spread out over a couple of days. I did get to
hear some interesting music, though.)

To be fair to the other search engines, entering that same
list of search terms into Altavista and Excite works just
about as well. To some extent, therefore, which search
engine you use is much less important than how you use it.
My own personal taste inclines towards fast and uncluttered
– I hate having ads and graphics blink at me when I'm
trying to think of search terms or read anything – and
experience over many searches has taught me that Google's
listing is far less likely to be full of time-wasting broken
links.

The '+' in front of 'on' in that search example is important. Google discards common words such as 'and,' 'the,'
and most prepositions. Preceding such words with a '+'
forces Google to include them in the search – important in
this case as all we had was a scrap of lyric. Tips like these
can make your searches far faster and more effective, and
much less frustrating. For that reason, any time you use an
unfamiliar search engine *read the help file*. Each engine has
its own quirks and design differences, and the ten minutes
you spend reading the help file and learning how to do a
more effective search saves you hours of time going through

10,000 irrelevant hits. From then on, any time you see anyone – a journalist in print, a commentator on TV, a marketer at a conference – saying that it's impossible to find what you want on the Internet because you get drowned in thousands of hits you can feel smug. The Internet is an enormously valuable research tool; but you should expect to have to learn how to use it effectively, just as you had to learn how to use a library when you were a child.

You can do all kinds of things with Google that people rarely realize. Enter a US stock ticker symbol (try INTC, for Intel) and get back a stock quote (from Yahoo!). Enter 'link:<Web address>' and see who links to a particular Web address. Click on underlined words at the top of the page of hits you get after a search, and go straight to their dictionary definitions. In addition, if you go to the page that explains Google's advanced features, you can drag buttons on to your browser's toolbar (literally, click your mouse on the indicated link and hold it down while dragging the mouse cursor to your toolbar – see http://www. google.com/options/buttons.html) that give you one-click access to Google's main search screen or to its 'similar pages' feature that goes out and finds you more pages similar to the one you're looking at. A different button lets you search the Web using Google on any phrase or group of words you highlight on the page you're looking at. Nifty stuff.

If you're in a hurry and you have become good at constructing effective searches, hit the 'I'm Feeling Lucky' button and you'll be taken straight to the top hit on the list.

There are a few limited circumstances under which you

might want to try a different search engine, although fewer
and fewer.

Yahoo!, which is often referred to as a search engine, is
more precisely a classified directory and a portal. For category searches – the kind of thing where you want to know,
say, the Web address of this week's pro women's tennis
tournament, or a listing of shopping sites selling Braun
household appliances – Yahoo! is the place to start. Google
has a directory, too, but it's newer and smaller, and Yahoo!
is still the best in this category. For category searches, you
use Yahoo! like any classified catalogue: start at the top and
select finer and finer subcategories. What's really helpful on
Yahoo! is that once you've moved into the classified pages
you can search only the category you're looking at (or, of
course, all of Yahoo!), making it easy to exclude irrelevant
hits. You might, for example, look for the site of the mid-
October Swisscom Challenge women's tennis tournament
by clicking in turn on Sports/Tennis/Tournaments. The
week the tournament was being played, it appeared at the
top.

One interesting experiment is the UK Web Library (http:
//www.scit.wlv.ac.uk/wwlib/searcht.html), a searchable,
classified catalogue of UK sites based at the Wolverhampton
Web Library. Attempting to marry classical library science
to the Web, the site assigns Dewey Decimal numbers to sites
in an effort to make it easier to find precise subject matches.
Useful for targeted searches when you want only UK sites
(and a few multinationals active in the UK), especially if
you're a whizz at the library numbers. Yahoo! does, of
course, much the same thing without assigning those num-

bers, and it has long had librarians working for it to improve its classification system.

Once you've been spoiled by these well-designed search engines, you can get very frustrated very fast by the mini search engines included on corporate and major news sites. Unfortunately, much of the time you do have to use them, as sites that require registration are essentially walling off their content from the major search engines. So, for example, although *Wired News*'s articles will pop up in a Web-wide search on Google or one of the others (a much better way of finding stories from the service, as its own search function only accepts single words as queries and only looks at headlines), stories from the registration-blocked *New York Times* and *Electronic Telegraph* won't. You will have to search those sites separately using their own built-in search functions.

Sometimes better search facilities are there, but you have to dig for them. Entering a term into the search box at the top of CNN's site (http://www.cnn.com), for example, gives you a list of hits and an Advanced link; the Advanced search lets you specify dates and multiple search terms.

Boolean operators

One set of techniques that pops up on many search engines, general and specific, is Boolean operators. Based on a branch of algebra, Boolean searching sounds more complicated than it is, and it is worth learning because it is so often used. The most common and simplest operators are AND, NOT and OR. Searching on 'Santa AND Claus' requires both terms to appear on a page for it to be returned as a hit. Searching on 'sanity AND clause' ought, for example, to get you back pages that mention both sanity and clause, of which the top entries will be Chico Marx's famous riposte, 'You cain' fool me. There ain'ta no Sanity Clause' from the 1935 Marx Brothers movie *A Night at the Opera*. Searching on 'sanity OR clause' will get you back pages that have either term or both. Searching on 'sanity NOT clause' will get you back pages that talk about sanity, but will exclude pages that include the word 'clause' – a Marx Brothers-free zone.

Boolean searches also allow you to specify a phrase by surrounding it with quotes; only pages with all the words, in the order specified, next to each other will be returned. Additional operators you don't find as often include ADJ, NEAR, FAR, and BEFORE, and all of these specify the relationship between the terms (ADJ stands for adjacent, so it means the words are next to each other, but in any order). A good explanation of Boolean operators and how to use them is at Lycos (http://www.lycos.co.uk/help/boolean. html), where you can use them to build quite complex searches that return very tightly targeted hits.

Understanding how to search effectively, therefore, requires you to spend a little time learning to use the tools, just as you had to learn how to use a library card catalogue when you were a child. Ultimately, picking a search engine you're comfortable with and learning the best strategies for that specific engine is probably the best bet for general searches. But you need to learn where to look for specific types of information, and ultimately that will come with experience and increased knowledge of both the Internet and the kinds of information you frequently search for.

One option is to consult a guide or comparison table that makes suggestions for specific topics (http://www.albany. edu/library/internet/choose.html), but often a general search will help you narrow things down to a few sources you can search more specifically. For example, if you're trying to find predictions on the size of the mobile commerce market in 2005, you might search Google on 'mobile commerce market size prediction 2005'. Going through some of the pages that pop up from that search should give you pointers to research companies (Gartner Group, Yankee Group – $200 billion) who have made such predictions; you'll probably have to search their sites separately for precise citations and to check figures.

A last caveat: not all of the Web is searchable. Besides registration-blocked sites, any site can be deliberately kept out of the search engine indexes by including a file called robots.txt in the directory where the Web pages are stored. Using a standard syntax (http://info.webcrawler.com/mak/ projects/robots/norobots-rfc.html) this file can instruct the search engines' indexing software ('spider') to ignore any or all pages in the site, rendering a page as invisible as an ex-directory phone number. In addition, interactive features such as calculators and dictionaries, databases and archived material are often not searchable by normal means. A number of specialist search engines claimed to have cracked this; the only one that seemed worth persevering with after a short trial is The Big Hub (http://www.thebighub.com), which searches a variety of these 'invisible Web' searchers.

Other search engines

Altavista (http://www.altavista.com): Altavista used to be the search engine of choice, but is now so cluttered I never use it. Constrain searches on Altavista by putting a '+' in front of words you want included in the search and a '-' in front of words you want excluded. To search for pages about Turkey but exclude holiday dinners and recipes, for example, you might try '+Turkey -Thanksgiving -recipe -Christmas'. To search on a phrase rather than individual words, put the phrase in quotes. Altavista also accepts * as a wild card (just like PCs); searching on 'Edd*' would return hits on both Eddy and Eddie.

Excite (http://www.excite.co.uk): the home site of a search engine you'll find in use on many corporate sites (for that reason alone, it pays to learn how to use Excite). On the main site, you can constrain your search to just UK sites, European sites or news, which is useful; it also has a search service for news wire photos.

Hotbot (http://www.hotbot.com): Hotbot began life as the in-house search engine for *Wired* magazine. Accordingly, it is now also owned by Lycos. Provides advanced search options (word, phrase, Boolean) from its front page, which is nice, but the lurid colours make it uncomfortable to look at for very long. Still, it sometimes indexes material that doesn't pop up elsewhere. Has helpful resources for finding MP3 music files, jobs and alumni (primarily useful in the US).

Lycos (http://www.lycos.co.uk): Lycos, now owner of *Wired News* and a number of other high-profile sites, has an irritating feature in that if you try to go to the US home page (http://www.lycos.com) and you're coming from a British ISP the site automatically dumps you on to the UK home page. In other words, it's too smart for its own good (type http://www-english.lycos.com/ to get to the US home page from the UK). Lycos does, however, have specialist search engines, notably one for MP3 music files, that can be useful (although you could, of course, just enter the song title or artist's name in Google and add MP3 to the list of search terms). (See **Yahoo and other Portals** for Lycos's other features.)

SECURITY

Quick tips

- Wherever possible, use a secure server for sensitive information such as credit card details. Look for the tiny locked padlock on the bar at the bottom of your browser window to confirm the connection is secure.

- Choose passwords carefully so that they are hard to guess but easy for you to remember.

- Use credit cards with higher levels of consumer protection, such as Barclaycard and American Express, or consider setting up a credit card you use only for Internet shopping and set the credit limit very low.

- Do not use Switch online. You have much less protection if the card information is copied or stolen.

- Never give out your password to any online service or Web site to someone who emails and asks for it, even if they say they're staff. If you think there's a genuine reason why they might be contacting you, call the company using its published phone number and check.

- Remember that in a security breach you have more to fear from someone's being able to impersonate you than you do from their simply being able to read your information.

- Install (free) firewall software to protect your computer.

- Read and follow the security advice supplied on online banking and credit card sites such as Barclays.

Anything new involves new risks. In the case of the Internet, the risks aren't as great as the mass media have made them out to be, but they still exist. There have been some well-publicized incidents that are quite disturbing. In January, 2000, for example, a Russian hacker stole credit-card information from online retailer CDUniverse and sold the details. In mid-summer of the same year, several men were arrested allegedly attempting to defraud the online bank Egg (security experts say that the fraud could just as easily have been carried out on paper). But the fact is that doing anything involves taking some risks, and part of the process of becoming familiar with a new technology is getting comfortable with its risk factors. We drive cars, even though many children are killed on the roads every year.

People's biggest concern seems to be that entering credit card or Switch details into the forms on shopping sites will

leave them wide open to being swiped by hackers. The first
defence against this is technology. Any ecommerce site
worth shopping at ensures that credit card details and other
sensitive information such as passwords are transmitted
across the Internet using technology called SSL, for Secure
Sockets Layer. Built into your browser, SSL encrypts the
data so that anyone intercepting it won't be able to read it.
The site's stored database of such information should also
be encrypted.

The second defence is the fact that in general hackers are
not the biggest risk to the public's credit cards. The kind of
security risk that Barclay's experienced in the summer of
2000, for example, when new customers logging on saw the
last customer's bank account details, is a technical problem
relating to the design of the software the company is using.
The fix for it is simple, a question of ensuring that the
computer cleared its short-term memory when a customer
logged off, and was quickly applied in Barclay's case. It
would be more comforting if we could blame hackers
instead of flaws in the bank's own software design, because
the hackers could be put in jail while software bugs can
happen to anyone at any time. Hackers do sometimes gain
access to a site and alter its front page to one of their own
choosing, but that is a long way from breaking into the site's
database of customer information. With stored credit card
details, you're more at risk from a disaffected company
employee with access to the system than from the archetypal
hacker without it. However, the risk is no greater than any
business these days; even High Street retailers have databases of past credit card transactions, and the waiter who

takes your credit card into the back room of the restaurant for processing has better access to your information than the fifteen-year-old geek in the back bedroom of popular mythology.

To give all this some personal perspective: I began shopping online the minute it became available. I've had one retailer fail to fill an order (I was never billed), one that waited so long to put the credit card charge through that the card had expired, and no theft at all. Some of that is luck, a lot of it is hanging around online with a lot of other people shopping at sites and swapping recommendations; some is being careful. Just as you need to develop 'street nous' if you live in a large city, you need to develop 'Net nous'. That said, it's also true that unfortunately you can't tell the quality of a site's security just from looking at it. One thing you can be sure of, though: they will get it right after there's been a well-publicized incident.

Checking up on online merchants

The most important thing you should do is check that when a site says it's linking you to a secure server it really is – look for the little closed padlock in the bar at the bottom of your browser window.

To some extent with experience you develop a 'feel' for sites. You visit them over time, you see how they work and how they compare to competitors, and you hear reports from friends or online acquaintances regarding their experiences. One reason Amazon.com became so successful so quickly, for example, is that once one person bought from them and liked their service, the word went out at Net speed. Online discussion areas, such as the message areas on Yahoo! or topic-specific newsgroups on Usenet are good places to ask about online vendors you're not sure about.

Beyond that, you can do as the online consumer guides recommend and look for logos signifying that the merchant complies with consumer protection schemes such as the one run by *Which?* You can also take your time or place a small order first to try out the service before committing to a large expenditure.

One big worry at the moment with so many dot-com companies going bust – Boxman.com, for example, was one of the leading CD/DVD/video/games retailers before it suddenly announced it was out of money in mid-October 2000 – is that the company may not be there to fill the order. Generally speaking, online companies, like mail order companies, should not debit your credit card until they fill the order. If they do, talk to your credit card company, which should be able to help.

Credit card companies, in fact, are among the organizations who are most anxious to improve security on the Internet, largely because as things are they are bearing a large part of the risk. The average credit card, after all, limits a consumer's liability to £50 once it's stolen, and Barclaycard doesn't even charge that. In the current climate, credit card companies have tended to give consumers the benefit of the doubt when they dispute Internet charges that appear on their bills. Visa is implementing a new secure system designed to offer real-time authentication for both customer and merchant, intended to enhance protection for both sides of the transaction. In the meantime, it's a good idea to check your statements carefully – but you should be doing that in any case.

Switch cards, however, do not give consumers the same protection credit cards do. Instead, they give a site direct access to your bank account. Avoid this scenario in general, although it's understandable that, for example, a travelling user might want to use his/her Switch card online to pay down a Barclaycard bill (http://www.barclaycard.co.uk) if it's getting near the limit during a trip.

Securing your computer

The same characteristics that let you see the entire Internet from your home computer mean that the Internet and its many computers can also see your computer. In some cases, such as the music-sharing service Napster (see **Music**), this is a benefit to you. But in others, such as when someone installs software on your machine without your knowledge, it can be extremely dangerous. The well-publicized attacks on leading eretailers like Amazon.com and Yahoo! in early 2000 came about because software was installed on 'innocent' machines that set them to sending out constant probes to those services, eventually flooding their servers (these are known as 'distributed denial of service' attacks). Blame Microsoft if you like: the lack of good security in its operating systems is a large reason why personal computers are so vulnerable.

For a graphic demonstration of exactly how much information a site can get about you just because you landed on one of its Web pages, try Privacy Net's analysis page (http://privacy.net/anonymizer/). If that hasn't scared you (it gets most people the first time they see it), test your computer for open ports (http://www.grc.com) and read the explanation of exactly what open ports can mean to you.

The more you are online, the more of the time your computer is available to the outside, making your risk greater. However, there are some mitigating factors. If you use standard dial-up, the chances are that you are assigned an IP number dynamically when you log on; this means that although someone might be able to gain access to your computer during an extended session, they are unlikely to be able to find it again as it won't be at the same address. Those using always-on services such as ADSL and cable modems should find that their ISPs have built security protection into the services. But don't assume – test your ports as above.

In either case, a solution is simple and free: install Zone Alarm (http://www.zonelabs.com). The company sells a fuller featured 'pro' version, but the free version is still pretty good. Once you've installed the software, you'll find that your first few browsing sessions are interrupted occasionally by little Zone Alarm windows asking if you want to allow this or that program to access the Internet. Check 'Remember' and 'Yes' for programs like Netscape, Real Player, your email software, and so on, and thereafter those questions will only pop up if you install new software. If someone else manages to install software on your computer without your knowledge, however, you'll be able to spot that it has happened and stop it from doing any damage by checking 'No' to block that program from accessing the Internet.

There are some other things you can do to make your computer less predictable – with 90 per cent of PCs running the same software, computers are like a field of cloned sheep, all prone to the same diseases. Some people pride themselves on using non-standard, non-Microsoft software, for example; if you don't use Word you're not vulnerable to Word viruses, and if you don't use Outlook email-borne viruses that spread by sending themselves to the names in your address book can't rely on that familiar format. Even if you can't do that, you can resist letting your software decide where to put your data and create a directory structure that suits you. For example, instead of letting every piece of Internet software create a 'My Downloads' subdirectory of its own, tell them all to use a central 'Receive' directory; instead of letting every piece of office software create its own data directory, create a central one. This has the additional advantage of making it easier to keep regular backups of those important files (see **Backup**). In addition, you can store the data on a disc in a removable drive, such as a Zip drive, and remove it from your computer, making it wholly inaccessible not just to overcurious hackers but to overcurious children in your own household.

If you share your computer, use the built-in function in your Web browser to clear your cache of stored Web pages after online sessions. In addition, turn off the option ecommerce sites offer to 'remember' you, so others can't use your account without your knowledge – many such sites keep not only your name, shipping and billing addresses, but your credit card information to make it quick and easy for you to put through future purchases. You will, of course, then have to log in yourself each time by typing in your ID and password, but that has a good side: it means when you're travelling and for some reason need to access the site you'll remember what they are.

While, again, the risks are relatively slight that someone out there will want to take over your specific computer and make it do their bidding, protecting your computer is good Net-citizenship, and takes only a small amount of time while you retrieve and set up the software, much of which is free.

For mobile users

It sounds paranoid, but make sure no one's reading over your shoulder when you enter ID numbers or passwords if you're accessing important accounts in an Internet café or other public area. If you've been on a trip where you've had to use terminals in such places, it wouldn't hurt to change your password when you get home.

Always make sure you correctly log off sites where personal financial information is stored, so that even if the terminal's next user finds a way to explore your just-completed transactions he/she won't be able to actually get into your account.

Email and other viruses

For most users, the biggest risk today is through email, particularly the files that sometimes come attached to a message. These may be anything from word-processed documents to pictures, music or even video files. You should ensure that your email software is set so that it does *not* automatically run such files without checking them for viruses first. Because email software varies, you will have to check the online help for your software to find out how to do this, but in general this should be covered in the settings for security preferences or options.

Whenever you receive an attached file unexpectedly even if it's from someone you know and trust, you should check very carefully before you run the file. The well-known Melissa virus that wreaked havoc in 1999 played on the trust people have in their friends and co-workers by sending itself out attached to an apparently innocuous and friendly email message. When people obeyed the instructions and checked out the document, thinking it was a work-related project they needed to look at, hidden instructions in the document sent out further copies to the first fifty entries in their Microsoft Outlook address book, clogging company mail servers.

As has already been mentioned, it is also important to run anti-virus software. Most anti-virus software packages these days are commercial packages, so they are not free; the exception is the program F-Prot (available from http://www.complex.is/f-prot/Download.html), which despite being free is considered to be one of the best. A commercial anti–virus package may have been included when you bought your computer. The important thing to remember is that it's not enough to install anti-virus software once; you must update it regularly in order to keep pace with the new viruses being released. Some software allows you to do this automatically, so that the software itself will check for an update when you're online, retrieve it, and install it without your having to do anything. With other packages, you will need to find and install the updates yourself. Either way, you should ensure that the software gets updated at the manufacturer's recommended frequency if you are in the habit of downloading or sharing files. The latest version of Zone Alarm (http://www.zonelabs.com) blocks email viruses.

Choosing passwords

Picking passwords for sites to use to protect your accounts, is a perennial problem, in part because a typical Web user eventually needs so many. The obvious strategy is to use one password for everything. Don't. The problem with doing that is that if someone learns your password to one site, they can get into all of your accounts. Remember, the risk is not just that they may see your information but that they can actually impersonate you, moving your money around (if it's a bank account), charging goods (if it's a retailer account), or sending out email as if they were you (if it's an email account). A better strategy, therefore, is to use individual, carefully chosen passwords for the relatively few really important accounts, such as those with your online bank and stockbroker, and use a different, single password or family of passwords for sites where you do not store personal data of any consequence and where you and/ or your reputation cannot be damaged if someone impersonates you.

The best passwords are easy to remember (so you don't have to write them down somewhere that a thief might see it) but difficult to guess. Avoid dictionary words, as there are software routines on the Net that can run through the entire dictionary in a matter of minutes to crack a password. Also avoid using easily associated passwords that could be guessed by anyone who knows you: spouse's, children's or pets' names, your address or birth date, or your mother's maiden name. Instead, pick something like the name of a restaurant with personal associations, a fictional character or childhood memory, and add a non-alphabetical character or two. On systems that use case-sensitive passwords (meaning that the system distinguishes between upper- and lower-case letters), you can make the password even more difficult to guess by capitalizing one or two of the letters.

Additional sites

The Encyclopaedia of Computer Security (http://www. itsecurity.com): compiled by security experts, explains every security term you're ever likely to come across. Click on a letter to go to that section of the alphabet; click on a word to see the definition.

Antivirus (http://www.av.ibm.com): IBM and Symantec have teamed up to produce this excellent site on viruses. Especially read the excellent common sense advice on how to avoid them and monitor the Hype Alerts page so you don't pass on hoaxes, which are almost as much of a nuisance.

Microsoft (http://www.microsoft.com/security): check back regularly for security patches for Microsoft software. They do make them – but you have to install them for them to do anything to plug up the holes in your machine.

RISKS Forum (http://the.wiretapped.net/security/textfiles/risks-digest/): best read as Usenet newsgroup comp.risks. Will confirm every idea you ever had about what's wrong with technology.

Security Portal (http://www.securityportal.com): check for news headlines about new security breaches and fixes.

SHAREWARE

Shareware is software that you can try for free before you buy it, letting you decide whether it's right for you. The fact that it is not commercial software shouldn't put you off: some shareware is the best software available in its category. Now that you're online, you have easy access to all of this. The list below is of a few must-haves.

Barclock (http://www.multimania.com/brocker/barclock/): a personal favourite, this little utility puts the time (if you like) or the amount of disk space and memory left, or a couple of application buttons (or all of the above) into the title bar on the active window on a Windows machine. Computing without this information in front of you once you're used to it is like driving without a speedometer or gas gauge. Actually free.

Paint Shop Pro (http://www.jasc.com): retouch, edit, repair photos and scanned-in images; capture screen shots; create graphics. Easily as good as any commercial package, and better than most. Thirty-day free trial, $99 to buy.

Winzip (http://www.winzip.com): zipping files is compressing them to save disk space and transmission time. Winzip is the best software available for managing all this within Windows; it integrates into Explorer so that extracting or archiving files is never more than two mouse clicks away. Free evaluation version on the honour system; $29 for single computer; worth it.

WS-FTP (ftp://ftp.ipswitch.com/Ipswitch/Product_Down loads/f_x86t32.exe): yes, you can do downloads through your Web browser. But once you gain some experience you'll appreciate the greater speed and flexibility of FTP – you can, for example, resume a download that got interrupted where with a Web browser you have to start all over again. WS-FTP LE is freeware with limited features; WS-FTP with the full complement offers a 30-day trial and then costs $37.50.

ZoneAlarm (http://www.zonelabs.com): free for individuals, ZoneAlarm firewalls your PC so that outsiders can't mess with your machine. Useful protection, especially for single users who spend a lot of time online. (See **Security**.)

Additional sites
C|Net Shareware.com (http://www.shareware.com) and Download.com (http://www.download.com): slightly dif-

ferent home pages (search is at the top of the Shareware page, browsing categories on the Download page), but the same huge database of shareware.

Stroud's CWS Apps (http://www.cws.internet.com): terrific collection of all types of Internet software. If you need a client for some new Internet application, this is the place to look. Search or browse by category.

TUCOWS (http://www.tucows.com): huge, searchable library of shareware, sound samples, desktop themes, you name it. If it exists, TUCOWs probably has it. Site has many mirrors around the world to make downloads as fast and efficient as possible.

SHOPPING

Quick tips

- Use a credit card rather than a Switch card or personal cheque (except for small items) for greater protection against fraud and lower liability in case of theft.

- Print out a copy of the final order confirmation as displayed on the site, and keep it until the order arrives and you're satisfied that the quality of the goods is as advertised and you have been charged the correct amount. Make a note on the printout of the company's name, address and customer service number – these may not be available if the company site or your Internet connection goes down.

- Consider designating one credit card for online use, giving it a limit no greater than you could stand to lose.

- Review all relevant credit card and bank statements carefully, so that in the unlikely event that your card does get stolen you become aware of it quickly. (You can check more frequently online if you like – see **Banking** for instructions.)

- Unless there's a really large price differential, go with the company with the best customer service, even if you have to pay a bit more. It's worth it in the long run.

- If you're buying clothes or shoes from outside the UK, check international clothing and shoe sizes (http:// www.kisc.co.jp/KIEA/onepoint10.html) before ordering from any site not based in the UK. (This chart covers British, American, Japanese and European sizes.)

Online shopping has a lot of advantages: no crowds, no queues, no traffic jams to get there, nothing to carry home. On the other hand: you don't get to see, touch or feel what you buy before you buy it. That, however, is not the biggest reason people give for being reluctant to buy online. Instead, the biggest deterrent is security worries (see also **Security**).

The best online shopping sites are often not the big high-street names, which tend to go for slow-loading graphical overkill or have trouble adapting to the level of customer service needed in the online world. In the absence of a shop to go into, companies must respond quickly and accurately to customer queries and sort problems out promptly. This is the secret behind the telephone-operated First Direct bank, long-running catalogue retailers Land's End and LL Bean and, the first-mover of electronic commerce, Amazon.com. Unfortunately customer service is difficult to test until you have ordered from a site – though one way is to make your first order a small one and see how the company responds. It is far more tempting to judge by the speed with which the site loads, how easy it is to navigate product listings and put through orders, and the quality of the information supplied. It is, of course, a persuasive idea that a company's attention to customer needs is reflected in the quality of its site design; but it is not a universal law.

Whenever you're buying from a new site, particularly if it's not based in the UK, the first thing to do is to check its shipping policy. These aren't always easy to find; use the site map, look under customer service or shopping information, or terms and conditions. It's irritating, but there's no point in spending a lot of time assembling an order only to find that the company doesn't deliver to the UK. While you're looking for the delivery information and price list (so you can add delivery charges to the advertised prices before deciding whether to buy), take a moment to read the terms and conditions. Pay particular attention to the policy on returns. Do they charge 'restocking fees' (an odious practice)? Are there surcharges for certain items or types of orders? Does the company say where it's based and how to report problems? Ask, in other words, all the same questions you would ask if you were ordering from a company you'd found in a magazine.

Once you've gone through this basic exercise, the process of ordering should be fairly simple; after all, you've got to know the site a bit while you were searching for the company policies. In general, any site with more than a few items for sale should have some kind of search function available so you can find the items you're interested in. Most sites follow a common pattern: you select the items you're interested in and drop them into a shopping cart, which you can review at any time, changing or deleting items as you see fit. Once your order is assembled, you click on a button labelled 'checkout' (usually) and follow the instructions for logging on to the company's secure server to place the transaction.

In many cases, using the secure server is recommended but not an absolute requirement. You should use the secure server wherever possible, and for the same reason that it's not recommended to send credit cards by email. Data crossing the Internet is like messages written on the backs of postcards. In general, you trust that no one in the post office has any reason to care what your uncle Mo had to say to you about his holiday on Crete. On the Internet, data in transit is in the same vulnerable position as the messages on those postcards. Most of the time, the data will get through without anyone's reading it. But just as you have your bank statements sent in envelopes, data is protected by being encrypted so that even if it is intercepted it can't be read. This is what the secure server does: encrypt the data while it's in transmission between your browser and the site using

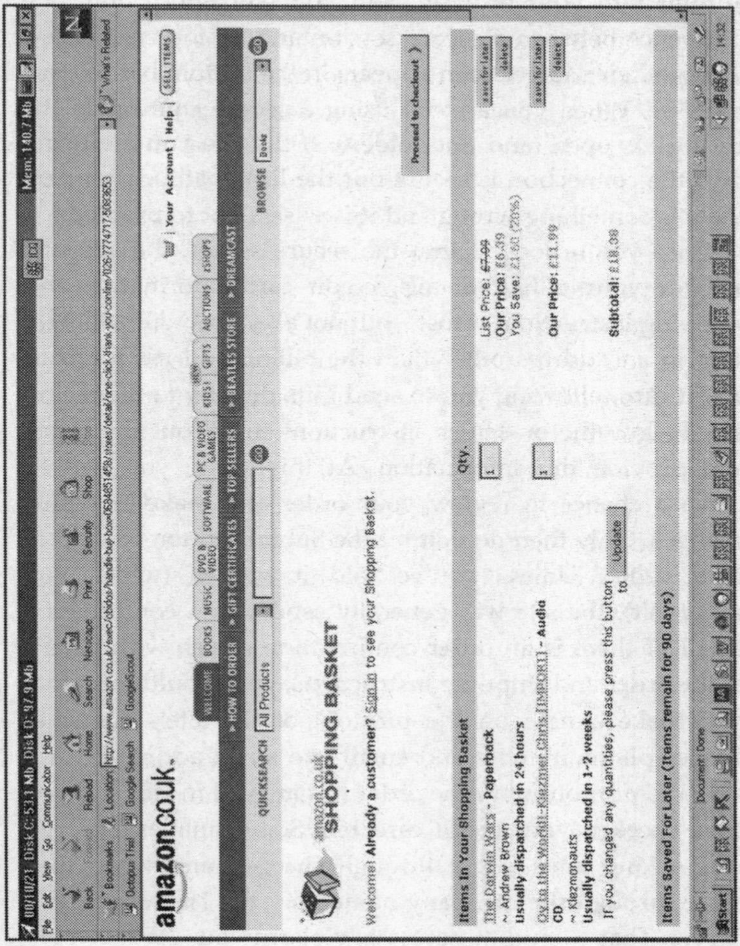

Figure 5. Constructing an order at Amazon.co.uk.

an open standard called SSL, for Secure Sockets Layer. This is built into your browser, and you will notice only one difference between a secure session and an insecure one: a little golden padlock icon appears in the bottom bar of your browser. When you are not using a secure connection the padlock is open (and not golden). If the site you are using says the connection is secure but the little padlock is open, there is something wrong and it is wisest not to proceed.

Once you're logged into the secure server, the site will ask for your billing details, credit card information and shipping instructions. Most – but not all – sites will willingly ship to an address other than the billing address for your credit card, allowing you to send gifts directly to the recipient. Follow the on-screen instructions to fill out the forms and provide this information. At this point, you will be given a chance to review your order and make any final changes. Only then do you hit the Submit button to send in your order. Unless you've told it not to (which you shouldn't), the site will generally send you a confirmation email. If there is an order confirmation screen with details of the order and shipping instructions, you should print that out. Make a note on the printout of the site's customer service phone number and email and street addresses, and save the printout until the order has arrived in full and you have checked your credit card bill. Some smaller sites can take a long time to put through charges, and when they come through the company name may not be the one you expect. That shouldn't necessarily alarm you – it may only mean that the site outsources that part of its operation.

And that's it. With any luck, you can sit back and the

merchandise will arrive when you expect it to and be everything you hoped for. In nearly six years of shopping online, that has almost always been my experience.

Oddly enough, the primary exception has been with **Groceries** (see entry), and that has been partly because the human grocery pickers who fill the orders tend to make mistakes with non-standard items (try ordering loose tea instead of teabags from Tescos), but even more because the level of information provided on grocery shopping sites is terrible. All the package labelling and other innovations consumers have fought for in real-world supermarkets disappear online, and you generally find yourself guessing which product you want from an inadequately designed list. Hopefully, this will improve – and it doesn't stop me from ordering groceries online because the advantages are so great – but in the meantime this is the trickiest online shopping to do well and the one most subject to vendor errors.

Buying from the US and beyond

Always check before starting that the site accepts international orders. You'd be surprised how many don't – despite the fact that the Web is global and the US has been leading the way in electronic commerce, many US businesses have been slow to adapt. The ones that do sell overseas, though, tend to do a reasonable job of it. Even so, this is an area that is very much buyer beware, in that you will be responsible for all customs duties and VAT as well as any extra administrative fees the delivery service decides to charge (Fedex is notorious for slapping on an extra £20 or so in fees) and the postal costs if you are unhappy with the goods and want to return them. If things go wrong, you will also have to deal with the fact that British laws will not protect you (although American consumer law is also quite strong), and that the data protection you enjoy here may not apply.

Some types of sites simply won't ship overseas, so don't waste your time trying. Online chemists (drug stores), for example, won't ship even non-drug items. Nor will grocery stores, and sites selling fresh fruit or meat won't be able to send those, either, though they may be willing to ship other parts of their range – an example is Harry and David (http://www.harryanddavid.com), famous in the US for its Fruit of the Month club, which it can't ship internationally, but also sells dried fruit, sweets and some gift items, which it can and will.

That said, plenty of people do buy from US sites without trouble. Besides the cheaper prices (often even after customs duty and VAT), the sites themselves tend to be better designed and many American companies are scrupulous about customer service. DVDs, CDs and books are, of course, the most popular items. All three are robust enough to survive the international post. CDs and DVDs are cheap to send. Books attract no customs duty or VAT, and nor do packages valued at less than £18 – which means a single CD or DVD will get through to you at little extra cost. The one caveat is regarding DVDs: unless you have a player that can handle Region 1 discs, you will not be able to play discs sourced from the US. Check your player before proceeding (see **Films**).

With clothing and shoes, the difficulty is sizing. Sites belonging to traditional mail order companies such as LL Bean (http://www.llbean.com) and Land's End (http://www.landsend.com) are meticulous about explaining their sizes and keeping them consistent, and also often have international sizing charts available. Bean will even let you send or fax in a tracing of your foot and match the size for you (see **Clothes**).

Further afield, there are all kinds of stores from around the world available online; it just takes a little confidence and willingness to experiment to find them. FNAC, France's largest department store, for example, operates a terrific online retailer (http://www.fnac.com/).

Additional sites

HM Customs and Excise (http://www.hmce.gov.uk/public/info/index.htm): this page gives basic information about VAT and customs duty payable on items imported into the UK, along with sample rates for the most commonly imported items. You should take these charges into account when pricing your order. In general, most small orders – for example, one or two CDs or DVDs – will come in free of charge. Books are the best deal of all, as they attract neither VAT nor duty.

SHOWBIZ

The Stage (http://www.thestage.co.uk) has put its recruitment ads online, along with features and gossip. Similarly, *Hollywood Reporter* (http://www.hollywood reporter), *Variety* (http://www.variety.com) and *Billboard* (http://www.billboard.com) all run sites covering their areas of expertise. *Billboard* has digitized its buyer's guide and talent and touring directory, though you have to buy a subscription for access to those.

Less familiar names offer rolling news coverage. Reporter TV (http://www.reporterTV.com/) does streaming – that is, live audio and video – show business news and uses agent software to let you put together a personalized news wire. Showbizwire (http://www.showbizwire.com/) runs a news wire covering most aspects of show business – TV, music, theatre, video and celebrities – drawing its stories from sources such as the BBC, E! Online, Reuters, *New Musical Express* and *Playbill*. The more populist *Entertainment Weekly* (http://www.ew.com) has a Web news service for entertainment stories, but elects not to put features from this week's issue online, waiting until the issue goes off the stands in the US to make them available. Once you get past the rather crude and unattractive front page, the features look fine.

(See also **Celebrities**.)

SKIING

See under **Sports**.

SNOOKER

See under **Sports**.

SPORTS

For some reason, the official sporting world has been slow to grasp hold of the opportunities provided by the Internet to give fans what they want: better access to statistics, historical facts and records, and player and team information, to say nothing of tips for playing ourselves. The upshot is that in just about every case the unofficial sites run by fans are far better than the official ones run by the organizing bodies of individual sports or even by international, well-funded outfits like the International Olympic Committee. Part of the problem is that where fans think in terms of sharing and getting information, organizations like the WTA Tour (women's tennis) think in terms of marketing.

Whatever sport you're fond of, probably the quickest source of daily news and results is to go to Yahoo!'s sports page (http://sports.yahoo.com), click on the sport you're interested in, and then bookmark (usually by pressing CTRL-D) the page that comes up. Thereafter, you can go straight to that page.

General news and information sites, all sports
BBC Sport (http://www.bbc.co.uk/sport).

Eurosport (http://www.eurosport.com): very cluttered and unpleasant to read, but covers just about every pro sport. TV listings for seven days, displayed by the day, are available from the link nearly all the way down on the left.

Quokka Sports (http://www.quokka.com): the company that created the comprehensive NBC Olympics site for the Sydney Games, Quokka aims to do a comprehensive job of presenting sports online taking advantage of new media. One of their first experiments was attaching sensors to top runners to show how their heart rate changes before, during and after races. Guess what? It's fastest before the race starts.

Sky Sports (http://www.skysports.co.uk): News and features on most major pro sports and many minor ones. The TV channels may be premium priced, but the Web site is free.

Sportal (http://www.sportal.com): sports plus portal, geddit? Again, a general news and features site for all types of sports.

Sportszine (http://www.sportszine.co.uk): built-in listings and search engine for just about every sport. Frustrating to use, though, if you're looking for a local club or organization as listings are not sorted by country.

CNN Sports Illustrated (http://www.cnnsi.com): joint venture between the US's leading sports magazine, *Sports Illustrated*, and the global satellite newscaster. Primarily coverage of major American sports such as American football, baseball, hockey, and basketball.

Athletics

World of Running and Track and Field (http://www.tflinks.com): although the site is worldwide in scope rather than oriented specifically to the UK, its links are comprehensive and easy to navigate. There are links to a page listing every track in the UK (http://www.runtrackdir.com/searchplace.htm), another listing UK athletics clubs (http://www.runtrackdir.com/ukclubs/), the various British marathons (see http://www.london-marathon.co.uk for the London one) and a main UK page with news headlines and national points tables (http://www.athletics-online.co.uk/running.htm).

Runner's World (http://www.runnersworld.co.uk/): the UK's largest running magazine's online site includes a runner's guide to cities around the UK, shoe guides and helpful advice for beginners.

Badminton

Badminton UK (http://www.badmintonuk.co.uk).

Bowls
Bowls Clubs (http://www.bowlsclubs.co.uk/).

Boxing
Boxing Monthly (http://www.boxingmonthly.co.uk): the site of Britain's best-selling boxing title isn't much but the links page (http://www.boxing-monthly.co.uk/links.htm) is worth scouring.

Seconds Out (http://www.secondsout.com): news, features and calendar.

Sky Sports (http://www.sky.com/sports/boxing/): boxing is one of Sky's better covered sports, unsurprisingly since the channel shows a lot of it.

Climbing
Climbers Net (http://www.climbers.net/): for owners of climbing walls, this site offers free Web pages and a listing of climbing walls in the UK, plus links to guidebooks and manufacturers.

UKClimbing.com (http://www.ukclimbing.com): comprehensive information about the sport, outdoor and indoor, links to manufacturers and suppliers and its own shop. Also includes a very useful search page (http://www.ukclimbing.com/walls/) to help you locate the climbing wall nearest you.

Cricket
CricInfo (http://www.cricket.org): 'the home of cricket on the Internet' has a network of six servers, one for each of

the main cricket-playing countries, and provides everything from current news and playing tips to a database of statistics, players and even photographs.

Cycling
See **Outdoors**.

Darts
British Darts Organization (http://www.bdodarts.com): rankings, news on past and current events such as the Embassy and county matches, links to player pages.

International Dart Players Federation (http://www.idpa. cwc.net/main.html).

Embassy Darts (http://www.embassydarts.com/application. htm): get tickets online for the main event of the year in Frimley Green.

World Darts Federation (http://www.dartswdf.com): nice history of the Embassy including drawsheets back to the early 1980s, along with archives from other events.

Equestrian
Kick On (http://www.kickon.com): no corner of the equestrian world is left unvisited, with magazine-style articles and advice from the likes of Mark Todd, Henry Cecil, Ginny Elliot and Mark Phillips, plus news and dates for equestrian events. Problems can be emailed to the Kickon vet, and there are chat rooms for more informal chat about your horse.

Football

Football 365 (http://www.football365.com): one of the 365 chain's of 365 sports sites, with scores, transfer gossip, statistics, audio and video, and even live coverage.

FIFA (http://www.fifa.com): unusually, football's governing body has put together an actually impressive site with almost everything a fan could want in the way of official information about competitions.

Usenet: Rec.sport.soccer Statistics Foundation (http://www.rsssf.com/): a great example of what dedicated fans can do if they try. Years and years of statistics gathered from every source they could get their hands on.

Golf

Golfzone (http://www.golfzone.co.uk): free ISP, dedicated to golf and intended as a comprehensive portal to the subject. If you sign up with the ISP, then every telephone call made through your modem donates some money to the Golf Foundation, the charity dedicated to the promotion of the junior game. Its GolfMart section lists second-hand clubs, trolleys and so on.

Horseracing

British Horseracing Board (http://www.bhb.co.uk/bhb/).

Horseracing in the UK (http://www.racetracks.com/UK.html): comprehensive set of British racing links.

The Racecourse Association (http://www.comeracing.co. uk/): complete schedules of fixtures and a beginner's guide to going racing.

UK Horseracing Links (http://www.darob.demon.co.uk/ links.htm): another set of racing links, better organized. Start with this one.

Motor racing

British Motor Racing Circuits (http://www.bmrc.co.uk): guide to British events, clubs, cars, championships, and TV and radio coverage throughout the UK, including satellite and cable, for the coming week.

Formula 1 (http://www.formula1.com).

ITV-Formula 1 (http://www.itv-f1.com).

Olympics

International Olympic Committee (http://www.olympic. org): the horse's mouth when it comes to the Olympics (and fussy about anyone else using its trademark). Links from the main site to the world anti-doping initiative and the official sites for past and future Games.

Rowing

River and Rowing Museum, Henley (http://www.rrm. co.uk/): as you'd expect, a site primarily intended to give information about the museum and its opening hours.

Rugby

Webrugby (http://www.webrugby.com).

World of Rugby League (http://rleague.com).

Skiing

1ski.com (http://www.1ski.com/): find a resort, book a holiday, get snow reports from a selection of 200 resorts around the world.

Snooker

Snooker Net (http://www.snookernet.com).

Squash

UK Squash (http://www.squashplayer.co.uk).

Swimming

SwimNet (http://www.swimnet.fsnet.co.uk/): not updated as often as it might be (in late October it was still showing Olympics headlines), probably SwimNet's best feature is its links page (http://www.swimnet.fsnet.co.uk/links.htm) – find any UK swimming club, swimmers' home pages, clinics, schools and manufacturers and their products.

Tennis

Association of Tennis Professionals (http://www.atptour.com): cluttered and over-produced, but it's the horse's mouth on the men's tour.

Lawn Tennis Association (http://www.lta.org.uk): just British tennis, professional, amateur and junior.

International Tennis Federation (http://www.itftennis.com): best feature is the players' match results and head-to-head database.

Tennis Corner (http://www.tenniscorner.com): the best place to find pro tournament draws, updated rankings and so on.

Tennis server (http://www.tennisserver.com): nice site, with its own features, links to unofficial fan sites, and playing instruction.

Women's Tennis Association (http://www.wtatour.com): the pro women's site is Java-laden, slow, lurid, annoying and often out of date.

Usenet: rec.sport.tennis. See you there.

SPYING

There are two kinds of spies: amateur and professional. The UK Public CCTV Surveillance Regulation Campaign (http://www.spy.org.uk/), 'Watching Them Watching Us' seeks to show just how pervasively we're being watched by the professionals. If you want to do your own surveillance, there's the Spy Store (http://www.spy-store.co.uk/) – pick up telephone bugs and video walkmans and all sorts of strange stuff. Just a shame there's so little informative detail on the site. There is, however, a fair bit of information about the UK's secret services (http://intellit.muskingum.edu/

intellsite/uk_folder/uktoc.html), including notes on famous cases, as well as a fair bit of information about Menwith Hill (http://www.dfg-vk.de/english/book73d.htm), the US National Security Agency's outpost in Britain.

If you think there really are people watching you, according to the Counterintelligence and technical security page (http://www.tscm.com/warningsigns.html) it could be anyone. 'Spouses bug each other on a regular basis,' it says helpfully, noting that you are in a high-threat personal situation if you're getting married, separated or divorced, if you're involved in political activisim ... in fact, basically, if you're alive and over eighteen. Finally, you may like to keep an eye on the development of Echelon (http://www.echelonwatch.org/), the global surveillance network. But that way lies paranoia (see **Truth**).

SQUASH

See under **Sports**.

SUPPORT GROUPS

Depression, Alzheimer's, alcoholism, autism, cancer ... these are just a few of the reasons people seek support online.

One reason online support groups thrive is that the

conditions themselves tend to make going out and socializing difficult, not just for the people who have the conditions but also for their carers. Online help is available even if you live in a rural area, have agoraphobia, and are only functional from 2 a.m. to 4 a.m. For people in small towns, online support can grant them an element of privacy, allowing them to talk about problems they aren't ready to discuss with the people in their everyday lives, just as people feel they can reveal their deepest secrets to strangers on a train with impunity.

Just like any other type of online community, support areas vary a great deal, encompassing everything from information-only Web sites to discussion forums, real-time chats and email lists. Because of the sensitive nature of the issues discussed, you should pay especial attention to the terms and conditions governing the use of the site, and spend more time than usual checking out the postings and getting a feel for the incumbent user base before posting.

To find support sites and groups for any particular condition do a search using the name of the condition or ailment, plus the words 'support UK' (see **Search Engines**). Doing that type of search brings up support sites for Fibromyalgia (http://www.lewolf.com/fms.htm), Wilson's Disease (http://www.wilsons-disease.org.uk/), and a list of UK dermatology patient support groups (http://www.kcl.ac.uk/depsta/medicine/dermatology/other/ukgroup.html). If the condition or disease's name is different in the US, remember to include the US version in the search – for example, the UK's glandular fever is the US's mononucleosis, and the UK's ADHD is the US's ADD. The help is out there.

Additional sites

Alcoholics Anonymous UK (http://www.alcoholics-anonymous. org.uk/econtent.html): you can't work the twelve-step programme just by accessing this Web site, but it includes a couple of questionnaires intended to help newcomers decide if they have a problem with alcohol and gives the support hotline number as well as the numbers and addresses for all the British offices. The US AA site (http://www.aa.org) is not much more comprehensive, and it's a shame: the sites could make it a lot easier to get copies of AA pamphlets and other material than they do.

Carers (http://www.carers.gov.uk): set up by the Department of Health, this site aims to help carers find the information and resources they need. Sections cover issues like money, education, work and available services. The site includes links to a number of support organizations, both local and national, that aim to provide assistance.

Health Centre list of self-help and support groups (http:// www.healthcentre.org.uk/hc/clinic/support.htm).

Mental Help Net (http://www.mentalhelp.net): comprehensive site with sections on most mental disorders, plus research news, information about treatments, book lists and discussion forums. Billed as the oldest and largest mental health guide and community on the Web, MHN is run by a psychologist from Dublin, Ohio, and many of the staff have advanced degrees in psychology or other related disciplines. A good starting point for any mental problem.

Usenet: start by looking for newsgroups on your topic in the following hierarchies: alt.support., soc.support., and uk.support. If that doesn't produce anything on your subject (for example, alt.transgendered, a support group for trans-sexuals, does not follow that naming convention, although your first search would turn up soc.support.transgendered), try searching the full list of newsgroups carried by your ISP. If that's not made easy for you to do, head for Deja News and search the list there. If you still can't find anything in the tens of thousands of Usenet newsgroups that's a precise match, try looking for closely related topics.

Victim Support (http://www.victimsupport.com): for victims of crime in the UK.

SWAPPING

Swapping is all about collectables: Pokémon cards, cars, houses and the strange wooden thing you found in the attic that only your great-aunt knew what it was. To some people, swapping goods seems safer than buying online, since no money or credit card information changes hands. At Webswappers (http://www.webswappers.com), this sense of safety is enhanced by the fact that throughout negotiations you never have to reveal even your email address to the other party. It's only when the swap is agreed that you exchange addresses in order to exchange goods. Apparently the big thing at Webswappers is Pokémon cards, but you'll find everything from DVDs to houses on this site, which was set up in late 2000.

SWIMMING

See under **Sports**.

T

TALK (OR RATHER, CHAT)

It may seem incomprehensible to anyone who has a telephone why you would want to do something as daft as use that telephone to set up an Internet connection and then sit there and type at people in real time. Nonetheless, there are a number of reasons why people do this. For one thing, because you can do more than one thing at once while you're connected to the Internet, you can run a chat session while Web pages are loading or while you're retrieving email, making more effective use of a connection you're already paying for. For another, chat can be like voicemail or mobile phones' SMS, letting you send a quick message without having to get involved in a lengthy phone call. If you are part of a widespread group all working on the same project, being immediately available can make the group function more as if you were all working in the same office.

There are two types of chat: public and private. In public chats, using technology such as Internet Relay Chat (IRC), you may have public areas where anyone can join at any time or private ones, where the numbers are strictly controlled. Private chats, using popular software such as ICQ or AOL Instant Messenger, are one-to-one and can't be accessed by anyone else.

If you run Netscape, you probably already have AIM on your system as AOL owns Netscape and bundles the two programs together. ICQ you download from the main ICQ site (http://www.icq.com); its installation routine is painless. You can search for friends on the ICQ site (and many people do have ICQ numbers), or give your number to people you know who already use ICQ. In either case, to communicate with someone you add them to your contact list by entering their number; most people set their software to require authorization before you can add them to your list, so typically you will have to wait for the OK to come back before you can communicate with them. Once they are authorized, you will see them on your contact list, and will be able to tell whenever they are online (there are some limits to this; you can set the software so you're invisible to other users). To send a message, you double-click on the user's name, type in a message and click or press ALT-Enter to send it. ICQ also supports live chat sessions, where you open up windows on each other's machines and see every-thing the other types in the chat window, and many other forms of one-to-one communication. It can be a very con-venient way of carrying on a telephone-like conversation in between doing other things – great for people who are working together on a project.

IRC, by contrast, is public. There are a number of IRC networks and servers, and this is where the geek part comes in: to join a particular channel (that is, a chat on a specific topic) you have to pick the network it's on. But don't worry too much about this. Start by downloading IRC Client software; the easiest to use is generally held to be mIRC (http://www.mirc.com). Read the instructions on the site and install the software, then go back and read the instructions on how to join a channel (http://www.mirc.com/irc.html).

The syntax for typing in IRC can seem quite arcane at first. But the reason to persevere is that it can be very useful – even a cheap replacement for telephone conferencing. If, for example, you have a group of people scattered around the country all working on the same project, on IRC they can all connect to each other (in a private channel you set up) for the cost of a local call. Better still, it's always clear who said what, because all contributions are identified, and everyone can reread the log later in case there's any doubt.

TAXES

The horse's mouth is, of course, the Inland Revenue's own site (http://www.inlandrevenue.gov.uk/home.htm), which gives you direct access to all the government leaflets and forms your cheque book could possibly desire. The site also accepts electronic tax returns (http://www.inlandrevenue.gov.uk/e-tax/index.htm); your first electronic return gets you a £10 discount. Even the international tax agreements (http://www.inlandrevenue.gov.uk/international/) are easily accessible.

VAT rates and leaflets are at HM Customs and Excise (http://www.hmce.gov.uk).

Money to pay the tax you'll have to supply yourself.

The Association of Online Accountants (http://www.aola.co.uk/find.html) has a site to help you find an accountant by postcode and speciality.

TECHNICAL SUPPORT
(For Stuff You Own)

Almost every manufacturer of computer hardware or software, and an increasing number of manufacturers of goods of other types, offers some type of technical support on its Web site.

Start by looking for the company's Web address in the manual that came with the product. If one isn't listed, look for a distributor's name, and if that doesn't work, try a search (see **Search Engines**) using the manufacturer, make and model number as search terms. Then look at the Web site to see if it offers technical support, either through a facility for answering questions by email or via a searchable database of technical fixes and problems. If there is an **FAQ** (see entry), read it before emailing in questions – your problem may be covered: that's why the questions are frequently asked.

It's also worth looking through the Usenet archives at Deja News (http://www.deja.com) and electronic mailing lists (http://www.liszt.com) to see if there's a discussion group covering the product or its general class – for example, breadmakers or coffee machines. It's very rare that you won't find some kind of user help with your problem somewhere on the Net. At the very least, you should be able to locate a current phone number.

TELEPHONE CALLS

Because of the cooperative way the Internet works (see **Introduction**, p. xvi) once you are online it costs no more to log on to a site in Australia than one that's housed in the garage next door. One consequence of this is that you can route telephone calls over the Internet at what are essentially wholesale prices – a few pence a minute anywhere in the world. (Be sure to compare this to today's discount services.)

To make phone calls over the Internet you will need: a computer with a sound board installed; an Internet connection; a microphone (to speak into) and speakers (so you can hear what's said to you) or a combination headset like telephone operators used to use; and client software for one of the Internet telephony services (Callserve, Net2Phone, TrulyGlobal Internet Phone, or ICQPhone). The software is generally free, since these services make their money from phone call charges.

Based on experience installing Callserve, you should start by making sure that your sound board works, for example by playing a music file. Then, pick one of the phone services and download the client software, checking first that your system has the resources necessary to run it. Install the software. At some point in the installation process you will be asked to fill in your real name and email address, along with credit card information so the company can bill you for calls. You should also be offered the chance to test your system to make sure everything is working. You will need to set up a microphone for this.

And then make a phone call by keying in the number using the keypad that pops up on your screen. Remember to use the international dialling code if instructed to do so. And hopefully it all works. Don't expect it to be BT quality yet – network congestion can cause lag in the phone connection, making it more like using walkie-talkies than a phone call. But the price is right.

TENNIS

See under **Sports**.

TOYS

Do not travel into London to get to the world's largest toy store; just click Hamleys (http://www.hamleys.co.uk), where you should have no trouble getting lost among the toys you want to buy yourself, insisting they're really for your kids. There are, of course, many other toy sites, but why bother? They'll deliver anything. Model trains, anyone?

On the other hand, if you're a hands-on sort of person, you might like to try some of the links to plans for children's toys and furniture from the woodworking page at About.com (http://woodworking.about.com/hobbies/woodworking/msubchild.htm); among other things, there's a set of instructions for notched boards kids can use to create their own play spaces.

TRAVEL

Travel services was one of the first ecommerce sectors to be successful, for reasons that ought to be obvious: the product (paper tickets) is lightweight and inexpensive to ship, and purchases tend to be information intensive. For many destinations it's now absolutely possible to book all parts of a holiday or business trip, from airline ticket to hotel rooms, rental cars, theatre and attraction tickets, and even restaurants online.

However, big caveat: if you don't travel that often and you already have a good travel agent you can phone who gives you good prices on tickets and trouble-free service, do not bother to try to book airline tickets on the Web. Do use the Web to look up schedules, though, as that may help you when you're talking to your travel agent. The exception is direct, low-cost airlines like Easyjet, which by October 2000 was selling 74 per cent of its seats online and which intends to phase out telephone bookings entirely in favour of lower-cost Web access.

The fact is that despite all the publicity given to last-minute deals and discounted prices online, buying airline tickets is still easier, faster and usually cheaper offline. The reason is that airline reservations systems are some of the most complex software known to man, and no amount of putting a Web interface on them makes them simpler. The complexity is due to variable pricing, which airlines have long since perfected: few passengers in the same section of an aircraft actually ever pay the same price. If you are a constant traveller, learning the codes and tricks that make the system jump through hoops for you is worth the trouble. Similarly, if you can't find a good discount travel agent offline or simply like hands-on serendipitous destination hunting, online air ticketing could be for you.

All the online ticketing services work pretty much the same way. You specify a city of origin, destination, date and rough time for the outgoing flight and the date and rough time for the return trip (if any), along with number of adult and child seats, and you get back a list of available flights with fares. Choosing from among those, you make a reservation and proceed to pay for the tickets much like any other online sale. Airlines that have electronic ticketing programs will give you a receipt page to print out with your booking number, and that's all you need: no waiting for tickets to arrive in the post, just turn up at the airport with the number in hand. Paper tickets can be sent the old-fashioned way or picked up at the airport. For security reasons, some sites may require the person actually purchasing the tickets to be one of the passengers (inconvenient if you're a parent buying a ticket for your teenager) and bring your credit card to the airline counter at the airport for identification.

General travel sites

Expedia (http://www.expedia.co.uk): owned by Microsoft, Expedia aims to be a one-stop shop for all your travel needs. If you fly frequently between the same pair of cities or you're planning a trip in advance, Expedia has a nice little function that will email you updates on current prices between those cities, giving you notice of special bargains to snap up.

Travelocity (http://www.travelocity.co.uk): owned by Sabre, the company that supplies the reservations system to most airlines. Travelocity, like Expedia, gives you access to a comprehensive range of travel services.

Airmiles (http://www.airmiles.co.uk): like other forms of loyalty points (see **Payments**), airmiles can be used to pay for a variety of goods, from flotation tank sessions to cinema tickets.

Flight Tracker (http://www.thetrip.com/ft/home/0,2096,1-1,00. shtml): only for flights within US airspace, but very precise.

Airline sites

Most airlines have some kind of site, even if it's only an information site giving basic travel guidelines. The best ones, however, all offer more than that, with timetables, flight bookings and access to your frequent flyer miles account. Diagrams showing the aircraft layout can let you make a more informed seating request, and on some of the more forward-looking airlines you can even sign up for mobile phone or pager notification if there are changes to your flight. One last popular and useful feature is flight tracking; in the airline site versions this feature isn't usually as detailed as the US-only Flight Tracker run by the Federation Aviation Authority, but it's good enough to tell you if your kids' flight has been diverted or give the people who are meeting you some idea whether you're going to be on time. In order to encourage people to book online, which is less expensive for the airline, many airlines are offering Web fare specials or bonus frequent flyer miles for taking advantage of these new services.

Access to frequent flyer miles accounts is typically done via your existing membership number and a PIN, which you normally apply for online but receive by postal mail. Since frequent flyer miles actually have value and personal travel details appear onscreen when you access these accounts, this cautious approach makes some sense.

For airlines not listed here, either try the obvious (for example, http://www.airindia.com for Air India) or use a search engine (see **Search Engines**). Once you've settled on a route or carrier, it's often worth checking the airline's Web site to see if there are any last-minute, online-only deals.

American Airlines (http://www.americanair.com or http://www.aa.com): full online booking for UK and US residents, access to frequent flyer account, fare specials, flight tracker, flight-specific seat maps, airport guides.

British Airways (http://www.britishairways.com): BA's site is catching up to those of the US airlines, although parts of it still load rather slowly. Fare specials, online bookings and flight schedules, airport information and package holidays, along with access to Executive Club accounts.

British Midland (http://www.britishmidland.co.uk): online bookings and timetable on a rather clunky site. Apply for Diamond club by downloading application and posting in with boarding cards and other documentation.

Continental (http://www.continental.com): downloadable electronic timetable, basic information, aircraft layouts, flight tracker, special offers and online bookings, plus hotel and rental car reservations.

Delta (http://www.delta.com): uncluttered, junk-free, and fast, Delta's site puts the two things you're most likely to want, flight lookup and status tracking, right in front of you on the first page. Frequent flyer account access, emailed weekly fare specials, and flight bookings, all streamlined and without excess graphics.

Easyjet (http://www.easyjet.com): painted on the side of every airplane in the fleet, Easyjet's Web site is its main source of sales. Easyjet's relatively small timetable makes it easy to find the flights you want and book them. The fares change with availability, so don't be surprised if the seat you price at one fare one day is selling at a different price the next.

KLM (http://www.klm.com): bookings from the US, the UK, and most European countries.

United Airlines: (http://www.ual.com).

Virgin Atlantic (http://www.virgin-atlantic.com): slow, over-produced and way too red, the Virgin site's design leaves a lot to be desired.

Destination guides

American Express (http://travel.americanexpress.com/travel/personal/resources/research/): really good travel planner covering everything from visas to inoculations, plus information about specific destinations.

Citysearch (http://www.citysearch.com/): entertainment guides for most US cities plus a few selected international destinations in Australia, Scandinavia, Canada, and Korea.

Lonely Planet Online (http://www.lonelyplanet.com): whatever your destination, start here. Information about almost anywhere you could possibly want to travel, with links to the most important local Web sites.

Smart Traveler (http://www.smartraveler.com/): current traffic conditions in thirty-six major US cities.

Package holidays

Island Holidays (http://www.sol.co.uk/islandholidays/index.html): specialist agency based in Scotland and offering guided tours to exotic destinations like Antarctica and the Seychelles, as well as trips to more familiar destinations like Crete and Cyprus that show those places in an extraordinary light. Book provisionally by email; confirm by post.

Lastminute.com (http://www.lastminute.com): well-known because of its heavy advertising and emphasis on branding,

Lastminute.com was nonetheless voted the worst travel site in a survey of six thousand *Daily Telegraph* readers in October 2000. A pain to use, many of the site's advertised holidays have to be booked by telephone. A Web site to handle last-minute bookings is a great idea; but this site simply doesn't execute it well. You will do better going straight to direct-sales airlines like Easyjet and online hotel chains.

Teletext (http://www.teletext.co.uk): just like on TV.

Thomas Cook Online (http://www.thomascook.co.uk): as the site says, 'find a great deal, book it online'. Scan holidays by price, map, resort reviews, or – and this is the fun one – the current weather report, like the couple in *A Touch of Class*. The selection of cheap last-minute deals is updated every morning. However, Cook's hasn't quite got the hang of this Internet thing: try checking prices at 2 a.m. and you'll be told to try back at 8 a.m. when the office is open. Sure, you can phone any time, but that's kind of missing the point.

Trains

Amtrak (http://www.amtrak.com): lots of people forget that the US actually has trains, even though they feature prominently in American song, legend and film. The Amtrak site gives you the nationwide timetables, reservation and booking facilities, and travel information for America's most forgotten transportation system. Unfortunately, you have to register just to get accurate fares for specific dates and journeys.

European Rail Timetable (http://www.eurorail.com/railsked. htm): pan-European timetable run by an air ticket consolidator that also produces rail passes on behalf of the European railroad committees. The site not only gives train times for the dates, routes and times you specify, but also gives prices on many routes, itinerary details and lets you book seats online as long as there's enough time to post the tickets out to you. The one downside is that because pricing isn't always available, in some cases you're buying tickets more or less blind – not really a comfortable idea. The site also handles hotel bookings and tours.

Eurostar (http://www.eurostar.co.uk): timetable, bookings.

Railtrack (http://www.railtrack.co.uk): in what can only be described as a shocking lapse in standards, Railtrack actually has a good, fast and well-designed nationwide British train timetable. Enter your station of origin, destination, and a time you'd like to arrive by or leave after, and get back a list of the three nearest matching train routes and times. You can page back or forward to earlier or later trains, and enter a return time and hit a button to get details for the return journey. The one thing you can't get is fares, because of the way the country's train companies have been divided up. But in every other respect, this is one of the best British sites out there.

The TrainLine (http://www.thetrainline.com): unlike the Railtrack site, the comparatively slow and clunky The Trainline will give you fares – but only after you register with an email address and password and enter all the travel information at least twice. However, the site will also book tickets and either post them out to you or have them ready for collection at the departure station. If neither of those options is available, it will still give you a list of the fares available and suggest you buy the tickets at the station.

Other transport

Ferry View (http://www.seaview.co.uk/Ferries.html): find the ferry you need – but you'll have to book it elsewhere.

Key Government Transport Statistics (http://www.greengas. u-net.com/transportinfo.html): compiled by Camden Council.

London Transport (http://www.londontransport.co.uk/): cluttered, but it takes you to maps and schedules for buses and tubes (http://www.londontransport. co.uk/tube/index. shtml) in the capital, as well as river services. If it moves and it's in London this site will help you work out how to get on it.

National Express (http://www.nationalexpress.co.uk): 10 per cent discount for booking online.

TROUBLE(SHOOTING)

Can't connect

Most of the time, if this is the problem it is going to be obvious to you. The difficulty is that there are many reasons why you might not be able to connect. There are many different pieces that make up an Internet connection, and if even one of them doesn't work you're in trouble. The trick is working out which piece is causing the problem (and it may be more than one). Ultimately, if the problem is anything complicated you're going to have to call the technical support desk at your Internet Service Provider. Debugging connections is beyond the scope of this book, if only because there are so many possibilities. But *before* making that possibly frustrating and time-consuming call, try these options:

- Check that everything is plugged in correctly: computer, modem cables (if the modem is external), monitor, phone line.

- Check that the phone line is working correctly. Either lift the receiver of a phone connected to the line and check that you get a dial tone, or make sure the speaker is turned on for your modem (this is a standard configuration option; check your manual) and listen for a dial tone, listen to it dial, and make sure that the call is going through correctly and being answered by a modem. (You can tell, because the modems sing to each other in a process known as 'handshaking' to establish the connection.) If the phone line is working but you get a phone company error message during or after dialling, call your ISP and check that you're using the correct number. If the phone line is not working, check the plugs again, and try plugging a phone directly into the wall socket (instead of the phone socket on the back of

the modem) and dialling out. If that doesn't work, call
your phone company and ask them to check the line.

- Check that your computer is configured correctly to use
  the modem and that the modem itself is responding
  correctly. Exactly how you do this varies according to
  the computer and modem you have and the operating
  system you're running.

- If you know you're connected correctly to your ISP, but
  you can't seem to reach any Web sites, try a couple of
  addresses you're familiar with and are absolutely certain
  are correct – for example, the top couple of bookmarks on
  your list. If those don't work and you're running
  Windows, open a DOS box (by choosing Command
  Prompt from the Start menu). At the C:\ prompt type
  ping <known address>. For example, you might type
  'ping google.com' or 'ping demon.net'. You should get
  back a list of replies and how long it took to receive them,
  usually no more than a few hundred milliseconds. This
  shows your Internet connection is working. In that case,
  the problem is likely to be your browser. Try shutting the
  browser down completely and restarting it. If you're in
  Windows, check in the Task Manager that the browser is
  completely shut down before you restart it. If you get
  back a reply saying the request has timed out, the
  problem is with your Internet connection: either you're
  not correctly connected or your ISP is having routing or
  other problems. In the first case, try the other things listed
  here; in the second, you will have to call your ISP to find
  out what the problem is and how long it is likely to last.

- If your browser hangs – that is, sits there apparently doing nothing for an extended period of time – close down and restart the browser using whatever override the system provides to let you kill a running program. In Windows, for example, you would do this through the Task Manager (press ALT-CTRL-DEL). Or, of course, close down everything and restart the computer (probably safest).

- All else having failed, call technical support. Have ready: your user ID (do not tell them your password; your ISP should not ask for it); the make and model of your computer and modem; the type of software you're using; the phone number you're dialling; a succinct description of the problem; and the list of things you've tried.

Can't get email

Make sure you log in to look for it. Email, unlike telephone calls or postal mail, doesn't just arrive.

If you have no problem browsing the Web but you can't collect email successfully and you are getting your email through your ISP (as opposed to a Web-based service), try sending yourself a test message, checking that the message has actually been sent successfully (your email software should provide a way for you to monitor this; check your online help). If you can't successfully collect that message in several attempts, try closing down and restarting your email software. Following the instructions regarding 'ping' above, try pinging the mail server (its address should be specified in the settings in your email software that tell it what server to use to send and receive email). If the server replies, the problem is likely to be with your email software. If there is no reply, go to your ISP's Web site and check the FAQs for the correct server addresses and make sure they match the ones specified in your email software – the online help provided with your software should explain how to do this. (Also see Figure 6 overleaf.)

If the settings are correct and you still can't get your email, either there's something still wrong inside your email software or your ISP's server is down. In either case, you will need to call technical support.

Browser crashes or hangs (stops responding)

Well, that's software for you. There are any number of reasons why browsers crash: the browser itself is badly written; there are conflicts between the browser and other software running on your computer; the site you're trying to load has elements that don't work correctly; you have several browser windows open and there are conflicts between them. To some extent, therefore, what you do to fix the problem is a judgement call. The first thing to try is shutting down your browser completely; then open it back up again and try to access the last site you were loading when the crash happened. If the site loads correctly, the problem was probably a conflict between two sites you had loaded or just simple browser overload. If the site crashes your browser again, there's a problem between the site and your browser; try upgrading or changing the browser if you really need to access the site.

If your browser crashes a *lot* – say, during every Web

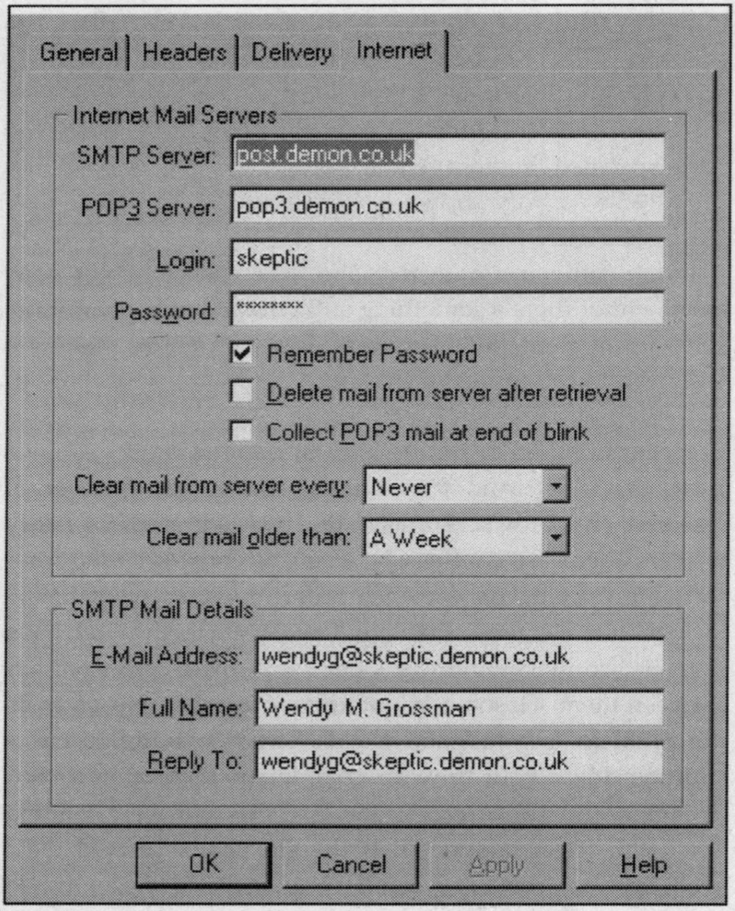

Figure 6. Example of mail server settings.
Do *not* copy – get the right ones from your ISP.

session – or if it crashes regularly on certain sites that you really need to visit, your best bet, again, is probably to upgrade or change the browser. Just because of that sort of problem, heavy Web users tend to have more than one browser on their systems, usually Internet Explorer – since it comes bundled not only with Windows but with a number of other products that insist they require it – and either Netscape or Opera (lean and elegant, if less well-known). If you design your own Web pages, you should have more than one browser available so you can check that you haven't included elements that only work in one browser or that look great in one but terrible in another.

Site says I'm using the wrong browser

Sadly, although everyone creating Web sites are supposed to be working to the same set of open standards, there are occasional variations. If a site says it's 'best viewed with Internet Explorer,' that's advertising, and if you're a Netscape or Opera user, you can use the site anyway. If, on the other hand, a secure site tells you that the encryption in your browser is too weak and you will need to upgrade it before proceeding, you will need to upgrade your browser as specified. In the middle ground, where the site tells you that certain elements of the site are only acessible via a particular browser or that you need a particular plug-in, it's up to you whether those elements are worth the trouble (see **Plug-ins**).

Back button doesn't work

Two possibilities. If you've been viewing a series of pages on a site and the Back button takes you to a different site that you visited earlier, chances are you're in a site that uses frames, a way of splitting up a Web page so that part of it remains constant (usually a bar at the top and left) and the rest changes as you browse the site. Go forward to get back to the page you were looking at, and right-click in the central portion of the page you were viewing. This should give you a menu with a Back option at the top. Left-click on that, and you should be taken back to the previous page within the site.

If, on the other hand, clicking on the Back button seems to keep reloading the page you're looking at instead of taking you back to the previous page, there's a page in between that is invisible to you because all it's doing is autoforwarding your request to the page you're seeing. You need to back up *two* pages; use your history list or the list of recent pages displayed via the navigation menu.

Bookmarked page, but saved URL took me to site's home page

Frames again. When you bookmark a page inside a frame, the address that gets saved is the one connected to the page the frame came from, not the page with the content inside the frame. To save the URL of the actual page with the information on it, right click inside the frame and pick 'Open frame in new window' from the menu that pops up, let the page load, and then save the bookmark. Problems like this are why a lot of people hate frames. Bear in mind that when you reload the page without the frame some of the site's functions won't work – but you will have the information.

The other way to find out the true address of a framed page is to view the page's information (in Netscape, you'll find this at View/Page info). The URL of the page is the one labelled 'Location'.

Printing page just gives me the menu at top and bottom
Frames yet again. Click in the area you want to print (making sure not to hit any links) and *then* hit the Print button.

Page loading slowly
Three possibilities. One, the site itself is overloaded, so it can't hand out data as fast. Two, your machine is over-loaded and it can't receive data as fast. Three, there's something wrong with your connection – ISPs and network connections can get overloaded, too, and when they do, they slow right down. Assume the first case first: kill the page that's loading by hitting the Escape key (this doesn't always work), and hit Reload or Refresh (CTRL-R in Netscape). If it's still slow, you might be in case two, so try shutting down some browser windows or exiting your browser and restarting it (if the rest of your computer is behaving like a snail stuck to fly-paper this is a good bet). You can also try disconnecting from your ISP and reconnecting – if your overall connection is slow, this often helps.

Reload/Refresh took me back to the site's home page, not the page I was looking at.

Aha. Frames yet *again*. See why we hate frames? You might be able to get back the page you were looking at from your history file, but more likely you'll have to navigate back through the site to the page you were looking at.

Can't find the file I just downloaded

Not nice to say so after the fact, but: bad planning. You probably have one of two problems, either not knowing which directory the file has been saved in or being unable to recognize the file's name. Both of these problems are easily preventable. First, however, to find the file you've lost, do the following. Open your Web browser and go to a page – any page – and click on a file – any file – to download. A 'Save As . . .' dialog box should pop up. Look in the field at the top labelled 'Save in'. The drive letter and directory name in that box is the directory the last file was saved in. Write it down if you can't remember it. Cancel the download. Now use your file manager (in Windows, that's Explorer) to look at that directory. If you can't remember the file name, try sorting the files by the time they were last modified. It should be the most recent one on the list. If that doesn't help, try sorting the files by type; at least that should cut down the number of possible matches to a manageable size.

If neither strategy works for you, download the file again, this time doing what you should have the first time: choose a meaningful directory name and filename you'll remember. You can rename a file in the 'Save As . . .' box to any name you like as long as the last three letters after the dot (known as a file extension) stay the same so that the file works the way it's supposed to. So, for example, if the Callserve site wants to give you a file called CS314IPP.EXE and your browser plans to save it in C:\WINDOWS (typically a very crowded directory), rename the thing CALLSERVE.EXE and save it in a directory you create for the purpose like C:\DOWNLOAD.

Mysterious charges on my credit card bill

Some sites use third parties to put through charges for them. Compare your statement against the records you've kept of the orders you've placed. If there really isn't a match, call your credit card company. One point lost on a lot of people: if you sign up for a free trial with an ISP or subscription Web service and gave a credit card number, more often than not you have to go back and actively cancel at the end of the free trial to avoid being charged. Make sure you actively cancel all unwanted free trials before charges kick in.

Order never arrived and now the site has shut down

Call the customer service number you wrote down when you placed the order (if you followed the instructions in this book) and ask them the status of your order. If customer service doesn't answer or if you've been billed for goods that aren't going to arrive, call the company whose credit card you used to pay for the goods and they should help you resolve matters.

TRUTH (IS OUT THERE)

Don't believe anything you read in this section. It, like the rest of this book, is part of a giant, world-wide mass media conspiracy to feed the public meaningless lies and sensationalist pap. The Truth is too dangerous to be told. Instead, we divert you with stories about toe-sucking and the state of Tony Blair's hair while the military-industrial complex/Corporate Amerika/national governments/MI5 get away with murdering people, raping the planet, and hiding the aliens who are, even now, among us. It's all on the Net (and a lot of other places), so it must be true.

Probably. Anyone who is churlish enough to notice that the people publishing all this dangerous information on their Web sites haven't actually disappeared, or that they cite plenty of newspaper stories, TV programmes and books in evidence, probably shouldn't tell anyone. You might be next.

But that's *good*. According to Lyndon LaRouche, the only presidential candidate to have been convicted in a Federal criminal case, 'the measure of a man's virtue is often the numerousness and savagery of his enemies.' If that's true, JFK was a winner. Even thirty-seven years after his death there's a whole newsgroup about it, alt.conspiracy.jfk, to rehash the the single-bullet theory, the multiple-assassin theory, and how the Warren Commission got it all wrong. The man is just as dead, but it was such a seminal moment in recent American history that many people can't let it go.

If you love conspiracy theories there are two sites you must try. Paranoia (http://www.paranoiamagazine.com/) is the site for *Paranoia Magazine*: the iatrogenic theory of AIDS, stolen consciousness, and, my favourite, a lengthy piece about Diana, Princess of Wales and the New World Order's role in choosing a new husband for her and alleging she was alive and largely unharmed after the crash. If you're not convinced, take a look at Conspiracy Nation (http://www.shout.net/~bigred/cn.html), which has more coverage of the subject, or Rumor Mill News (http://www.rumormillnews.com/), which has even more, or UFO Mind (http://www.ufomind.com/para/conspire/), which tries to collect conspiracies without judging them.

Then get your head back together by visiting Disinfo (http://www.disinfo.com), where everything you know is wrong.

Good conspiracy theories never die, whether they're on the Net or elsewhere: humans love mysteries, as anyone who has studied the history of paranormal claims knows. Like other material on the Net, most of the conspiracy theorizing is derived from books, pamphlets, speeches, media coverage and other information available offline. What the Net does is what it always does: makes it easier for like-minded people to meet and distribute their ideas. But cheer up. Read Gary North's 1998 site (http://www.garynorth.com) on TEOTWAWKI (The End of the World As We Know It), which he expected would result from the Y2K bug after 1999. Check your calendar. Breathe.

Additional sites

Speaker of the House Newt Gingrich is working to destroy the US, 'with applause from backers in London'. From Lyndon LaRouche (http://www.clark.net/larouche/welcome.html).

TV

At the moment, most people wouldn't want to watch TV on the Internet: on anything but the fastest connections you get a tiny, grainy, jerky box. Watch TV on a TV.

Except . . . you can't always. Some things don't get on TV. Like the full 24-hour feed from the Big Brother house. Or NASA TV, which broadcasts a few hours a week. Most of the sites that follow are listings sites for familiar UK channels.

Sites

BBC (http://www.bbc.co.uk/whatson/).

Channel 4 (http://www.channel4.co.uk/): click on Listings (way down at the bottom of the screen) for the week's schedule.

Digiguide (http://www.digiguide.com): TV listings up to 14 days into the future on a user-configurable set of channels. The Digiguide software, downloadable from the site, updates itself automatically when you go online according to the channels and interests you've selected.

ITV (http://www.itv.co.uk/).

TV Ark (http://www.bognor.force9.co.uk/): online British TV museum. Clips, chat, discussion area and what's new on most channels.

TV Licensing Authority (http://www.tv-l.co.uk): yes, you can pay for your TV licence online using a credit or Switch card. You will need the number of your current licence.

UmmissableTV (http://unmissabletv.com).

Web Television (http://www.goan.com/tvi.shtml): huge list of live TV-broadcasting sites, from ABC News in the US to Germany's *Der Spiegel*'s online wildlife programme.

U

UNDERGROUND

Underground has, of course, many meanings, from the London Underground (http://www.londontransport.co.uk) to the underground press (http://www.undergroundpress. org). A personal favourite is the Underground Grammarian (http://www.sourcetext.com/grammarian/), Richard Mitchell, whose books are now brought back to availability on the Web for free, along with the text of the newsletter he published quarterly until 1991.

V

VIEWS (CITYSCAPES, PANORAMAS)

We mean Webcams: little cameras connected to the Internet that send constantly updated pictures, some video, most still. Try this list (http://chili.rt66.com/ozone/countries. htm), which will get you almost anywhere in the world.

Also: watch the London Eye (http://www.london-eye. com) go round. Not that you'll see much in the rain.

VIRUSES

See **Security**.

W

WAP

WAP isn't an end in itself; instead, standing for Wireless Application Protocol, it's a way of letting people use Internet services via mobile phones, pocket computers, personal digital assistants, and, soon, other types of wireless devices. WAP is currently at the stage the Web itself was at in 1995: lots of people have heard of it, but most haven't tried it and have little idea why it's useful or what to do with it.

At the moment, because data connections via the GSM network in common use for mobile telephony across Europe are rather slow – limited to roughly one-sixth the speed of newer modems on home PCs – WAP services tend to be slow and unsatisfying. However, as the next-generation mobile networks are rolled out, speeds will improve and the services will become much more usable. No one is suggesting that the wireless Web will replace the 'fixed', or PC-based, Web, but that mobile phones will be a convenient additional form of access for bank accounts, up-to-the-minute sports scores and stock prices, certain types of electronic commerce, and even games to keep people who have run out of reading material from being bored on the move. What we're seeing now are only the earliest versions of these things, but the potential is there.

To access a WAP site, you must use a WAP-enabled device. Usually, this will be a mobile phone or pocket computer; WAP emulators are available for PCs (go to http://www.wapwednesday.com to find one you can use through your standard browser). Exactly what sites you'll be able to access depends on your network operator. The practice is beginning to die now, but the earliest WAP services, notably that provided by Orange, limited users to a selected set of sites managed by the operator itself, an approach often referred to as 'walled garden'.

To get to a WAP site, you start the same way you do on the Web at large: you type in a Web address. This is, of course, more difficult using a mobile phone's limited number pad than using a PC keyboard, but it's as easy as sending an SMS message. The phone will connect to the site and you will see a tiny menu of options, some of which may be off the screen. Use the scroll button to move up and down the menu and select the option you want. Two navigation buttons, right and left, let you access further options or back up a page. It can take a little while to get the hang of how it works, but once you do it's surprisingly effective. Most WAP phones have bookmark facilities, so you don't have to keep painfully typing in the same addresses over and over again.

The list below includes some of the earliest successes. You will need a WAP phone to access these, rather than a Web browser.

WAP sites

Google (http://wap.google.com): searches the entire Web
and translates pages for display on WAP devices.

Kizoom (http://www.railtrack.co.uk/i.wml): complete rail-
way timetables for all of Britain, in cooperation with Railtrack.
Enter your point of origin, your destination, and a time, and
get back the time and details of the next train. From there,
you can move backwards and forwards to earlier or later
trains.

Figure 7.   WAP emulator showing train times from Kizoom.

Mviva (www.mviva.com/wap/index.wml): British WAP portal with access to mobile commerce and many other services including games (only try nGame's Alien Fish Exchange if you're willing to become an addict). You will need to register first via the Web at http://www.mviva.com.

Sports.com (http://mobile.sports.com): sports headlines and scores including Premier League football and most other major events.

UK-iNvest (http://wap.ukinvest.com): news headlines, research, and stock quotes from the London Stock Exchange.

Ummissabletv (http://www.unmissabletv.com): the best part of checking up on what's been happening on your favourite soap opera via your mobile phone is that no one else has to know about it. Personalized listings, recommendations, and gossip.

Sites about WAP
WAP.com (http://www.wap.com): WAP site reviews, WAP phone reviews, WAP tools, WAP news, and a catalogue of WAP services. In other words, the whole WAP and nothing but the WAP. Includes a WAP viewer for the WAP-deprived.

ZDNN WAP Access Guide (http://www.zdnet.co.uk/news/specials/2000/03/wap/zdnn.html): phone reviews, explanations of the technology, downloadable WAP emulator, events listing, guide to UK network operators, and news.

WEATHER

Everyone, as Mark Twain famously observed, talks about the weather, but no one does anything about it. One advantage of the Web is that you can get far more detailed and extensive weather information than you can in any other medium.

You can find basic weather forecasts at almost any news site – certainly, all the ones belonging to British broadcasters or newspapers carry at least minimal national and regional weather forecasts. Usually, 'weather' will appear as one of the options on the site's list of sections, and its a simple matter to click and go straight there. There is, however, far more detailed and exotic data available than simply the temperatures you can expect and whether or not it's likely to rain.

The first port of call should probably be the Meteorological Office (http://www.meto.gov.uk), which supplies the weather to the BBC and many other media organizations, including the *Guardian* (http://www.guardianunlimited.co.uk/Weather/), ITN (http://www.itn.co.uk/) and the BBC (http://www.bbc.co.uk/weather/). On this site, you can find maps, charts, satellite photographs, and five-day forecast for an extensive range of British cities, along with similar, though somewhat more limited, services for the rest of the world. In addition, the site offers information about the research carried out by the Met Office and lengthy explanations of how weather forecasts are created.

For more detail on weather further afield, a good start is

the Web site run by the US's Weather Channel (http://www.weather.com), a non-stop TV channel aimed at weather junkies (which turns out to be pretty much everybody). The site's primary speciality is, of course, American weather, but besides carrying an excellent range of forecasts for other parts of the world (including Britain), it runs features on different types of storms (a recent example is maps of lightning strikes), and specialized forecasts for activities like golf and travel. The Web site belonging to the global news channel CNN is also helpful, offering five-day forecasts for cities all over the world. The main page (http://www.cnn.com/WEATHER) offers access to maps, features and other items of interest such as the allergy report (US only).

Sites

BBC (http://www.weather.co.uk): five-day forecasts for many cities around the UK and the world. UK and US satellite and radar pictures, shipping forecasts, features, and an explanation on how the BBC produces the weather.

Met Office (http://www.meto.gov.uk): five-day forecasts for most UK cities, weather warnings, world weather, and news. Has a useful system of guessable URLs in the following format: http://www.meto.gov.uk/ukcity/<city>.html. Replace '<city>' with the city name of your choice, and most of the time you should go straight to the report for that city. For example, Belfast is http://www.meto.gov.uk/ukcity/belfast.html.

Weather Channel (http://www.weather.com): US-based site belonging to the TV channel of the same name, both aimed at weather junkies. Probably the most comprehensive site about the US, it also covers the rest of the world with maps and forecasts designed for travellers. Also runs features such as weather's impact on emergency situations and sports like skydiving, and environmental issues.

The UK Weather Site (http://www.weather.org.uk/): forecast data, comprehensive listing of UK weather-related sites from the British Antarctic survey to weather stations and academic meteorology departments, and a great listing showing where to direct complaints about weather forecasts to the various TV channels.

WEB PAGE
(Make Your Own)

The news talks only about major commercial sites, but the great secret of the Web is that a huge percentage of the billion pages indexed by Google are grass-roots affairs, maintained by individuals for fun or (small) profit. You can become one of them with surprising ease.

If you really want to keep things simple, the easiest way to create a home page for yourself is to use one of the free Web hosting services, the two best-known being Geocities (http://geocities.yahoo.com) and Tripod (http://www.tripod.co.uk). Both of these started as independents and were taken over by larger portals, Geocities by Yahoo! and Tripod by Lycos. Both services offer facilities to make it easy for first-timers to build simple Web pages with text and photos. You start by creating a user ID on the service, and then follow the online instructions to create your page and publish it on the site. Most likely, however, you will already have Web space included with your Internet access acount, and it may well make more sense for you to use that. In that case, you will need to create your own pages using either a plain text editor or a dedicated HTML editor such as Homesite (http://www.allaire.com/products/homesite/).

The fact is, though, that people are more intimidated than they need to be by HTML (for Hypertext Markup Language), the coding used to create Web pages. Essentially, HTML is just a set of tags – bits of text – you use to tell a Web browser how to display the page. Say, for example, you wanted to format a line of text so that this book's title was displayed in italics. You might type

This book, <i>The Daily Telegraph Internet A to Z</i>,
is intended to help newcomers find their way around the
Internet.

The angle brackets identify the letter(s) inside them as tags; the <i> and </i> tag the text inside them as italicized, so the browser 'knows' to display them that way. Almost all HTML tags come in pairs – the '/' marks ending tags – and the number you need to learn to create a simple Web page is really very small.

One function built into Web browsers is View Source (look for it on the View menu), that lets you see the exact syntax that was used to create the page you're looking at. This is one of the most fundamental decisions making the

Web a medium everyone can use: see an effect you like, view the source, and copy the way it was done. As Web pages have become more complex, with Java scripts, style sheets and complex formatting, this has become harder to do, but if you start with simple pages it's still the best way of understanding how it all goes together.

Here is a template for a simple Web page.

```
<html>
<head>
<title>Simple Web page template</title>
</head>
<body>
<h1>Making a simple Web page</h1>
Making a simple Web page doesn't have to be that
hard. It's a matter of learning a few simple codes and
making sure they're used in the <b>right</b> places.<p>
    We could even put in a picture <img
src="picture.jpg"> without that much difficulty, or a <a
href="http://www.pelicancrossing.net" >link</a> to the
author's home page.<p>
    Believe it or not, it's just as easy to put in a <a
href="roseville.mp3" >sound file</a>.<p>
    And that's a page.<p>
</body>
</html>
```

The syntax of that page shouldn't be too difficult to analyse. First of all, you'll notice that the <p> tag doesn't have a </p> equivalent. In fact, it did once, but no one uses it. That tag is known as the paragraph tag, and putting it at the end of a chunk of text tells the browser to skip a line and start a new paragraph. Otherwise, the browser places only a single space between words; it ignores any extra spaces or blank lines you may insert when you're writing the page. The <HTML> and </HTML> tags tell the browser that what it's displaying is a Web page. The text that appears inside the TITLE tag pair will be displayed in the title bar at the top of the browser window. The HEAD and BODY tag pairs set off sections within the page. In the header section, for example, you'll typically place not only the document's title but, as you get more advanced, settings for background colours and font colours and sizes. The body of the document is usually the actual text, pictures and other elements that make up the page. The B tag pair tells the browser to display the text it surrounds in boldface.

The tags to create links are a bit more complex. First of all, you have a tag pair – <a> and </a> – that mark the enclosed text as a hotlink to another page or file. Inside those, the string of text beginning HREF is the address that the highlighted text is to link to. In the case above, there are two links. The first links to another page, elsewhere on the Net. The second, the sound file, links to a file in the same directory as the page itself. Both use the same syntax; the only real difference is the length of the address.

Finally, the IMG tag is an instruction to the browser to display an image, and the following information until the closing angle bracket tells the browser where to get the picture from (imagine the tags as reading IMAGE SOURCE= and perhaps it will all make more immediate sense). Most of the time, the source of the picture will be the same location as the Web page itself and all you'll need will be the file name. However, as the pages you construct get more complex, you may find you want to link to an image across the Web on another site – perhaps a photo of a friend's child or your company's logo. The Web doesn't care where the image is; the browser just needs to know where to find it. Once you become aware of this, you'll find yourself noticing surprisingly often that the Web page you're loading is calling up images and other elements from elsewhere on the Web. Banner advertising is almost always delivered this way, sourced from third-party ad agency servers across the Net; the ad agencies themselves can therefore track how many ads they're serving up and supply the ads to many hundreds of sites, targeting the ads according to the visiting users' interests.

None of this is intended to be comprehensive; if you want to design your own Web pages you will wind up learning a great deal more about HTML than this, probably even if you use an HTML editor that hides it all from you. But it's intended to give a flavour of how it's done, and to get across the point that despite the fact that Web pages *can* be very complex, they don't *have* to be. If what you want to do is just shove a few pictures of the grandchildren up for your family to admire, you don't need to do anything more complicated than the example above. It's only when you decide you want to run a business and accept online orders and provide clever interactive features that you start getting into more difficult areas involving programming and a lot of buzzwords. My own Web pages (http://www. pelicancrossing.net), for example, are entirely written in a plain text editor (Windows Notepad), sound, pictures, imagemap and all, and, although they're unlikely to win any awards, they are very easy to update with new information and they are readable by just about anyone.

Additional sites

Allaire (http://www.allaire.com/products/homesite/): Allaire's Homesite is generally considered to be the best and easiest to use HTML editor – that is, software that does for creating Web pages what word processors do for plain text. Unlike some other HTML generating programs you may have heard of, like Microsoft's Front Page, Homesite will generate code that needs no special features on your ISP's server to run correctly. Costs $89 if you download it from the site (an evaluation version is available).

Color Center (http://www.hidaho.com/colorcenter/cc.html): nifty and useful site that lets you pick colours for background, text, and links, see what the combination looks like on the screen, and copy the correct BODY tag to make them your page's background and text colours. This site can save you hours of figuring out hexadecimal codes so you can try different colour schemes.

Web Pages That Suck (http://www.webpagesthatsuck.com): what not to do. Trust him. Vincent Flanders, who owns the site, has no trouble finding a Daily Sucker – a page bad enough to point out to his regular readers as a turkey. Here you will find every type of bad Web design, from clashing colours to bad image maps to text that overspills unreadably on to graphics to menus so unrecognizable they need little user manuals and arrows pointing to them. Great entertainment even if you aren't malicious enough to submit the sites you visit and can't stand. This site also has a helpful tutorial on creating your own Web pages, and links to many useful design resources for developers of all levels from the most basic to the intricate stratosphere of Java programming. Strongly recommended.

World Wide Web Consortium (http://www.wc.org): the home site of the World Wide Web, owned and operated by its inventor, Tim Berners-Lee, who continues to mastermind its development via this non-commercial group. Based at the Massachusetts Institute of Technology and independent of any single company, the W3C works on developing new standards and continuing to extend the Web's functions. While much of it is technical proposals, the W3C site is the ultimate authority on everything from what is (or is not) a proper HTML tag (http://validator.w3.org/) to the best way to design a Web page for maximum accessibility (http://www.w3.org/WAI/gettingstarted).

WEDDINGS

The only person I've ever met who thought planning a wedding was easy was someone who'd organized a marathon race. Everyone else might like the Wedding Planner (http://www.weddings.co.uk/info/wedplan.htm), which gives a detailed guide down to where and how to get a special licence – the sort of thing characters never know in books.

The even bigger help, at least for guests, on the Internet is the emergence of online wishlists and gift registries. At a site like Amazon or many other retailers, you can create a wish list of all the items you'd like and open it up to friends and relatives; of course the list gets updated as the items get purchased. Kind of spoils the surprise, but it works. The more traditional wedding gift list at the Wedding Day Services site (http://www.weddingdayservices.co.uk), based in Essex, will help you know what to ask for if you set up a register at one of the older department stores. In fact, Debenhams (http://www.debenhams.com) will let you register online; an adviser will contact you, the site says, 'within a few days'.

WEIRD

Truth is stranger than fiction ... as News of the Weird (http://www.newsoftheweird.com/) proves every day, and so does *Fortean Times* (http://www.forteantimes.com). The Web is even weirder, but one person's weird is another's ordinary existence, so to a large extent weird will just happen to you as you explore the vastness that is the Web.

BUFORA (http://www.bufora.org.uk), the British UFO Research Association, has enough of a sense of humour to include an animated flying saucer on its Web site to illustrate its explanation of what UFOs are. They are: unidentified. According to BUFORA, about 10 per cent of the UFO reports the association receives can't be investigated due to insufficient information. Another 70 per cent can, after careful investigation, be explained by natural causes. So the squabble between UFOlogists and sceptics is largely over that last 20 per cent, half of which BUFORA says are related to other, unrelated, paranormal phenomena (sceptics can argue that one, too).

If you want the other side of that particular argument, try *The Skeptic* (http://www.skeptic.org.uk), which gives a rationalist look at not just UFOs but a lot of other weird stuff, like astrology and Feng Shui. Mostly a print magazine, but also a Web site that tells your rationalist fortune and an AOL area (keyword: skeptic). I founded it, so it had to go in here.

Further out on a limb (perhaps about to fall off the end) is the Church of the Subgenius (http://www.subgenius. com): join the Reverend Ivan Stang and enjoy an hour of Slack radio under the image of Bob Dobbs. If none of that makes any sense to you, don't worry about it too much. Stang is also author of *High Weirdness by Mail*, now out of print, a compendium of the strangest junk mail. His site is tame by comparison.

More fascinating is the entire world of urban legends, as discussed with great passion daily on the Usenet newsgroup alt.folklore.urban. The group's Web site (http://www.urban legends.com/) holds archives and many stories categorized by topic. It's not our fault if the stories you read here are the same ones your friend's friend swore were true. Definitely the place to check out that story about the guy waking up in the bathtub full of crushed ice missing a kidney, though.

WINE

Wine is one of those things that ought to be ideally matched to the Internet: information-intensive and generally hard to sample offline. Most wine sold is similar to the range available in the shops, bearing in mind that the range available to British consumers has expanded dramatically in the last ten years. Much is sold by the case, logically enough. For really exotic wines, you will have to search carefully, and may have to buy directly from the vineyard's own site.

Information sites
The Wine Lover's Page (http://www.wine-lovers-page.com/): news, recommendations, discussions.

Wine Spectator (http://www.winespectator.com/): daily news, weekly features, discussion boards, library, and even the odd feature on choosing food to go with your wine.

Retailers
Bordeaux Direct: extension of a mail-order company. Not just limited to Bordeaux, own vineyard Chateau Laithwaite. ave a number of trading names, doing wine clubs for the *Sunday Times*, *Radio Times*, and others.

Majestic Wines (http://www.majestic.co.uk/): the leading by-the-case retailer; its site lets you search by region, type of wine, and price, and features special sales.

Oddbins.co.uk: selling only champagne at the end of 2000, somewhat odd since the real-world shops specialize in carefully trained and knowledgeable staff. There is, however, lots of information on their site – if you can get past the Flash bottle saying hello (why does the world need this?). The staff is a little variable about updating the site: discount vouchers for the physical-world shops expiring September 30, 2000 were still being offered in mid-October.

Winerack.co.uk: publicizes the Wine Rack shops, and with its partner, Enjoyment, sells over the Web. Requires too much Flash.

Veuve Clicquot (http://www.veuve-clicquot.fr/index_gb. html): champagne, basically, with a detailed history of the old widow Clicquot and tasting notes on how best to care for and drink it.

Virgin Wines: originally known as Orgasmic Wines until Virgin bought it. Sells customized or standard mixed cases, and makes recommendations based on the information you give it.

WineWineWine (http://www.winewinewine.co.uk): fairly primitive site, but owned by a small importer who sells wine by the case at Borough market at a discount for in-person sales.

X

XML AND OTHER JARGON OF THE FUTURE

The thing about the Internet is that just about every year it spawns a new technology that is going to 'change the way we live, work and play'. Looking over the past few years' worth of buzzwords, judge for yourself.

2000: WAP. Wireless Application Protocol. Surf the Web and read email on a mobile phone.

1999: Y2K. TEOTWAWKI.

1998: XML. Extended version of the Web's language, HTML, that will make the Web readable by machines and make the interchange of data much easier.

1997: Push. Instead of making users go out and get information, let's push it to them over channels. Sound like TV? Or junk email? Useful inside businesses for deploying software updates.

1996: Portals. See **Yahoo! and Other Portals.**

1995: Java. Let the Web run programs on your computer.

1994: the Web.

Has your life changed yet?

SEXXX

An entire site selling nothing but condoms, Condomania (http://www.condomania.com/) has probably more styles than anyone wants to think about. Discreet packaging (it promises here).

Or try checking out the Safe Sex Web site – (http://www.safesex.com).

Y

YAHOO! AND OTHER PORTALS

Yahoo! (http://www.yahoo.co.uk) is probably the best known of a class of Web site known as portals. These all-purpose sites are intended to make it easy for people to use the Web and find the things they are looking for. In fact, Yahoo! started in 1993, when two graduate students at Stanford University decided to compile a directory of their favourite Web sites. At the time, before search engines and the ability to save bookmarks in a Web browser, the only way to find a Web site on a particular topic was through word of mouth, and if you wanted to remember the location you had to write it down and save it somewhere. Yahoo! changed all that. By now, Yahoo! has many sites around the world with localized content, all offering a mix of stock quotes, news headlines, free email, discussion boards, auctions, personalized home pages, ads, and electronic shopping on top of the directory services it started with.

Yahoo! is frequently referred to as a search engine, but this is incorrect, even though it does include a (Google-supplied) function for searching the Web and/or its own database of sites. Instead, it's first and foremost a classified index to the Web compiled by Yahoo! staff, which includes librarians experienced in cataloguing. If, for example, you want to find a list of all the British newspapers with Web sites, Yahoo! is a good place to start. To find the list, start from Yahoo!'s main page (above), and pick newspapers from the short list under Media. The list should come right up. (Or, if you're too impatient to follow those instructions, go straight to http://uk.dir.yahoo.com/Regional/Countries/United_Kingdom/News_and_Media/Newspapers/). Yahoo!'s directory structure (widely copied) makes it easy to browse categories and get a feel for what's out there.

Its shopping service includes a mini search engine (http://shopping.yahoo.co.uk) that scans its retail partners for the items you're looking for; the UK list of such partners is still fairly small, so your choice is, unfortunately, limited. Its finance section (http://uk.finance.yahoo.com) also gives access to insurance and mortage quotes, market news, and links to articles of note from other online publications.

By now, many ISPs such as Freeserve (http://www.freeserve.co.uk), AOL (http://www.aol.co.uk), and MSN (http://www.msn.co.uk) operate portals intended to make getting started online easier for their subscribers as well as promoting their own services and ecommerce partners. In addition, **Search Engines** (see entry) such as Excite (http://excite.co.uk), Lycos (http://www.lycos.co.uk) and Altavista (http://www.altavista.co.uk) are also portals. Chances are, however, that the portal you will have seen first is the page that loads automatically when you start your browser, usually either Netscape's Netcenter (http://www.netscape.com) or MSN (http://www.msn.com).

Most experienced Web users rarely use portals. For a

newcomer, however, taking a few minutes to look at all the choices and set the one you like best as your Home Page can pay dividends in making it easier to find your way around.

Z

ZEN

You might not think of the Net as a place to go to meditate or get in touch with your inner soul, but the Zen MOO (http://www.zennet.com) is one place that aims to let you try. Peaceful contemplation is rewarded by this site, which tells you to stop the infernal 'racket' if you type too often. The temptation may be to get on with other things in other windows on your machine, but because the system periodically poses questions to check that you are still there meditating rather than asleep or inattentive, you risk getting thrown off if you aren't paying attention.

Glossary

Active-X: technology that, like Java (see below) lets a site run small programs on your computer to make it interactive.

Applets: mini-applications. Applications are programs that run on a computer, such as a word processor or spreadsheet. Applets are tiny programs; on the Web, the word typically refers to small programs a Web site may send your browser to make the Web more interactive. Scrolling headlines are one example.

Banner ads: graphical ads that appear on Web pages.

Bits: a measure of digital data. Think atoms in the physical world.

Browser (or Web browser): piece of software that accesses and displays Web pages. The best known are Microsoft Internet Explorer, Netscape, and Opera, but there are many more, including microbrowsers for WAP phones and other pocket devices.

Cache: directory (folder) in which Web pages and related files are stored temporarily while you're browsing. Caching the files allows them to load faster as you move back and forth among pages.

Client: in client/server computing, the client and server are complementary. The client is the software that runs on the user's machine and requests data or services from the server on the remote machine.

Cookie: string of gibberish characters Web sites store on a user's computer that the site can use to identify a user, keep track of orders being created, and personalize pages.

Dial-up connection: method of accessing the Internet over an ordinary telephone line. A device known as a modem, connected to a computer, dials up your Internet service provider and makes the connection.

Domain name: the name, such as the *Daily Telegraph*'s telegraph.co.uk or Wendy M. Grossman's pelicancrossing. net, by which businesses and other organizations are known on the Internet, making it possible to send them email and access their Web sites.

Download: retrieve computer files from a remote system.

Ecommerce: short for electronic commerce. Usually used to refer to any type of online transaction involving money, such as online banking, shopping, or financial services.

Email: short for electronic mail. (See also A–Z entry **Email**.)

Encryption: the art of scrambling data so that it can't be read by unauthorized third parties. Because encryption played a vital role in World War II, until recently encryption software has been classed as a military weapon and there have been restrictions on its import, export and use. These are easing because of its vital importance in protecting information such as credit card details in transmission across the Net.

Flame: term for intemperate, abusive communication, whether it's private email or a public discussion area posting. A certain amount of flaming seems to be par for the course in electronic media.

Flash: plug-in that enables fancy graphics and often noisy animations on Web sites. Look for the button that says 'skip intro'.

FTP: abbreviation for File Transfer Protocol. A standard utility to allow users to access remote stores of files across the Internet and upload or download files. FTP pre-dates the Web, and for most users is indistinguishable from retrieving a file via a Web browser. However, FTP has some facilities lacking in Web browsers, such as the ability to resume a download that was interrupted partway through. For people who need to download very large files frequently, therefore, seeking out a separate FTP utility (http://www.stroud.com is a good source) isn't a bad idea.

GIF: abbreviation for Graphic Interchange Format. Originally developed by the early online service CompuServe (now owned by AOL) as an efficient, compressed way for users to exchange images. GIF is one of three image formats automatically readable by Web browsers (the other two are JPG and PNG). However, it's used less than it was, as the large computer manufacturer Unisys claims patent rights in a portion of the compression technology involved, and in the process of demanding licensing fees has alienated a good chunk of the Net.

Gopher: menu-based system for retrieving Internet archives, usually organized by subject.

History file: your browser keeps a record of the sites you have visited, and calls the list your 'history file'. To see the list, click on History (or hit CTRL-H on the keyboard).

Home page: most commonly, the opening page of the speaker's Web site. Also, the page a Web browser goes to if you press the Home button or choose Go Home from the menu bar (you can set this to any page you like).

Hosting: storing data or online services. A Web site is hosted by your Internet service provider, for example.

HTML: abbreviation for Hypertext Markup Language.

ICQ: say it fast, with the emphasis on the 'C'. Now owned by AOL, ICQ is instant messaging software that runs across the Internet. ICQ users can send each other messages, engage in real-time typed chats, and see when their friends are online.

Hypertext: text presented in such a way as to allow the reader to jump directly to related information. On the Web, hypertext is implemented with links that allow the user to jump not only between bits of related information on the same page but on multiple pages spread across many computers in different countries.

IRC: abbreviation for Internet Relay Chat. Another service that pre-dates the Web, IRC lets users type to each other in real time. There are a variety of regular public channels that cover a wide range of topics of discussion, as well as many more private ones that you can join by invitation only. The original IRC interface is text-based, but several graphical versions of the client software are available today (one example is at http://www.mirc.com).

IP number: each machine connected to the Internet has an Internet protocol number assigned to it. The computers that route traffic use these numbers. Humans use words, known as domain names (like telegraph.co.uk), to stand in for the numbers for usability reasons; behind the scenes, every time you type in a Web address or send an email message a computer looks up the number corresponding to the domain name you've typed. Customers with fixed connections such as leased lines or ADSL usually have a permanent IP number allocated to them by their ISP. Dial-up customers use IP numbers too, but the number varies from session to session: every time you dial in and log on your ISP's computers assign your machine an IP number from the pool of numbers it has available.

ISP: abbreviation for Internet service provider.

Java: often referred to as a language, but actually a system composed of four elements. These are: a programming language, a virtual 'machine' that runs on a piece of hardware and provides an environment that Java programs ('applets') can run in without change from any other type of hardware, a set of libraries that Java programs can draw on for standard routines, and a Java compiler (that is, a computer program that turns the programming code humans write in near-readable language into machine code only computers can read). Any device that can run a virtual machine and has a set of the libraries installed should be able to run any Java program without alteration. Java was developed by Sun Microsystems and released in 1995.

JPEG: a highly compressed but reasonably high quality graphic file format. Files in this format end with the extension .JPG. Probably the most commonly used graphical file format on the Web.

Links: the highlighted text in a Web page that, if clicked on, takes you to related information elsewhere, be it on the same page, another page, or another computer.

Log on/off (in/out): on restricted-access systems, you log in by typing in your user ID and password, much as you might swipe a card through a reader to unlock the door to a building. Logging off is usually no more complicated than typing 'quit' or 'bye' or clicking on a button. It is, however, an important security measure, as doing so notifies the remote computer that you're gone, so that anyone trying to use your account will have to log in correctly to do so.

Microbrowser: Web browser designed for WAP phones or other devices with a minimum of computing power.

MIME: because email and Usenet carry only text, to send anything else, such as a music, picture, or program file, it has to be converted to text for submission (and then converted back after it arrives). MIME is a standard for performing this encoding.

Mirror (site): an exact copy of a site. Mirror sites are usually set up for one of two reasons: (1) to spread the load because the original site is getting more traffic than it can handle; (2) to defeat attempts at censorship by storing copies of the original site on hosts in many different countries.

MP3: a type of music file, actually known as M-PEG 2, layer 3. Highly compressed (to roughly 1/10 the size of a music file extracted from a CD) but high quality, MP3 is the most popular online music format, allowing users to trade files via services such as Napster.

MUD: abbreviation for Multi-User Dungeon. The dungeon in question refers to the original role-playing game *Dungeons and Dragons*, of which MUDs are a direct descendant. The first MUD was invented at the University of Essex in the late 1970s by students Roy Trubshaw and Richard Bartle, and even though MUDs are generally text-based there are still thousands of them around the world accessible via the Internet. A good list of MUDs and related resources is at http://directory.google.com/Top/Games/Internet/MUDs/.

Net: abbreviation for the Internet.

Newsgroup: discussion group on Usenet.

Newsreader: software for reading Usenet.

Password: a word or string of numbers used to restrict an online account to authorized users, much like the PIN codes you use in cash machines.

PDF: Adobe Acrobat file format, standing for Portable Document Format. PDF is used frequently for documents where the owner wants to ensure that all the original formatting – tables, charts – is preserved. Because software that will read these files is available for almost every type of computer imaginable and because the files are relatively small in size (compared to the original files formatted in, say, Microsoft Word), and also because the files can't carry viruses, you will see PDF used a lot. Download the reader (it's free) for your machine at http://www.adobe.com/products/acrobat/readstep.html.

Plug-in: piece of special-purpose software you add to a larger computer program such as a Web browser. Popular plug-ins for the Web include music and video players or animation software such as Flash. Most of the common plug-ins are installed automatically when you install your Web browser. If you land on a page that requires one you don't have, typically the page will give you a link straight to a page where you can download it.

Port: a port on a computer is a means of access. The computer and modem use the serial port, for example. The software (TCP/IP) that makes it possible for your computer to talk to others on the Internet also makes it possible for them to create channels by which they can install and run software on your computer. Checking for open ports, therefore, is making sure that there are no such open channels you don't know about.

Portal: all-in-one Web site that intends to act as an organized gateway to the Internet. Most include a search engine, news headlines, free email and Web pages, a shopping directory, and stock quotes. Examples are Yahoo!, Lycos, MSN, and Freeserve.

Refresh: update. Even if you're connected to the Internet, most pages do not update themselves automatically if new content is added. Refreshing (or reloading) the page will let you see, for example, if the price on the auction you're following has changed.

Server: in client/server computing, the client and server are complementary. The server is the software that runs on the remote machine and responds to requests for data or services from the client on the user's machine.

Shockwave: plug-in that enables fancy graphics and often noisy animations on Web sites. Look for the button that says 'skip intro'.

SMS: short message system. Enables teens to send each other messages on their mobile phones under the table while they're having dinner with their boring parents. Among other things.

Spam: named after the famous Monty Python sketch, spam is widespread, abusive advertising on Usenet. There is a small clutch of people who delete spam, which they define in part as messages posted to a wide variety of newsgroups regardless of relevance. Sometimes also used to apply to junk email, but technically that's more correctly known as UCE (for unsolicited commercial email) or UBE (for unsolicited bulk email).

SSL: secure sockets layer. Technology that encrypts sensitive information as it travels across the Net from you to the site you're doing business with so that the information isn't readable if it does get intercepted.

Streaming media: the Internet version of broadcasting. That is, if you have the right client software, such as Real Audio, you can tap directly into a live 'Webcast' or play music or video files stored on a remote computer. The streaming software does not store copies on your computer.

TCP/IP: Transfer Control Protocol/Internet Protocol, the technology that allows all the different types of computer to 'talk' to one another.

Telnet: text-based Internet utility that allows a user to operate a remote computer as if he were sitting at a terminal directly connected to it. Used directly these days primarily to access MUDs and older, text-based bulletin boards and electronic conferencing systems across the Net.

Upload: sending a file from your system to a remote computer.

URL: uniform resource locator. Or, more simply, a Web address. These always begin with 'http://'.

Usenet: a global set of online discussion groups on a wide variety of topics. Usenet pre-dates the Internet, and can be transmitted via other means (such as computers phoning each other directly and copying files). You can read Usenet via the newsreader built into your Web browser, but to read newsgroups efficiently it's best to get hold of a type of software known as an 'offline reader,' which will let you run quickly through subject headings, skipping the ones that don't interest you, and also minimize the amount of time you spend connected to the Net, important if you're paying per-minute phone charges. Most ISPs give direct access to Usenet's tens of thousands of newsgroups; if yours doesn't you can also read or search newsgroups online via services like Deja News (http://www.deja.com). (See also A–Z entry **Argue**.)

UUencode/UUdecode: because email and Usenet carry only text, to send anything else, such as a music, picture, or program file, it has to be converted to text for transmission. UUencode handles this; it should be built into your email and/or Usenet software. Often now programs use the more recent **MIME** instead.

Virus: a computer program designed to replicate itself (and thereby spread from one computer to many others). It may or may not have other functions, which may be harmless or malicious.

WAP: abbreviation for Wireless Application Protocol. Functions being built into new mobile phones and other wireless devices from 1999 onwards that will allow access to the Web and other Internet-based services.

Web: abbreviation for World Wide Web (see below).

Webcast: like a live TV broadcast, only over the Web. Many large US companies now, for example, Webcast their telephone conference calls to discuss earnings with financial analysts. As broadband – permanent, fixed, high-speed connections – becomes common, Webcasting many different types of live events will become routine.

Weblogs: daily diaries that may include personal information but that have more in common with ships' logs, in that they record the most interesting results of daily travels around the Internet. If you find a Weblog whose owner's tastes somewhat match yours, you can be assured of an ongoing supply of interesting, new sites.

World Wide Web: the best-known part of the Internet. Invented by Englishman Tim Berners-Lee during a stint at CERN in 1989, the Web began to reach mainstream consciousness in 1994, when the first commercial services became available. Essentially, the Web provides a unifying, easy-to-use graphical interface to what was previously a complex set of text-based programs requiring a lot of technical knowledge to use.